Economics: An Honors Companion

to accompany David Colander's Economics, Second Edition

written by

Sunder Ramaswamy
Middlebury College

Kailash Khandke
Furman University

Jenifer Gamber
Eastern Economic Journal

David Colander
Middlebury College

Project Editor: Jenifer Gamber
Copy Editor: Helen Reiff
Compositor: Jenifer Gamber
Art Director: Jenifer Gamber
Printer and Binder: Science Press, Ephrata, PA 17522

MaxiPress, Box 152C, Dog Team Road, New Haven, VT 05472

Economics: An Honors Companion
© MaxiPress, 1995

Printed in the United States of America

ISBN 0-256-16813-X

Acknowledgments

We would like to thank Sandro Wulff and He Shen for their valuable research and editorial assistance in preparing the manuscript. We would also like to thank our families for their support and patience which helped to make this project a reality.

Brief Contents

Contents

Part II   Macroeconomics

Part III

Preface

Teaching Principles of Economics is challenging, to say the least. Classes are usually composed of students who have varying educational backgrounds, abilities and desires. The Colander text, like most introductory texts, is designed to avoid intimidation—so as not to scare off the students with presentation of mathematics or technical issues for which they may not be prepared them to deal. Thus, for exposition of ideas it adopts a verbal and simplified graphical approach. The advantage is that it makes the complex issues understandable to nontechnical students, the disadvantages are excess verbiage and not introducing the technical tools, the beauty, and the limitations of the technical analysis to those students who do have the requisite background.

This book is designed to offset those disadvantages. It loosens the constraint under which the text was written and assumes a working knowledge of algebra, geometry and introductory calculus. It presents selected topics in which showing the student a more elegant presentation of the same idea that has been presented in words in the text can add to the student's understanding. Freeing the presentation from the nontechnical constraint allows those students with the appropriate background to go a bit deeper into the theories and techniques and get more out of the learning process.

Exposing students to mathematical techniques as early as possible has many virtues. It permits the argument to go beyond the narrow confines of a two-variable world; it allows a more precise statement of the underlying assumptions of an economic model and it allows an elegance of presentation that is beautiful in its own right. At the beginning of his classic *Foundations of Economic Analysis*, Paul Samuelson quoted J. Willard Gibbs in writing, " Mathematics is a language." We are in complete agreement. For people who are comfortable with the language, mathematics is an efficient way of conveying information. For those who are not , it is a hindrance—and directs them away from ideas, ideas that are ultimately what economics is about.

Students Who Can Benefit From This Book

We call this book an honors companion because it is particularly suited for
economics majors and honors sections. It will better prepare students who
wish to go on and major in economics and make economics easier to grasp
for technically oriented students. All students with the suitable background, however, whether or not they are planning to go on and take more
economics courses can benefit from the intellectually satisfying exercise
of thinking about economics mathematically.

Economics courses taught at engineering and technical colleges, at
MBA programs that combine introductory and intermediate courses in one
course, and at highly selective liberal arts colleges where it is reasonable to
presume that students have a solid algebraic and geometric background
and some introduction to calculus are the most likely candidates to use this
book.

Topics Covered

We chose topics with the general outline of the Colander text in mind. It
does not go chapter by chapter but instead focuses on those topics of
interest that are most conducive to mathematical exposition. Some of the
chapters extend topics only mentioned in the Colander text; others take the
same issue discussed in the text and present them technically.

The book is broken into three sections. The first section, "Mathematical Tools" reviews basic geometric, algebraic and calculus tools used in
the book. It is brief and only meant to be a refresher. If the material
presented in these chapters is totally new to the students, they probably
should not be using this text. The next two sections deal with specific
topics in macroeconomics and microeconomics.

Each of the chapters presents an idea, goes through a numerical
example, and finally presents problems for the student to do. Brief
answers to these questions are provided at the end of the text. Although
this book is most effective integrated into a course by the professor, this
pedagogical method is meant to allow students to work through the book

on their own progressing at an individual pace to learn the usefulness of mathematical tools in economics. We have taken this approach recognizing that integrating this book into a course is not always possible.

Whether working alone or in a class, students who use this companion volume in conjunction with the introductory text will gain more of an appreciation of the complexities in economic thinking and modeling, and the way in which economic concepts relate to the world.

Technical Work and the Art of Economics

A text such as this written in conjunction with Colander's text may surprise some people. After all, Colander's text argues that what we should be teaching students is the art of economics—applied policy economics—not techniques and mathematical models. We see no contradiction. As long as the technical models are kept in perspective, teaching them and doing abstract problems is a great way to learn economic concepts. Keeping them in perspective means that we remember that the models are an exercise—a prelude to the art—not the art itself, and that the exactness of the models does not carry over into the real world.

Part I
Mathematical Tools

1

Mathematics, Algebra, and Economics

Mathematics is generally divided into topology and analysis, although the division is not foolproof. *Topology* is the study of space and spatial relations; geometry is that branch of topology with which you are most familiar; graphish falls within geometry. *Analysis* includes the study of numbers; arithmetic, which deals with operations on numbers (addition, subtraction, etc.), is familiar to all college students; and algebra, which deals with relations between numbers and operations performed on those operations. Functions and operations are important elements of algebra. Infinitesimally small changes in variables or functions fall within a subsection of analysis called calculus. The relations of changes in variables to other variables are the simplest of the many variations of calculus and fall within traditional introductory college calculus courses. (When you do differentiation you're doing this.)

An extension of calculus done in the introductory course is the study of integration (taking antiderivatives). A further extension is the study of differential equations—equations which involve differentials. Differential equations combine algebra with calculus—it's usually taken after one has completed the full calculus sequence. Differential equations can be linear or nonlinear, and nonlinear dynamic systems of equations can become very complicated indeed.

It isn't only changes in variables that can be related to each other; changes in functions can also be related to changes in other functions. The study of such issues is called control theory or the calculus of variations. (Once you're into this you're getting into some real math.) You'll be happy to know that in this honors companion we are sticking to the simple stuff—but to keep the math we are using in perspective, it's important to know that a whole other world of math is out there.

Serious theoretical debates in economics are going on in this higher realm of math. They concern nonlinear dynamic systems and the chaos that can result when all the interrelationships are allowed take place. So if you're planning to study economic theory in graduate school, get ready for lots of math.

For purposes of introductory economics, even in this technical book we will forget the fine points of the math and the high level stuff. We stick with basic algebra, geometry, and calculus. In this chapter we discuss some operative basics of algebra used in economics. Then in Chapter 2 we discuss some geometry, and in Chapter 3 we discuss introductory concepts in calculus.

Algebra

Central to those operative basics of algebra are the sense and meaning of equality and function.

Equality

Think of doing algebra as operating a scale—or a child's teeter totter with the equals sign as the fulcrum. Algebra allows you to manipulate one side or the other and maintain balance. These manipulations give you different pictures of what's there—some are more in focus than others. For example, say you have

$$x^2 - x\ln[(e^x)^{1/x}] + 9/x\{\ln[(e^x)^{1/x}]\} = 9.$$

Following the rules of algebra, we can reduce this to

$$x = 1.$$

This second formulation doesn't look as impressive as the first, but it tells us a lot more than does "$x^2 - x\ln[(e^x)^{1/x}] + 9/x\{\ln[(e^x)^{1/x}]\} = 9$"—it's a different, more easily understood, picture. So the purpose of operating the scale —algebra— is to switch things around so you get a better picture of the relations you are looking at.

Function

The other term that is helpful to know in algebra is *function*. Loosely, a *function* is a relationship between two or more variables. The equation $y = 2x$ (or, more generally, $y = f(x)$) is a function. It expresses the relationship between the variable x and the variable y. The specific relationship shown above involves a numeric operation— "multiplying by 2."

Functions that relate two variables exist in two dimensions: in the previous case, dimensions x and y. Functions can also relate three, four, five or more variables. In these cases, those functions would exist in three, four and five-space. Although it is difficult to imagine more than three dimensions, there are tricks that will let us see portions of higher level dimensions. Frequently in economics, variables depend upon more than one other variable so these tricks will be handy in your study of economics.

Functions can be either explicit or implicit. The function $y = 2x$ is explicit because the variables x and y can be separated out. The equation can be reduced to $y = 2x$ or $x = (1/2)y$. The operator can be expressed as operating on only one of the variables at a time.

Alternatively, functions can be implicit. That is, the x cannot be isolated; the equation cannot be reduced to $x =$ ___; The equation, $x^3 + y^3 = 3xy$, is an implicit function in which the variables cannot be isolated. The variable x is related to y in this implicit function but the variables cannot be expressed in any explicit way. The functions that we will use in this text will be limited to explicit function.

Continuity and Smoothness

An important concept in economics when using functions is continuity. A function is *continuous* if a small change in one variable corresponds to a small change in the variable to which it relates. Graphically, continuity means that the function can be drawn without taking the pencil off the paper in the range over which the function is continuous.

A second characteristic of functions is smoothness. A function is *smooth* if the direction of the geometric curve of that function doesn't change abruptly, i.e., have any sharp edges. Continuous smooth functions are nice because they allow one to use marginal analysis and calculus techniques without noting all kinds of exceptions.

Many economic arguments depend on assumptions of smoothness and continuity, and direct explicit functions chosen to represent economic relationships place continuity restrictions on the type of indirect functions we can assume relate to them. Specifically, specifying a general law assumes that an analytic function lies behind it. This means that the law is some type of explicit function.

Operators on Variables

A function is a specific operation or combination of operations on a variable or set of variables.

There are many types of operators that can be used in functions. Some of the types most commonly used in economics are:

Addition	$x + 2$;	Exponent	$x^2, x^3, \ldots$ etc. (square, cube, etc.);
Subtraction	$x - 2$;	Logarithm	$\log x$, $\ln x$;
Division	$x/2$;	Derivative	dx, d^2x, $\ldots$ (first, second, etc.)
Multiplication	$2x$.		

Equations are often classified by their highest exponent: *cubic* if the highest exponent is three; *quadratic* if the highest exponent is two; *linear* if the highest exponent is one.

One of the biggest uses of functions in economics is to specify an observed relationship. You do this continually throughout both microeconomics and macroeconomics. The first task in economics is generally to reduce observed relationships among variables to functions.

For example, in macro, say you are considering the relationship between income and consumption. You might posit that consumption (C) is a linear function of income (Y):

$$C = a + bY.$$

Interdependent Relationships

After relationships among variables are specified functionally, one can use the laws of algebra to combine various functions into composite or reduced-form functions that maintain the interrelationships among variables in the original functions.

The Laws of Algebra

The following are the laws of algebra:

1. The Law of Reflexivity $a = a$
Any number is equal to itself.

2. The Law of Symmetry   If $a = b$ then $b = a$.
Any equality may be reversed.

3. The Law of Transitivity   If $a = b$ and $b = c$, then $a = c$.

Also known as the substitution principle. If one number is equal to a second number, and the second number is equal to a third number, then the first number is equal to the third number.

4. *The Commutative Property of Addition* $a + b = b + a$
The order in which two numbers are added does not change their sum.

5. *The Associative Property of Addition* $(a + b) + c = a + (b + c)$
Numbers can be grouped in different ways without changing their sum.

6. *The Commutative Property of Multiplication* $ab = ba$
The order in which numbers are multiplied does not change their product.

7. *The Associative Property of Multiplication* $(ab)c = a(bc)$
The product of the first two numbers times a third equals the product of the second two numbers times the first.

8. *The Distributive Property of Multiplication over Addition* $a(b + c) = ab + ac$
The product of one number times the sum of a second and third number equals the product of the first and second number plus the product of the first and third.

The laws of algebra can be used to reduce or solve a system of equations that represent economic relationships among variables.

A Macroeconomic Example

Let's consider a macroeconomic example of the use of algebra. Say that you had the consumption function stated above:

$$C = a + bY.$$

Say also that you know by definition that income is the sum of consumption and investment:

$$Y = C + I.$$

We have two linear functions. Using the substitution principle (substituting the first function into the second), we can combine the two equations into one:

$$Y = a + bY + I.$$

Using the law of reflexivity we can subtract bY from both sides to get

$$Y - bY = a + I.$$

Using the distributive property of multiplication over addition, we can factor out a $1-b$ from the left- hand side:

$$Y(1-b) = a + I.$$

Dividing both sides by $1-b$ gives

$$Y = (1/1-b)\ (a + I).$$

We have now defined income, Y, as a function of b, a and I. This is called a *reduced-form* equation; it combines the information in the two equations into one.

A Microeconomic Example

The same can be done with relationships in microeconomics. In this case, we want to solve for output, X and price, P. Say you have the following two functions:

$$\text{Supply: } X = 4 + 2P;$$
$$\text{Demand: } X = 6 - 3P.$$

First, let's solve for P by substituting the demand equation $X = 6-3P$ into the supply equation. This results in

$$6 - 3P = 4 + 2P.$$

To isolate the P, subtract 4 from, and add $3P$ to, both sides. Then divide both sides by 5. The result is

$$P = 2/5.$$

We can solve for X easily now by substituting in 2/5 for P into either the demand or supply equation. Doing so yields

$$X = 24/5.$$

The above method of solving systems of equations is known as the *substitution method*. It's the one most used in undergraduate economics and the one we will generally use. It's important to remember, however, that there are many other methods, some of them rather complicated.

Notice that in this reduction process the equation is like a child's teeter-totter, with the "equals" sign as the fulcrum. Anything you do to change one side, you do to the other, and eventually, if you're crafty and lucky, you get the reduced-form functions in a form that you want.

Exercise 1: Try the same reduction with general parameters: Supply is $X = a_1 + b_1 P$; Demand is $X = a_2 - b_2 P$. What is the equilibrium price and quantity?

Combining More Than Two Equations

The above example involved only two equations and two unknowns to keep the presentation simple. However, it's important to remember that the number of equations and unknowns can be increased at will. The process remains the same, but carrying out the process becomes harder and harder. At some point, fancier methods than substitution become necessary. That's why there is a separate matrix algebra that allows one to perform specific operations on groups of variables. It's also why courses on linear algebra are very useful for those students thinking about graduate work in economics.

One thing economists often look for is a unique solution for each of the variables in a set of equations. For there to be a unique solution there must be an equal number of independent equations and unknowns. (Independent means that some combination of equations don't say essentially the same thing as other combinations of equations.) In our second example, there were two equations and two unknowns, so there was a unique numerical answer for X and P. If there are fewer equations than unknowns, you can't find numerical solutions; there are multiple solutions. If there are more equations than unknowns, there may be no solution.

Limitations of Algebra in Economics

It is important for a student of economics to learn not only the techniques, but also the limitations of those techniques. The first thing to remember is that the algebra presented above places severe restrictions on the relationships we allow. The limitations must be kept in the back of one's mind. For example, throughout introductory economics we often assume continuous functions, which allows us to specify optimization—maximizing welfare, say—with marginal conditions only (subject to appropriate second-order conditions). But if continuity doesn't exist, and interdependent relationships are often discontinuous, that is no longer possible. One must also look at each point of discontinuity separately.

As soon as equations become complicated and involve differential equations and nonlinear equations, the likelihood of discontinuity increases enormously. Economists usually avoid such complications for tractability, but that is an enormous limitation on the applicability of mathematical results to economics—even math that to you looks enormously complicated.

Translating from Ideas and Words to Equations

Probably the hardest part of algebra is translating an idea expressed in words into an equation. For example, say that producing 4 widgets costs $3, producing 6 widgets costs $4, and producing 8 widgets costs $5. Under certain assumptions, including continuity and linearity, we could translate those words into the following function:

$$C = \$1 + \$.50W,$$

where C = costs
        W = the number of widgets produced.

That is the only linear continuous function that fits all the observations.

If we don't limit ourselves to linear continuous functions, many functions could fit. In economics we generally limit allowable functions enormously. In introductory economics we generally limit the allowable functions to cubic, quadratic, exponential, and linear functions, and in introductory macroeconomics we limit ourselves almost entirely to linear functions. Thus, we assume consumption is a continuous linear function of income.

Complex Systems, Chaos and Path Dependency

A recent movement in economics has been to stop making those limiting assumptions and to try to represent economic processes as more complex systems. This has brought about significant changes in the way in which some economists analyze problems. They no longer look for analytic solutions, but instead turn to computer simulations to find patterns of shifting equilibria.

What they often find is a continual unfolding of new interrelationships. The direction the system goes in is highly sensitive to initial conditions, and sometimes a small change in one part of the system that seemed totally removed from another part of the system can cause large effects in another part of the system. This is sometimes known as the *butterfly effect* to refer to the analogy that it is possible that a butterfly flapping its wings in China can change the weather in the United States.

When there's lots of butterfly effects in a system, the system is considered *chaotic*. In a chaotic system events and variables are related but it is almost impossible to find out what that relationship is and to use any past relationship to predict a future one. One explanation of why economists have been so poor at predicting is that economic systems have a relatively large chaotic component.

Another complexity that economists have recently been trying to incorporate into economics is *path dependency*. That's a fancy name for a simple idea: history is important. What is so hard about adding history, you ask. Consider a simple equation: $C = a + bY$.

Where's history in it? To add history we must add a time component, t, which in general form gives us

$$C(t) = a(t) + b(t) \, Y(t).$$

Each variable becomes an equation which can be affected by other variables, changes in other variables, or the like. That's all easy to say informally, but it's difficult to specify formally.

Because the math becomes very messy very quickly with complicated differential equations, economists have generally avoided the issue of time dependency in the models we present students. But many economists believe such issues are fundamentally important and that models that do not incorporate path dependency miss many of the important aspects of economic events. For example, in answering the question why the unemployment rate in Europe exceeds 10 percent in the mid-1990s, these economists would say that the answer can be understood only by considering the events of the 1980s leading to it. History becomes central when path dependency exists, and you can understand where we are only by knowing where we've been.

Conclusion

We'll stop here. As you can see, the algebra necessary to deal with even simple relationships can become complicated quickly. That's one of the main reasons many bright students have so much trouble with algebra, and math in general. Their minds intuitively picture a set of very complicated interrelationships, and far exceed the algebraic relationships that are allowed given the assumptions. They are on a higher dimension and they simply can't make the jump from reality to the simple algebra used in the models to describe that reality.

So we strongly urge you to study the formal models in economics for what they are—and to deal with them on their own terms. If you do that, learning them will be a lot easier. If you want formal models that truly correspond to reality and our minds' picture of it, we suggest you learn a lot more math than we cover in this book.

Problems

1. Consider an economy described by the following set of equations. Wages and prices are fixed.

(1) $C = C_0 + c_1 Y$
(2) $I = I_0$
(3) $G = G_0$
(4) $X = X_0$
(5) $M = M_0$
(6) $Y = C + I + G + (X - M)$

where
 $c_1 = 1/3$; $C_0 = \$300$ billion; $I_0 = \$100$ billion; $G_0 = \$50$ billion;
 $X_0 = \$60$ billion; $M_0 = \$75$ billion.

What is the equilibrium level of income (Y)?

2. Consider the decision of a firm that wants to hold costs down. Its production function can be expressed as

(1) $2z - x - 2y = 6,$

where x and y are inputs to the product z. The inputs must be added in the following ratio: $x/2 + y/2 = 12$ and x can be no greater than 12. In other words, the production function is subject to the following constraints:

(2) $x/2 + y/2 = 12$; and

(3) $x \leq 12$.

What is the maximum amount of z the firm is able to produce?

Answers to In-Text Questions

1. $X = (a_1 b_2 + a_2 b_1)/(b_1 + b_2); P = (a_2 - a_1)/(b_1 + b_2)$.

2

Geometric Tools and Economics

Perhaps the most used branch of mathematics in introductory economics is geometry. Graphs facilitate our understanding of economic relationships. In your textbook you have a brief introduction to graphish, a small portion of geometry. Before we go further, let us consider where geometry fits into mathematics.

Geometry is a branch of a broader area of study in mathematics called topology. *Topology* includes the study of number theory, set theory and the functional and visual representation of numbers and sets. Geometry is a small part of that visual presentation of numbers and sets. In lay terms, *geometry* is the study of relationships exhibited through shapes and pictures. This means that geometry gives us a way to consider pictures of the functions that we discussed in the last chapter. In this chapter we show you what some of those pictures look like and how they can be related to the various curves discussed in the text.

Polynomials

A function relates two or more variables in a specific way. The relationship between two variables x and y is generally specified by $y = f(x)$. A common functional form is the *polynomial* which can be specified in general terms by the expression:

(1) $$y = a_n x^n + a_{n-1} x^{n-1} + \ldots\ldots\ldots + a_1 x^1 + a_0,$$

where n determines its degree, a_0 is a constant and all other a's are coefficients of respective x's.

As introduced in the previous chapter, functions are usually categorized by their highest exponent, n. When $n = 1$, the polynomial is called a *linear function* and is specified by $y = a_0 + a_1 x$. When $n = 2$, the polynomial is called a *quadratic function* and is specified by $y = a_0 + a_1 x + a_2 x^2$. When $n = 3$, the functional form $y = a_0 + a_1 x + a_2 x^2 + a_3 x^3$.

13

Terminology of a Graph

Functions can be represented by graphs (or pictures) defined by axes. *Axes* are just number lines that are perpendicular to one another to produce an n-space. Two axes define 2-space. Functions with 3 variables need three axes and can be fully drawn only in 3-space. Three-dimensional and higher-number space are discussed later in this chapter. To draw a picture of a function, just place a dot at all points that are in the solution set of that function. For functions with two variables, each dot represents a set of ordered pairs and can be determined by selecting values of one variable and solving for the other.

Linear Functions

With a linear function, if a_1 is positive then the line represented by the function is upward sloping; if a_1 is negative then it is downward sloping. A linear demand curve can be written as a linear function.

An example of a linear functional form is $y = 6 + 6x$. The solution to this function includes the set of ordered pairs, or points on the x-y grid, (0, 6), (-1, 0), and (1, 12); each of these ordered pairs balances or makes both sides of the equation $y = 6 + 6x$ equal. We can easily graph this function, and we do this below.

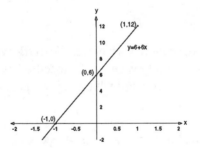

Figure 2.1

Figure 2.1 is the visual picture of our equation $y = 6 + 6x$. It is a simple straight line that passes through the point (-1,0) on the x-axis and (0,6) on the y-axis. Note that the slope of the line is 6 and the y-intercept in this case is also 6. If a_1 were negative, the slope would be negative.

Graphs of Quadratic Functions

Graphs of equations with degree greater than 1, ($n > 1$) are not so simple and start behaving strangely especially when x is negative. The shape of this general form depends on the signs and sizes of the a parameters. If all a's are positive then it is U-shaped.

An example of a quadratic function is the equation $y = 6 + 6x - x^2$. This is just a specific form of equation (1) with $a_0 = 6$, $a_1 = 6$ and $a_2 = -1$. Notice this function just adds the term $-x^2$ to the linear equation $6 + 6x$ we chose earlier. How does this change the picture we drew? Before we draw a picture, let us see what happens as we change the value of the x variable. For simplicity, consider only the positive quadrant or only the positive values for the variables x and y.

When $\quad x = 0, \quad y = 6 + 6(0) -(0)^2 \ = \ 6,$
when $\quad x = 1, \quad y = 6 + 6(1) -(1)^2 \ = \ 11,$
when $\quad x = 2, \quad y = 6 + 6(2) -(2)^2 \ = \ 14,$ and
when $\quad x = 3, \quad y = 6 + 6(3) -(3)^2 \ = \ 15.$

When we try to draw a picture with the combination of points $(0, 6)$, $(1, 11)$, $(2, 14)$ and $(3, 15)$, we cannot draw a straight line that passes through all these points. When we add the square term $-x^2$ to our linear equation, the picture now has a gentle upward curve as shown in Figure 2.2. What happens as we move to $x = 4$ and $x = 5$?

When $\quad x = 4, \quad y = 6 + 6(4) -(4)^2 \ = \ 14,$ and
when $\quad x = 5, \quad y = 6 + 6(5) -(5)^2 \ = \ 9.$

Did you notice what just happened? Beyond $x = 3$, the value of y seems to get smaller and smaller. Figure 2.2 shows the picture for $y = 6 + 6x - x^2$, for the set of points $(0,6)$, $(1, 11)$, $(2, 14)$, $(3, 15)$, $(4, 14)$ and $(5, 9)$. We can connect these points only by means of a freehand curve as shown below.

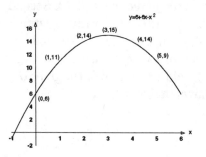

Figure 2.2

As you can see, when we add the square term $-x^2$ the resultant picture Figure 2.2, is quite different from the linear picture in Figure 2.1. The y-intercept is still 6, but when we begin to increase the value of x, the value of y increases along a curve up to a point. The curve reaches its highest point when $x = 3$. Beyond $x = 3$, the value of y drops, causing our functional form to slope downward. Adding the term $-x^2$ to our function gives the graph the shape of an *inverted U- shaped curve*.

Exercise 1: Graph the quadratic $y = 6 + 6x + x^2$ for all values of x. Confirm that the picture you get now is not an inverted-U but just a simple U-shaped curve. (Plot the graph for both positive and negative values of x.)

To give you an idea of how shapes and pictures change in geometry, let us consider another form of the quadratic function. Consider the equation $y = x^2$. Again, this is a polynomial of order 2 (i.e. $n = 2$). But with $a_0 = 0$, $a_1 = 0$ and $a_2 = 1$, the function is reduced to just $y = x^2$.

When $\quad x = 0, \quad y = (0)^2 \ = \ 0,$
when $\quad x = 1, \quad y = (1)^2 \ = \ 1,$ and
when $\quad x = 2, \quad y = (2)^2 \ = \ 4.$

Thus we have a set of points for (x, y) which include the pairs $(0, 0)$, $(1, 1)$ and $(2, 4)$. What would happen if we considered negative values of the variable x?

When $\quad x = -1, \quad y = (-1)^2 \ = \ 1,$ and
when $\quad x = -2, \quad y = (-2)^2 \ = \ 4.$

Note two things with this quadratic form. One, there is no intercept term and the equation passes through the point $(0, 0)$. Second, the square term, x^2, converts any negative x-terms into positive y-terms. The quadratic, $y = x^2$, is a curve which is symmetrical about the y axis, i.e., both negative and positive integer values of x give us the same y integer value. For example both $x = 3$ and $x = -3$ yield a y-value of 9. The graph of $y = x^2$ is a symmetrical *U-shaped curve* shown in Figure 2.3

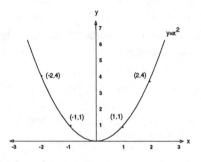

Figure 2.3

Exercise 2: Graph the function y = 6 - 6x - x² for all values of x and show that it is also U-shaped.

Cubic and Higher Level Polynomials

In the course of your study of economics you will often come across other higher-order forms of equation (1). Consider a slight variation of the linear and quadratic functions we have considered so far. The equation $y = 6 + 6x - 6x^2 + x^3$ is an example of a cubic ($n = 3$) functional form. Once again observe that this is but a specific form of our general polynomial (1), with $a_0 = 6$ and $a_1 = 6, a_2 = -6, a_3 = 1$ and $n = 3$. Its picture for positive x's is shown in Figure 2.4 below.

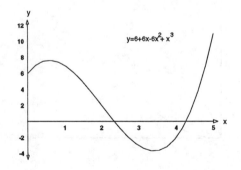

Figure 2.4

When we add a cube term ($+x^3$ in this case) the curve has some dips in it. Thus, it is unlike the quadratic function where we observed a U-shape or inverted U-shape. We get an inverted U-shape initially, but as the value of x increases, y decreases to a point as it did with the quadratic form and then again begins to increase. It is as if we have two parts to the picture, an initial inverted U followed by an attached U shape. Cubic functions often take on the shape. As with the linear and quadratic functions, the y-intercept is once again 6. The function then steadily rises, reaches a maximum (a maximum within a range of x values) and begins to decline until it reaches a minimum after which it begins to rise once again. After that it rises indefinitely.

Exercise 3: Confirm on graph paper that the picture for the cubic equation $y = 6 + 6x - 6x^2 + x^3$ is indeed as we have drawn it above.

We'll stop there, but we could present fourth and fifth-order equations. If we did, the results would be more and more squiggly curves. (In statistics you will learn that the degrees of freedom decrease as the order of the functional form used to fit the curve increases; that's because they are more squiggly and can accommodate points that are out of line. In the limit five (or n) points can be perfectly fit to a fourth-order (or n-1) polynomial).

The Geometry of Cost and Revenue Curves

In the textbook, the total revenue and total cost curves of a firm looked like those shown in Figure 2.5, while the marginal cost and average cost curves were like those in Figure 2.6.

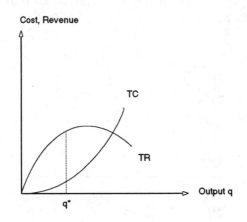

Figure 2.5

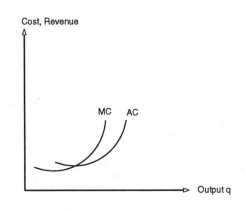

Figure 2.6

What functional forms would give us curves that look like the cost and revenue curves drawn in Figures 2.5 and 2.6? Let us define q as the units of output produced by a firm. If you carefully graph the cubic function $q^3 - 8q^2 + 40q$, it would look similar to the total cost curve (TC) drawn in Figure 2.5. Similarly, a quadratic functional form such as $45q - 3q^2$ would look very much like the U-shaped total revenue curve (TR) drawn above.

When specifying total revenue and total cost functions, we generally use cubic rather than quadratic equations. The reason has to do with getting the marginal cost curve to look like what we have drawn in Figure 2.6. As we will discuss in the calculus review in the next chapter, marginal cost is derived by taking the first derivative of the total cost function. Taking the derivative of a function reduces its order by one, so if we want a U-shaped marginal cost curve, the function representing marginal costs has to be quadratic which requires a cubic total cost curve. Since we're not so picky about the shape of the marginal revenue curve, we can use quadratic total revenue functions. That gives us a straight-line marginal revenue curve.

Often one has an average, not a total cost, function and a demand curve which is an average revenue function. No problem: by multiplying average costs or average revenue by quantity we can change those average cost and revenue functions into total cost and total revenue functions. That's because by definition, $AC = TC/q$.

Once we know the total cost equation ($TC = q^3 - 8q^2 + 40q$, in this case), the marginal cost and average cost curves can now be easily sketched for different values of output.

Exercise 4: Sketch the AC and MC curves for output levels 1 to 6 for the above TC equation and confirm that the shape of the curve is indeed as shown above.

The Profit Function

The firm is interested in making maximum profits. Profits are just the difference between the total revenue the firm makes and its total costs. If we define profits as Π, then $\Pi = TR - TC$. Any time the firm's revenue exceeds its cost, it makes a profit. But there is usually only one level of output q where the firm makes the maximum possible profit. Geometrically, this occurs when the vertical distance between TR and TC in Figure 2.5 is largest, which is at an output level q^*. One can determine q^* and the resulting profit at q^* by carefully plotting the cubic and quadratic equations on graph paper; however, this is a tedious and inaccurate method which is seldom used. Instead we generally use calculus to determine the profit maximizing position. We'll talk specifically about calculus and its uses in the next chapter. The application of calculus to cost and revenue curves is dealt with in Chapter 15 of this text. In this chapter we are just exposing you to shapes of curves that you are likely to come across in economic problems.

Other Functional Forms

Although the quadratic and cubic functional forms are among the most common functional forms you are likely to come across in your study of economics, there are other useful forms, and in this next section we take a moment to look at some of these.

The Rectangular Hyperbola

The polynomials discussed above all had the x variable in the numerator of the equation. Another functional form that is often seen in economics is a rectangular hyperbola. It occurs when the x variable is in the denominator of the equation. The equation $y = a/x$ where a is a constant greater than zero is the general form of a rectangular hyperbola.

The equation $y = 6/x$ is an example of a rectangular hyperbola. This may also be written with x and y both on the left-hand side as $xy = 6$. Before we draw the graph of our equation, think about how the value of y changes as x changes. As we increase the value of the variable x, y becomes smaller and smaller. Why? Because the numerator is a constant 6 which never changes. If we continue dividing the number six by larger and larger numbers, the value of y becomes smaller and smaller. The value of y comes close to zero as x becomes larger although it never quite becomes zero. In mathematics we refer to this as *asymptotically* approaching zero. Hence the graph of $y = 6/x$ takes the form shown below.

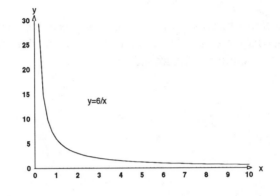

Figure 2.7

An asymptotic curve comes close to the x-axis but never touches it. Similarly as y becomes larger, x approaches zero but never quite touches the y-axis. It appears to become nearly parallel to the y-axis. Nonlinear demand curves are often expressed as rectangular hyperbolas. For example a demand curve showing the relation between price, P, and quantity demanded, Q, may be specified by the equation $P = 6/Q$, which would have the same shape as the curve in Figure 2.7.

Exponential and Logarithmic Functions

Two final functional relations which we sometimes come across in principles of economics are the *exponential function* and the *logarithmic functions*. The general form of the exponential function is $y = a^x$. The general form of the logarithmic function is $y = \log_a x$. The exponential function differs from the functions that we have seen so far in one main respect. The x variable is in neither the denominator nor the numerator of the equation, but is expressed as a *power* of the constant term. What do we mean by *power*? Consider a specific exponential function, $y = 10^x$. When $x = 1$, y is 10 raised to the power 1, which is 10 When $x = 2$, y is now 10 raised to the power 2 or 10 squared, which is 100. The table below gives us the values for x and y in the solution set of this exponential function.

x	y
0	$10^0 = 1$
1	$10^1 = 10$
2	$10^2 = 100$
3	$10^3 = 1000$

Notice that as x increases, the value of y begins to increase rapidly and becomes much larger relative to the value of y. If you plot this on a graph the picture will look similar to Figure 2.8.

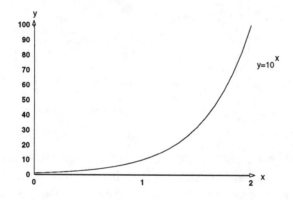

Figure 2.8

The logarithmic function $y = \log_a x$ is referred to in mathematics as the *inverse* of the exponential function we just described. For example the inverse of $y = a^x$ is $x = a^y$. All we have done is replace the x by y and vice versa in the exponential function. Instead of writing the logarithmic function as $x = a^y$, it is most commonly written as $y = \log_a x$. In words, this is read as the logarithm in base a of a number x.

The inverse of our exponential function $y = 10^x$ is therefore simply $x = 10^y$, which is more easily written as $y = \log_{10} x$. The equation $y = \log_{10} x$ is an example of a logarithmic function in base 10. The relationship between x and y for the logarithmic function is exactly the opposite of the exponential relation. As x increases, y increases as well but in very small increments. The graph of $y = \log_{10} x$ is shown in Figure 2.9. Observe that the exponential and logarithmic functions are merely mirror images of each other through the line $y = x$.

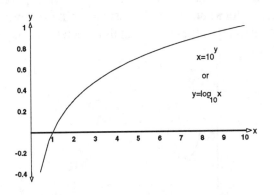

Figure 2.9

Exercise 5: For the logarithmic function $y = \log_{10}x$, determine the values of y as x increases from 1 to 10, using a scientific calculator. Plot the values for x and y and confirm the shape of the logarithmic function drawn above.

Visualizing Pictures in Three or More Dimensions

Our discussion so far has concerned two-dimensional graphs in which we can see the relationship between two variables. But what if we had three related variables? Then we would need a three-dimensional graph, as in Figure 2.10 below.

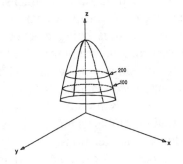

Figure 2.10

You have to be an artist (or have a good computer program) to draw three-dimensional graphs and most economists aren't good artists. But by using a trick we can visualize three-dimensional shapes through a variety of two-dimensional relationships.

Consider the following curves in Figure 2.11 which represent levels of equal satisfaction for a consumer. A consumer is indifferent between points A and B. (We'll analyze these in much more detail in Chapter 13.)

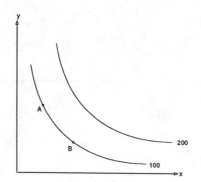

Figure 2.11

These curves could be seen as a two-dimensional "cut" of the three-dimensional mountain in Figure 2.10. Similarly the second curve, labeled 200, could be seen as a higher slice.

By looking at the various slices in two dimensions we can get a full sense of what the three-dimensional mountain looks like in two dimensions.

The same general argument holds for four dimensions. By picturing ourselves taking a slice of a four-dimensional object we can visualize three-dimensional objects as slices of those four-dimensional objects. And by taking a slice of a slice, we can in principle visualize n-dimensional objects.

Such many-dimensional stuff is for higher level courses. We mention it here because we will be using the technique a lot to reduce three-dimensional relationships into two-dimensional graphs. Thus, indifference curves and isoquants used in microeconomics to study production, and IS/LM analysis used in macroeconomics to study the effect of monetary and fiscal policy, will all use variations of this technique. They are two-dimensional projections of three-dimensional relationships.

The issue is more general. For example, the demand curves that have been introduced to you in your textbook specify an inverse relation between only two variables, price and quantity. A more complete demand curve may, however, be one in which quantity demanded is influenced not only by price but also by other variables, which in the textbook we called *shift variables*. Consider, for example, the demand curve

$$Q_d = 20 - 20\,P + 0.1Y + 3P_s + 4T + 0.5E,$$

where P is the price of the good, Y is income, P_s is the price of a substitute good, T is taste and E is expectations. This demand curve has six variables and is of course difficult if not impossible to represent geometrically. To get the demand curve presented in the textbook we assume that all other variables except for price and quantity are held constant. This leaves us with a two-dimensional graph. Suppose, for example, that we are told that income $Y = \$200$, the price of the substitute good P_s is \$3.00, tastes are quantified as $T = 10$, and a qualification of expectations of $E = 100$. The demand curve now reduces to $Q_d = 99 - 20P$, which can be easily graphed.

Therein lies a significant limitation of two-dimensional geometric interpretations of economic problems. If other variables change, the curves are shifting all over the place. Consequently, in economics as in other sciences, we have to be cautious in our interpretation of the equilibrium concept emerging from such a multivariate n-dimensional space.

Conclusion

That last discussion gets pretty esoteric, but recognizing the limited dimensionality of our two-dimensional graphs helps to keep them in perspective. Often we extend our reasoning in two dimensions to n-dimensional reality, forgetting to add back the other dimensions before we apply the analysis to reality. That's a mistake. Alfred Marshall, the economist who made supply and demand analysis central to economics, was clear that his analysis is two-dimensional and that it is important to keep all other dimensions in the back of one's mind. We urge you to follow in Marshall's footsteps.

Problems

1. Draw a picture of the quadratic function $y = x^2 - 9x + 12$, for positive values of x. Does this quadratic have the U-shaped property associated with quadratic functional forms? If x is the output produced by a firm, is it likely that this function could describe the total cost curve of a firm? Why or why not?

2. Sketch the graph of the cubic function $y = 2x^3 - 12x^2 + 50$, for x values 0, 1, 2, 3, 4 and 5. At which point (x, y) does the curve reach its maximum? At which point does it reach a minimum?

Answers to In-Text Questions

1. To graph this equation select values of x and solve for y. We do this for whole numbers $-6 \leqslant x \leqslant 0$. The solution set of the equation includes the points (-6, 6), (-5, 1), (-4, -2), (-3, -3), (-2, -2), (-1, 1), (0,6). Graphing these points, we see that the curve representing this equation is a simple U with a minimum at -3.

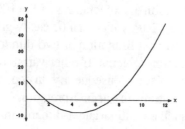

It is no mistake that we included -3 in the sample for x. Using some calculus presented in the next chapter we knew that -3 was the only minimum of this function.

2. We select values of x and solve for y. We do this for whole numbers $-6 \leqslant x \leqslant 0$. The solution set of the equation includes the points (-6, 6), (-5, 11), (-4, 14), (-3, 15), (-2, 14), (-1, 11), and (0,6). Graphing these points, we see that the curve representing this equation is an inverted U-shape with a maximum at -3.

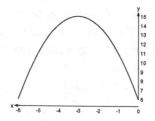

3. Select values for x and solve for y. We do this for whole numbers $0 \leqslant x \leqslant 5$. The solution set of the equation includes the points (0, 6), (1, 7), (2, 2), (3, -3), (4, -2), and (5, 11). Graphing these points we see that, indeed, the graph is as presented in the text.

4. The marginal cost curve in this case is $3q^2 - 16q + 40$ and the average cost curve is $q^2 - 8q + 40$. The solution set for the marginal cost curve for values $1 \leqslant q \leqslant 6$ is (1, 27), (2, 20), (3, 19), (4, 24), (5, 35), (6, 52). The solution set for the average cost curve for the same range values for q is (1, 33), (2, 28), (3, 25), (4, 24), (5, 25), and (6, 28). They have the expected shapes. Notice that the marginal cost curve cuts the average cost curve at the minimum of the average cost curve from below.

5. The solution set for the function $y = \log_{10} x$ for values of x from 1 to 10 is (1, 0), (2, .30), (3, .48), (4, .60), (5, .70), (6, .78), (7, .85), (8, .90), (9, .95), and (10, 1). Graphing these points we see that, indeed, the graph is as presented in the text.

3

Calculus and Economics

The economic decision rule discussed in the textbook focused on the concepts of marginal benefits and marginal costs. If marginal benefits exceed marginal costs, do it, if marginal costs exceed marginal benefits, don't. This marginal analysis forms the core of neoclassical economics, and is at the heart of the mainstream analysis of both the consumer and the producer. Marginal analysis is closely related to a branch of mathematics known as calculus, and, not surprisingly, both developed around the same time. As economists became adept at calculus, they used it to frame their analysis. But the neoclassical framework has limitations that are imposed upon it by calculus. In particular, it cannot consider decisions that are not marginal decisions; often the conditions necessary to apply the neoclassical marginal rule do not hold. To really understand the limitations, as well as the strengths of microeconomic analysis, one must understand the underlying calculus.

Differentials

Calculus is *the systematic consideration of the rates of changes of functions.* In this chapter we focus on *differential calculus*—that branch of calculus which considers the effects of the rates of changes in functions. Another branch is *integral calculus* which reverses the process: given the rates of changes, one must determine the function. Here we will stick to differential calculus. The *derivative function,* a function that measures responses to changes, is an important tool for the study of economics. For example, consider the utility function, $U(x)$. What is the change in utility that results from a change in x? In this case, the derivative would relate the change in x with the change in U.

Limits and Continuity

The derivative function can be applied only to a limited set of functions. In particular, to be differentiable, a function must be continuous and smooth over the relevant range. To be differentiable, (1) the function must be defined at all points, (2) the function must have a limit at all points and (3) the limits from the left and the right must equal the value of the function at each point. In a calculus course you spend much of the initial part of the course discussing limits and continuity of functions. Where there is no continuity, calculus doesn't apply. For example, say we had the function

$$y = 1 - 1/x.$$

Notice that the y value approaches infinity as x approaches 0 from the left. The function is not defined at 0. The first condition of continuity is not met, so the function is not differentiable at $x = 0$ and there is no calculus to apply.

Consider another function $y = |x - 4|$. (The lines around a number mean absolute value which means you change the sign of the number inside to be positive.) This function is graphed below.

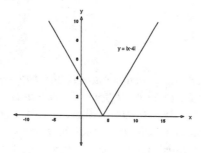

Figure 3.1

The function is defined and continuous at all points, but is not everywhere differentiable. That is true because at 4, the limits as the function approaches 4 from the right and from the left do not equal the value of the function at 4. The third condition is violated so the function is not differentiable at $x = 4$.

Terminology

In our discussion of functions in the last chapter we emphasized that the type of functions we would consider are continuous over the relevant range. This means that we can talk about a differential calculus for these functions. We will stick with those here (which is why we don't spend much time on limits and continuity). Thus we focus on appropriately limited cubic and quadratic functions of the form

$$y = f(x).$$

Although the derivative function is related to the old function, it is an entirely new function with characteristics of its own. Generally the concept *change in* is written with a *d* (which comes from the Greek letter D (delta, Δ) which in mathematics represents *change in*:

$$dy = df/dx.$$

Another way to write a derivative function is by $f'(x)$, which is read as *f prime of x* or *y'* (*y prime*).

Rules of Differentiation

To simplify the application of the derivative function to another function, mathematicians have developed a whole set of rules. These rules apply the general concept to create a whole set of new functions. We don't have enough space to go through all of these rules in this book, so we'll just review the central ones to jog your memory. If you don't remember seeing them before, it's probably best to get some help. We are assuming that you are already familiar with the general ideas.

1. *Differentiation of a Constant*
Suppose the functional relationship is $Y = K$, where K is a constant. Then $dY/dx = 0$. (e.g. $Y = 4$, $dY/dx = 0$).

2. *Differentiation of Power Terms*
Suppose the functional relationship is $Y = x^n$, then $dY/dx = nx^{n-1}$ (e.g. $Y = x^5$, $dY/dx = 5x^4$).

3. Differentiation of Sums and Differences
If $Y = h(x) + g(x)$, then $dY/dx = dh(x)/dx + dg(x)/dx$ (e.g. $Y = 3x + x^2$, $dY/dx = 3 + 2x$).

4. Differentiation of a Product
If $Y = h(x) \cdot g(x)$ then $dY/dx = h(x) \, dg(x)/dx + g(x) \, dh(x)/dx$ (e.g. $Y = (4x+3)$ $(5x)$, $dY/dx = (4x+3)(5) + (5x)(4) = 20x + 15 + 20x = 40x + 15$).

5. Differentiation of a Quotient
If $Y = h(x)/g(x)$, then $dY/dx = \{g(x) \cdot [dh(x)/dx] - h(x) \cdot [dg(x)/dx]\}/g(x)^2$. (e.g. $Y = (5x + 1)/4x$, then $dY/dx = [4x(5) - (5x+1)4]/16x^2$).

6. Differentiation of a Negative Power
If $Y = x^{-n}$, then $dY/dx = -nx^{-n-1}$ (e.g. $Y = x^{-5}$, $dY/dx = -5x^{-6}$).

7. Differentiation of a Function of a Function (The Chain Rule)
Suppose $Y = h/2$ and $h = x/4$, then $dY/dx = (dY/dh)(dh/dx) = (1/2)(1/4) = 1/8$.

Some Standard Results of Differentiation

Certain types of general functions have relatively simple derivatives which are hard to derive but once known, can prove useful. Two of these are the log and exponential functions which have the following derivatives:

Logarithmic: If $Y = \ln x$, $dY/dx = 1/x$.

Exponential: If $Y = e^x$, $dY/dx = e^x$.

An Example

Just to make sure you can apply the rules of differentiation, here is an example. Let's determine the derivative of the following function:

$$Y = (x^7 + 5x^5)/(3x^2 + 5x).$$

To find the first derivative, we use the quotient rule:

$$dY/dx = [(3x^2 + 5x)(7x^6 + 25x^4) - (x^7 + 5x^5)(6x + 5)]/(3x^2 + 5x)^2.$$

And multiply out and collect like terms:

$$dY/dx = (15x^8 + 30x^7 + 45x^6 + 100x^5)/(3x^2 + 5x)^2.$$

Exercise 1: Find the first derivative of the function, $f(x) = (5x^2 - x^3)^4$.

An Economic Application

One of the concepts that you will use while studying the theory of consumer demand is the concept of *elasticity*. It is a measure of how responsive changes in one variable are to changes in another variable. For example, the price elasticity of demand is the percentage change in quantity demanded divided by the percentage change in price; i.e., if price of a product changes by 1%, does quantity demanded change by more than, less than or equal to 1%?

We write the price elasticity of demand as

$$E_d = \%\Delta Q/\%\Delta P.$$

The percentage change in Q (and P) can be written using a derivative as dQ/Q (and dP/P), so E_d can be written as

$$(dQ/Q)/(dP/P),$$

which can be further written as

$$d\ln Q/d\ln P.$$

Higher-Order Differentiation

The derivative function can be applied more than once. Consider the following functional relationship, $Y = x^7$. Measuring the rate of change in Y due to a small change in x, we differentiate to get $dY/dx = 7x^6$. If we differentiate this expression again, we get $d/dx\,(7x^6) = 42x^5$. In calculus, this expression is called the *second derivative* of Y. Given $Y = f(x)$, the second derivative tells us how the change in the function Y' changes in response to changes in x. We can continue to take third, fourth differentials, until we get the derivative of a constant which will be zero. If $Y = f(x)$, then derivatives are denoted by $f'(x)$ for the first derivative, $f''(x)$ for the second derivative and so on.

Higher-order derivatives are also important in economics. For example, in production functions, we are interested not only in marginal products (first derivative of total product) but also in whether marginal products are rising or falling (second derivative of total product).

Exercise 2: Find the first, second and third derivatives of the function, f(x) = x⁴ + 5x²+ 10.

Graphical Depiction of Derivatives

The derivative of a function at a point can be graphically shown by the slope of the line that is tangent to the curve at that point. We won't prove that to you here. Just keep in mind that the derivative and the slope of a line tangent to the function share the same formula.

The Nature of Functions and the Sign of Derivatives

To give you a visual sense of what calculus is telling us, look at the six figures below. In the Figure 3.2a, y decreases as x increases. This is shown mathematically as $f'(x) < 0$. Further, the change in y remains constant, so $f'(x)$ is some constant less than zero. Alternatively, Figure 3.2b shows a function in which y rises as x increases, and at a constant rate. Here $f'(x)$ is positive and constant. In Figure 3.2c, y increases as x increases, but here the rate of increase increases as x increases; that is, $f'(x) > 0$ and $f''(x) > 0$. Alternatively looking at Figure 3.2d, we see a function in which y increases with an increase in x, but the incremental increase in y falls as x rises. Thus, while $f'(x) > 0$, $f''(x) < 0$. The first derivative of the function tells us the direction of the value of a function whereas the second derivative tells us its shape in that direction.

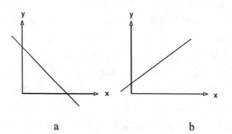

a   b

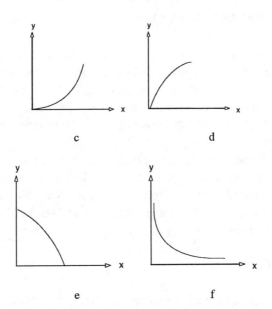

c   d

e   f

Figure 3.2(a-f)

Exercise 3: Explain Figures 3.2e and 3.2f in terms of derivatives.

We can summarize the possible cases as following:

If $f'(x) > 0$ and $f''(x) = 0$, then the value of the function is increasing at a constant rate as x increases.

If $f'(x) < 0$ and $f'(x) = 0$, then the value of function is decreasing at a constant rate as x increases.

If $f'(x) > 0$ and $f''(x) > 0$, then the value of the function is increasing at an increasing rate as x increases.

If $f'(x) > 0$ and $f''(x) < 0$, then the value of function is increasing at a decreasing rate as x increases.

If $f'(x) < 0$ and $f''(x) < 0$ then the value of the function is decreasing at a decreasing rate as x increases.

If $f'(x) < 0$ and $f''(x) > 0$ then the value of the function is decreasing at an increasing rate as x increases.

Optimization of Functions

Economic decisions frequently involve getting the most for as little as possible, or using the least to get a specified amount. The techniques of calculus, of optimization or finding an optimum value for a function, is fundamental to economics. *Optimization* basically implies maximizing or minimizing a function—finding that point at which the function is at its highest (or lowest) point.

Here are some examples: A consumer maximizes utility, a producer maximizes profits or sales, a government maximizes revenue from taxes or welfare for its citizens; A firm minimizes costs. The two assumptions of rationality and self-interest dictate maximizing and minimizing behavior—behavior of the *homo economicus* or the *economic person*.

First-Order Conditions

Economists constantly deal with functions that rise and fall. In considering these functions, they are interested in finding out the maximum or minimum values of various functions, be they utility, production or cost functions. Derivatives can be used to determine the maximum or minimum values of a continuous function. Mathematically, to find the maximum or minimum value of a function, take the derivative, set it equal to zero and solve for x. This is called the *first-order* or *necessary condition* for maximum or a minimum.

Let's consider two continuous functions:

(1) $$y = x^2 - 4x + 2,$$

(2) $$y = -x^2 + 4x + 2.$$

Taking the first derivatives of equations (1) and (2) respectively we get

$$y' = 2x - 4,$$

$$y' = -2x + 4.$$

Setting these equal to 0 we can solve for x and find that the optimum values of both functions is at $x = 2$.

To see whether these are maxima or minima, we can draw the curves and observe. The functions are depicted in Figures 3.3a and 3.3b respectively.

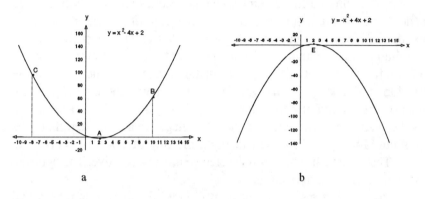

a   b

Figure 3.3(a, b)

Notice that function $y = x^2 - 4x + 2$ is at a minimum when $x = 2$ and function $y = -x^2 + 4x + 2$ is at a maximum when $x = 2$.

Why does setting the first derivative equal to zero work to find the maximum or minimum? Because the derivative of a function tells us how much the value of that function is changing. At the maximum or minimum points, the value of a function is not changing.

You can see this graphically by remembering that the derivative of a function is the tangent to the curve at the relevant point. Consider point C in Figure 3.3a, $x = -8$. Here $f'(x) = -20$, a negative value, so we know the function is decreasing. B is not a minimum or maximum point because at B, $x = 10$, $f'(x) = 16$, a positive value; the value of the function is increasing. At A, $x = 2$, however, $f'(x) = 0$. Here, the slope of the tangent is zero; y does not change with a change in x. Logically, when the first derivative of a function equals zero, the function must be either at a maximum or a minimum.

Second-Order Conditions

Setting the first derivative equal to zero ensures that we have either a maximum or minimum, but it doesn't tell us which. One way to find out is to draw the picture as we did above to see that the function shown in Figure 3.3a has a minimum at $x = 2$ and function in Figure 3.3b has a maximum at $x = 2$. Another is to substitute in numbers right around the point where the first derivative equals zero.

Both these methods can be a pain, and an easier way exists: see whether the second derivative is greater or less than zero. If it's greater than zero, you have a minimum; if it's less than zero, you have a maximum.

Why does this work? Remember that the second derivative is the change in the change of a function, or a change in the slope of a function. Since the first derivative is zero, the slope at that point is zero and the point is either a minimum or a maximum. For that optimum to be a minimum, all values to the left or the right of that point must be higher than the value of the function at that point. For the values to the left and right to be higher, the function must be falling from the left and rising to the right. That is, the first derivative of the function to the left is negative and to the right of the optimum is positive. From left to right, the first derivative is becoming larger. That means the change in the change must be positive. The opposite argument goes for a maximum.

In graphical terms, for point A in Figure 3.3a to be a minimum, all points to the left and right of A must be higher than A. The slope must be negative to the left and positive to the right. For that to happen, the slope must always be rising. Again, in terms of derivatives, the second derivative is positive.

To summarize the first and second-order conditions, an optimum is found where

$$f'(x) = 0.$$

The optimum is a maximum if

$$f''(x) < 0.$$

The optimum is a minimum if

$$f''(x) > 0.$$

These are called *second-order* or *sufficient conditions*. They tell us whether we are at a maximum or a minimum.

An Example

Let's go through an example. Suppose $y = x^3 - 3x + 1$. Does this function have a maximum or a minimum? If so, what is it? To answer this, take the first derivative of $f(x)$:

$$f'(x) = 3x^2 - 3.$$

Set it equal to zero and solve for x, to get

$$3x^2 = 3 \text{ or } x = \pm 1.$$

To differentiate between the maximum or minimum values, apply the second-order condition. First take the second derivative of $f(x)$:

$$f''(x) = 6x.$$

Next assess the second derivative at the possible minimum and maximum points. At $x = -1, f''(x) = -6 < 0$, and at $x = 1, f''(x) = 6 > 0$. To find the exact value of the function at the optimum values, substitute 1 and -1 into the original function. Thus the function has a minimum value of -1 at $x = 1$ and maximum value of 3 at $x = -1$. We can graph the function and see that this is indeed the case. We do this in Figure 3.4.

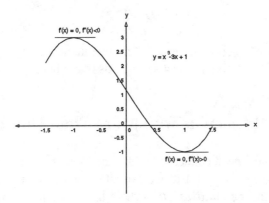

Figure 3.4

Exercise 4: Does the function y = x³ - 4x² + 9 have a minimum or maximum? If so where?

An Economic Example

Now let's go through an economic example. A demand function is of the form

$$P = 60 - Q,$$

where P is the market price for the product, and
 Q is the market output.

A firm's total revenue from sales is given by the expression

$$TR = PQ.$$

What is the firm's total revenue equation given the above demand equation? First, we must substitute P from the demand function into the total revenue function.

$$TR = 60Q - Q^2.$$

Next we set the derivative of this equation equal to zero and solve for Q:

$$dTR/dQ = 60 - 2Q = 0,$$

$$Q = 30.$$

This tells us that at $Q = 30$, TR is either at a maximum or a minimum. The second-order condition, $f''(Q) = -2$, tells us that where $Q = 30$, TR is at its maximum.

Differential Calculus with More Than One Variable

Thus far we have been concerned with functions of one independent variable, of the form $Y = f(x)$. But we can cite many examples in economics where functions are *multivariate*—where they depend on two or more independent variables: $Y = f(x_1, x_2,..., x_n)$. For example, a consumer's total utility is dependent not on the consumption of one good but on many goods and services. For the firm, production plans utilize multiple inputs. There are many other examples.

In these cases, we want to see how Y changes in response to changes in only one of many variables on the right-hand side. If we want to know how Y changes in response to a change in x_1, we would find the *partial derivative* of Y with respect to x_1. It is *partial* because the level of all other variables $(x_2, x_3,...,x_n)$ are held constant. The partial derivative is denoted with a ∂ (a lowercase Greek d) to distinguish it from derivative notation d. In particular, the partial derivative of the function $Y = f(x_1, x_2)$ with respect to x_1 holding x_2 constant would be denoted as $\partial Y/\partial x_1$. This can also be represented by Y_{x1}. Alternatively, to see how Y changes in response to a change in x_2 holding x_1 constant, we would find the partial derivative of Y with respect to x_2, $\partial Y/\partial x_2$. The same rules of differentiation apply here remembering that all other variables are treated as constants.

Taking partial derivatives relates to the discussion of reducing dimensions that we discussed in Chapter 2; a partial derivative gives us a sense of what's happening on one plane. By taking all partials we have a sense of a multidimensional relationship. The problem comes if the dimensions are interdependent so that a movement in one dimension changes the relationships in another dimension. Then the relationship we're picturing is constantly changing and drawing intuitive implications from calculus can be almost impossible.

An Economic Example

To see how calculus relates to economic issues let's consider a production example, in which the firm's output level depends not only on a labor input but also on a capital input. Thus,

$$Q = f(K,L).$$

The firm is interested in asking the question, what happens if it hires more workers given the existing capital stock? We seek the partial derivative of Q with respect to L: $\partial Q/\partial L$ or Q_L.

We specify the exact production function as

$$Q = 10L - 6K + 9KL.$$

Taking the partial derivative of Q with respect to L,

$$Q_L = 10 + 9K.$$

This tells us how much output will change with a given change in labor inputs, or the marginal product of labor. In this case, the first derivative is a constant: a unit change in labor inputs will produce the same increase in output no matter the current level of labor; the marginal product of labor is constant. A good exercise is to go through the same procedure for capital, K.

We can also find partial derivatives of a higher order which in this case tells us how the marginal products vary with respect to changes in that input or other inputs. For example, say

$$Q = L^3K.$$

The first partial derivative $Q_L = 3L^2K$ is greater than 0. The marginal product of labor is positive. The second partial of the function, i.e., the partial derivative of the first partial derivative, denoted by $Q_{LL} = 6LK > 0$, tells us that the marginal product is always increasing. You could also take the second partial derivative of L with respect to K: Q_{LK} which is known as a *cross partial*. It tells us how the marginal product of labor changes with respect to changes in capital inputs.

Total Differentiation

In the previous section, when we took partial derivatives, we held all other variables constant. But suppose both L and K changed, what happens to Q? For that we introduce a concept known as the *total differential*.

In our example, suppose the firm hires more machinery and more labor. $\partial Q/\partial L$ is the change in Q when there is small change in L, with K held constant. Suppose that L changes by a small amount, ΔL, the change in Q is

$$(\partial Q/\partial L) \cdot \Delta L.$$

Similarly the change in Q due to a change in K is

$$(\partial Q/\partial K) \cdot \Delta K.$$

Thus the total change in Q (or ΔQ) due to small changes in L and K is

$$\Delta Q = (\partial Q/\partial L) \cdot \Delta L + (\partial Q/\partial K) \cdot \Delta K.$$

Alternatively, when these small changes tend to approach zero,

$$dQ = (\partial Q/\partial L) \cdot dL + (\partial Q/\partial K) \cdot dK.$$

Total derivatives are useful when one wants to take into account all the interdependencies of dimensions.

Maxima and Minima of Multi-Variable Functions

With at least two independent variables, the graph of the function $Q = f(L,K)$ becomes a surface in three-dimensional space. You may refer back to the graphs drawn for a maximum and minimum in the one-variable case and visualize a three-dimensional hill or a trough respectively. We can write the first and second-order conditions for the multivariate case which are similar to the conditions we laid down for the univariate case.

To find a maximum or minimum of a function that is dependent upon two variables, you follow essentially the same procedure as in the univariate case. First solve the first-order conditions, $Q_L = Q_K = 0$, for values of both L and K. Second, assess the second-order conditions. If, $Q_{LL} < 0$, $Q_{KK} < 0$ and $(Q_{KL})^2 < Q_{KK} Q_{LL}$, then you have found a maximum. If $Q_{LL} > 0$, $Q_{KK} > 0$ and $(Q_{KL})^2 < Q_{KK} Q_{LL}$ then you have found a minimum.

An Example

Let's find the maximum or minimum of a function:

$$Z = 2Y^3 + 2Y^2 - 2XY + X^2 + 8.$$

First, we take the first derivative with respect to each variable and set the resulting equations to zero:

$$Z_Y = 6Y^2 + 4Y - 2X = 0,$$

$$Z_x = -2Y + 2X = 0.$$

We have two equations and two unknowns. Solving for X and Y we get possible mimima or maxima: (0,0) and (-1/3, -1/3).

To find out whether these are minima or maxima we must assess the second derivatives at these points. First take the second derivatives:

$$Z_{YY} = 12Y + 4,$$

$$Z_{XX} = 2,$$

$$Z_{YX} = -2.$$

Then assess at (0,0) and (-1/3, -1/3). We find that $Z_{YY}(0,0) = 4 > 0$. Further $Z_{XX} = 2 > 0$. Lastly, $(Z_{YX})^2 = 4 < Z_{YY} Z_{XX}$. This point (0,0) is a minimum. Z_{YY} (-1/3,-1/3) = 0 which means this point is neither a minimum nor a maximum.

We now have the basis for studying one of the most important tools used in microeconomics: maximization subject to constraints. This is only a minor subtopic in calculus and is often covered only in second semester courses, if at all. But it is central to economics and is a primary reason calculus is used so heavily in the study of economics.

Optimization: Maximization Subject to Constraints

When the maximization problem is the maximization of a function subject to a constraint—another function holding true—we have an optimization problem. The solution to the optimization problem belongs to the solution set of both functions. For example, a consumer has to maximize utility while satisfying his budget constraint; a firm has to maximize production while satisfying its cost constraint. A constraint typically narrows the domain of the function to be optimized.

For example, suppose a utility function is defined as a function of two goods:

no diminishing
marginal utility

$$U(x, y) = 3x4y.$$

A consumer wants to maximize utility, but is constrained by her budget. This constraint can be written as

$$P_x x + P_y y \leq M.$$

How much of each good will she purchase? The problem she faces is to maximize an *objective function*, $U(x,y)$, subject to a *constraint*, here a budget constraint, $P_x x + P_y y \leq M$.

Substitution Method

One way to find a solution to an optimization problem is first to solve the constraint for one good, say x, and substitute that into the objective function to create a combined function. Thus by substitution we change an optimization problem into a maximization problem and we are sure the solution will belong to the solution set of both the objective function and the constraint. Solving the budget constraint for x we get

$$x = (M - P_y y/P_x).$$

And substituting this into the objective function we get

$$U(x,y) = [(3M - 3P_y y)/P_x]4y.$$

Now, maximize the combined function by using the first and second-order conditions. The first derivative of $U(x,y)$ with respect to y is

$$U_y = 12M/P_x - 24P_y y/P_x.$$

Setting this equal to zero,

$$0 = 12M/P_x - 24P_y y/P_x.$$

Solving for y,

$$y = .5M/P_y.$$

Substituting back into the budget constraint and solving for x we get

$$x = .5M/P_x.$$

Second-order conditions require that we find U_{yy}, U_{xx} and U_{yx}:

$$U_{yy} = -24P_y/P_x,$$

$$U_{xx} = -24P_x/P_y,$$

$$U_{yx} = 0.$$

Since price (P_x and P_y) is greater than zero, $U_{yy} < 0$ and $U_{xx} < 0$. Further, $(U_{yx})^2 = 0$ which implies that $(U_{yx})^2 < U_{yy} U_{xx}$. We have indeed found a maximum.

The Lagrangean Method

In order to solve a constrained optimization problem, many methods have been put forward, and one of the most widely used methods in economics is the *Lagrangean method*. It is an alternative to this cumbersome method of combining functions.

The steps are as follows. First, create a new function called the *Lagrangean function* which is a combination of the objective function (function being maximized or minimized) and the constraints. Thus,

$$L = \text{objective function} + \Sigma\lambda_i \text{ constraints.}$$

The λ terms (lamda, Greek L) are called the *Lagrangean multipliers*. Their economic interpretation are the costs of relaxing the constraint by one unit. You can see this mathematically by taking the derivative of L with respect to the constraint. We are left with λ. Also notice that when the λs equal zero, it is like maximizing the unconstrained objective function. The economic intuition of the Lagrangean multiplier will become clearer as you see the utilization of this technique in the subsequent chapters.

After setting up the Lagrangean the next step in the process is to maximize L. The first-order conditions require that

$$L_x = 0,$$

$$L_y = 0,$$

$$L_\lambda = 0.$$

Now this system of three equations and three unknowns (x, y, and λ) can be solved to determine those values that maximize L subject to the given constraint. These will be the values that also maximize U subject to the given constraint. To be sure this is a maximum we should assess the second-order conditions for the Lagrangean. This, however, is beyond the scope of this book.

An Economic Example

Let's consider another utility function with a budget constraint and this time use the Lagrange method. The problem here is to maximize the utility function subject to a budget constraint. Consequently, the problem can be written as follows:

Maximize $U(x,y) = 4x^2 - 2xy + 6y^2$

subject to the income constraint of $72.

Thus the constraint is

$$P_x x + P_y y = 72.$$

To keep the analysis simple, let's say that both x and y have a price of $1. We can write the Lagrangean function as

$$L = 4x^2 - 2xy + 6y^2 + \lambda(72 - x - y).$$

The first-order conditions for maximizing this function with respect to x, y and λ are

(1) $$L_x = 8x - 2y - \lambda = 0,$$

(2) $$L_y = -2x + 12y - \lambda = 0,$$

(3) $$L_\lambda = 72 - x - y = 0.$$

Solve equations (1) and (2) for λ and set the results equal to one another. Doing so we get

(5) $$8x - 2y = \lambda = -2x + 12y.$$

This simplifies to

(6) $$10x - 14\,y = 0$$

This gives us two equations, (3) and (6), and two unknowns, x and y. Solving (3) and (6) simultaneously we get $x^* = 42$ and $y^* = 30$. We now calculate λ^* from (1) or (2) by substituting in x^* and y^* and finding $\lambda^* = 276$. The λ^* can be interpreted that if the budget constraint were relaxed by one unit, the Lagrangean function and therefore the objective function would increase by 276 units. The Lagrangean is a measure of the value of reducing the constraint—what it would be worth to us to have it loosened. We can also use $x^* = 42$ and $y^* = 30$ to find that U is maximized at a value of 9936 units.

Exercise 5: Maximize U(x,y) = xy *subject to the budget constraint* $P_x x + P_y y = $100 *assuming* $P_x = P_y = $1.

Conclusion

We'll stop here; we've covered a lot in this chapter and this is only a beginning of a consideration of the role of calculus in economics. What we have
presented should give you a sufficient base in calculus to follow the mathematical presentations in later chapters. There's a lot there and it's only
learned through doing exercises. They are, we believe, important exercises
and understanding them can give you a deeper understanding of the discussion in the text. But a word of caution too. Calculus is great, but it is not a
substitute for thinking. Often, the problems economists face don't fit the
conditions needed to use calculus (i.e., continuity and simplicity of relationships). So a good understanding of calculus is as important to understanding when marginal arguments apply as when they don't.

Problems

1. Determine the first derivatives of the given expressions:
a. $Y = (10x^5 - 6x^3)/2x$.
b. $Y = (5x - 10)^5$.
c. $Y = 6x(4x - 5)^3$.

2. Find the maximum or minimum point of the total cost function
$C = 2/3Q^3 - 11Q^2 + 48Q + 62$.

3. Maximize the following total profit functions and solve for the optimal
level of output:
a. $\Pi = 16Q - 0.8Q^2$.
b. $\Pi = -4Q^2 + 48Q - 96$.

4. Find the partial derivatives of the following functions with respect to x
and z:
a. $Y = 6x^2 z^3$.
b. $Y = (6x + 10)(2x + 6z)$.

5. Use the Lagrangean multipliers method to optimize the following function subject to the given constraint: Maximize $f(x,z) = 12x^2 + 6xz + 12z^2 +
240$, subject to $2x + 2z = 112$.

Answers to In-Text Questions

1. $f'(x) = 4(5x^2 - x^3)^3(10x - 3x^2)$.
2. The first derivative is $f'(x) = 4x^3 + 10x$. The second derivative is $f''(x) = 12x^2 + 10$, and the third derivative is $f'''(x) = 24x$.
3. In Figure 3.1e, $f'(x) < 0$ and $f''(x) > 0$ and in Figure 3.1f, $f'(x) < 0$ and $f''(x) < 0$.
4. The first and second-order conditions require $f'(x) = 3x^2 - 8x = 0$ and $f''(x) = 6x - 8 = 0$. Solving for x we find that $x = 0$ or $x = 8/3$. To differentiate between the maximum or minimum values, apply the second-order condition: At $x = 0$, $f''(x) = -8 < 0$ and at $x = 8/3$, $f''(x) = 8 > 0$. Thus the function has a maximum value at $x = 0$ and minimum value at $x = 8/3$.
5. The Lagrangean function is $L = xy + \lambda(100 - x - y)$. The first-order conditions for maximizing this function with respect to x, y and λ are, $L_x = y - \lambda = 0$; $L_y = x - \lambda = 0$; and $L = 100 - x - y = 0$. Solving the first two equations for λ and setting the result equal to one another we get $x = y$. Now we have two equations and two unknowns. Solving them simultaneously we get $x^* = 50$ and $y^* = 50$. $U(x, y)$ is maximized at 2500 units.

Part II
Macroeconomics

4

The Multiplier Model

In the appendix to the textbook we presented the basic Keynesian model algebraically. In this chapter we explore that model a bit more carefully. Let's start with the model of the economy presented in the appendix of the textbook.

(1) $\quad C \;=\; C_0 + bY_d$
(2) $\quad Y_d \;=\; Y - T + R$
(3) $\quad I \;=\; I_0$
(4) $\quad G \;=\; G_0$
(5) $\quad R \;=\; R_0$
(6) $\quad T \;=\; T_0 + tY$
(7) $\quad X \;=\; X_0$
(8) $\quad M \;=\; M_0 + mY$
(9) $\quad Y \;=\; C + I + G + X - M$

Equation (1) is the consumption function. C_0 is autonomous consumption; the endogenous component, bY_d, is the marginal propensity to consume multiplied by real disposable income (Y_d).

Equation (2) defines disposable income as a function of real income, taxes, and transfers.

Equation (3) is the investment function. I_0 is autonomous investment.

Equation (4) is the government expenditure function. G_0 is autonomous spending.

Equation (5) is the government transfer function. R_0 is autonomous transfers.

Equation (6) is the tax function. The autonomous component, T_0, is unaffected by income. The endogenous component, tY, is the marginal or proportional tax rate, represented by t times real income (Y).

Equation (7) is the export function. X_0 is autonomous exports.

Equation (8) is the import function. The import function has two components. The autonomous component, M_0, is unaffected by income. The endogenous component, mY, is the marginal propensity to import represented by m, times real income(Y).

Equation (9) is the national income accounting identity. At equilibrium, total or aggregate expenditures (AE) = total income (Y).

Solving the Model

You can solve this model by substituting equations (1) through (8) into equation (9) to obtain a reduced-form equation. If you correctly solve it for Y using algebra, you should get

$$(10) \quad Y = [1/(1 - b + bt + m)](C_0 - bT_0 + bR_0 + I_0 + G_0 + X_0 - M_0).$$

Recollect that the term $1/(1 - b + bt + m)$ is our multiplier in the Keynesian model. It is a useful exercise to check to see if you do in fact obtain the above reduced-form equation before proceeding further with the rest of this chapter. To do so you combine the terms and solve; use the appendix to Chapter 11 in the textbook to check your work.

Extensions of the Multiplier Analysis

Now, let's consider a variety of ways in which this basic Keynesian model can be extended. Let's first consider what the addition of endogenous transfer payments does to the model.

Endogenous Transfer Payments

Transfer payments may be thought of as payments that are made to consumers from the government. Examples of transfer payments include pensions, unemployment compensation and social security benefits. Transfer payments differ from government expenditures in that they do not count as an expenditure when they are initially paid but instead as an increase in people's disposable income. Thus, they do not have the first-round effect that government expenditures have.

The appendix to Chapter 11 in the textbook works out the algebra of the basic Keynesian model when transfer payments are assumed to be autonomous, given by the equation $R = R_0$. There is no reason to assume that transfers are limited to just an autonomous component. Just as we had a consumption function with two components, autonomous C_0 and endogenous bY_d, we could have a transfer payments function with two components:

(5A) $$R = R_0 - rY.$$

In equation (5A), the autonomous component R_0 is unaffected by income while the endogenous component rY is inversely related to income. Why inversely related? Transfers tend to fall with a rising level of income in the economy. Consider the effect of a boom on unemployment in the economy. An expanding economy usually lowers unemployment. This would explain why autonomous transfer payments are positive while income-dependent transfers are negative in equation (5A).

Let's now solve for the new multiplier. We first substitute equation (2) into equation (1):

(1A) $$C = C_0 + b(Y - T + R)$$

Next we substitute equations (1A), (3), (4), (6), (7), (8) and (5A) into equation (9) to yield

$$Y = C_0 + b(Y - T_0 - tY + R_0 - rY) + I_0 + G_0 + X_0 - M_0 - mY.$$

Multiplying out and moving all the Y terms to the left-hand side as before,

$$Y - bY + btY + brY + mY = C_0 - bT_0 + bR_0 + I_0 + G_0 + X_0 - M_0.$$

Factoring out Y gives

$$Y(1 - b + bt + br + m) = C_0 - bT_0 + bR_0 + I_0 + G_0 + X_0 - M_0.$$

Dividing by $(1 - b + bt + br + m)$ gives

(11) $$Y = [1/(1 - b + bt + br + m)](C_0 - bT_0 + bR_0 + I_0 + G_0 + X_0 - M_0).$$

When we include endogenous transfers, equation (11) is the reduced-form equation which solves the equilibrium level of income in the Keynesian model. Comparing equation (10) and equation (11), notice that they are similar in all respects except for the transfer payments terms. Equation (11) has an extra term br in the multiplier.

Putting the algebra aside, it is important to realize that the tax function and the transfer payments functions are merely leakages and injections to our Keynesian system of equations. A leakage reduces income and is therefore not used to purchase domestic goods and services. Taxes, savings, and imports are leakages in our Keynesian model. Leakages reduce the value of the multiplier. The term *bt* in the denominator of the multiplier makes the value of the multiplier smaller. On the other hand, injections or inflows add to the level of income in the economy. You have already seen how investment, government spending and exports increase the demand for domestic goods and services and hence increase the overall GDP in the economy. Transfer payments may be viewed as a pure injection into the economy since they increase disposable income of individuals which in turn is spent on domestic goods and services.

Exercise 1: The equilibrium level of income in the economy is currently $500 billion. Suppose the government increases autonomous transfer payments by $10 billion. What is the new equilibrium level of income? You know the marginal propensity to consume is 0.8, the marginal tax rate is 0.2, the marginal propensity to import is 0.1 and the endogenous transfer payments coefficient (r) is 0.3.

Endogenous Investment Function

While the simple model in the textbook assumes investment is autonomous, given by $I = I_0$, again, it would be perfectly acceptable to let investment be a function of income Y. We can expect investment by firms to increase when income or GDP in the economy increases. When the economy is growing firms will increase their investment in current stocks of capital and build up their stocks of inventories. This would mean that there is a relationship between investment and changes in income which involves some complicated dynamic relationships which you will see below. For now, let's keep it simple and assume that there is a direct relation between investment I and income Y. Hence investment can be written as

(3A) $$I = I_0 + vY.$$

With this investment function what is the multiplier and the reduced-form equation likely to be? Even before proceeding to derive the final reduced-form equation by substituting equation (3A) into the equations for the model of the economy as we did before, you should recognize that the equilibrium level of income with this new investment function is

$$Y = [1/(1 - b + bt + br + m - v)](C_0 - bT_0 + bR_0 + I_0 + G_0 + X_0 - M_0).$$

But let us proceed as before. Equation (3A) has two components. The first component, I_0, is unaffected by income. The second component, vY, is dependent on income. We have therefore defined an investment function much like the consumption function. The parameter v may be thought of as the *marginal propensity to invest*. We can now substitute equations (1A), (3A), (5A), (4), (6), (7) and (8) into equation (9) to obtain the reduced-form equation for income Y:

$$Y = C_0 + b(Y - T_0 - tY + R_0 - rY) + I_0 + vY + G_0 + X_0 - M_0 - mY.$$

Moving all the Y terms to the left-hand side,

$$Y - bY + btY + brY + mY - vY = C_0 - bT_0 + bR_0 + I_0 + G_0 + X_0 - M_0.$$

Factoring out Y gives

$$Y(1 - b + bt + br + m - v) = C_0 - bT_0 + bR_0 + I_0 + G_0 + X_0 - M_0.$$

Dividing by $(1 - b + bt + br + m - v)$ gives

$$(12) Y = [1/(1 - b + bt + br + m - v)](C_0 - bT_0 + bR_0 + I_0 + G_0 + X_0 - M_0).$$

As long as the equations for different variables are clearly defined and if you have understood the general form, obtaining a reduced-form equation with other functional forms can be easily worked out. Equation (12) is similar to equation (11) in all respects except the multiplier term. Our multiplier now has an additional term v subtracted in the denominator. If we assume that the marginal propensity to invest v lies between zero and one (the same assumption we made with the marginal propensity to consume b), then the value of the multiplier from equation (12) is larger than before. Why? Because we are subtracting v from the rest of the terms in the denominator of the multiplier, thus making the denominator smaller.

Exercise 2: Suppose the marginal propensity to invest is 0.2. Using the same numbers as in exercise 1, (a) calculate the multiplier for a change in investment and (b) if firms increase their investment by $50 million, what is the change in equilibrium income?

Deriving the Tax Multiplier

Let us now shift gears and look at some other multiplier concepts that were briefly alluded to in your textbook. The multiplier we have obtained above, $1/(1 - b + bt + br + m - v)$, is similar to the multiplier in equation (10) except for the br and v terms. Suppose that there were no foreign sector, no marginal tax rate, no transfer payments and no income component for the investment function. The multiplier clearly reduces to just $1/(1-b)$. Hence, $\Delta Y/\Delta I$ or $\Delta Y/\Delta G = 1/(1-b)$.

Your textbook tells you that the multiplier for a lump-sum or exogenous change in taxes $\Delta Y/\Delta T$ is $-b/(1-b)$. This is referred to as the *tax multiplier*. Note that the tax multiplier which has the $-b$ term in the numerator is slightly different from the simple government multiplier, $1/(1-b)$. Why is this so and from where does the tax multiplier come?

Rather than assuming this to be true, in this section we proceed algebraically to derive the tax multiplier. We will discuss only the simple case of a Keynesian model in the presence of a lump-sum tax, T. The tax function in the economy is therefore a given constant $T = T_0$.

With an exogenous level of investment and government spending, I_0 and G_0 respectively, you should be able to derive the reduced-form equation for the equilibrium level of output easily. We simply state it here as

(13) $Y_0 = [(1/(1-b)](C_0 + I_0 + G_0 - bT_0)$.

Suppose that the lump-sum level of taxes is increased in the economy. Let the new level of taxes be T_1. What happens to the equilibrium level of income in the economy? An increase in lump-sum taxes reduces disposable income of the economy and hence reduces the equilibrium level of income in the economy. Let the new level of income (after the increase in taxes to T_1) be Y_1. With no change in consumption investment or government spending, the new level of equilibrium income is given by

(14) $Y_1 = [1/(1-b)](C_0 + I_0 + G_0 - bT_1)$.

Subtracting equation (13) from equation (14),

$Y_1 - Y_0 = (1/1-b)](C_0 + I_0 + G_0 - bT_1) - [1/(1-b)](C_0 + I_0 + G_0 - bT_0)$.

Factoring out $[1/(1-b)]$,

$Y_1 - Y_0 = [1/(1-b)](C_0 + I_0 + G_0 - bT_1 - C_0 - I_0 - G_0 + bT_0)$,

and combining terms,

$Y_1 - Y_0 = [1/(1-b)](-bT_1 + bT_0)$.

Factoring out the $-b$ the equation can be rewritten as,

$$Y_1 - Y_0 = [1/(1 - b)][- b (T_1 - T_0)],$$

or, $$Y_1 - Y_0 = [-b/(1 - b)](T_1 - T_0)$$

Now $(Y_1 - Y_0)$ is just the change in equilibrium income Y and $(T_1 - T_0)$ is the change in lump-sum taxes ΔT. Hence, $\Delta Y = [-b/(1-b)](\Delta T)$ or $\Delta Y/\Delta T = [-b/(1-b)]$ which is the tax multiplier.

To illustrate the algebraic approach consider the following values:

the marginal propensity to consume, $MPC = 0.8$;
the change in government spending, $\Delta G = 100$;
the change in taxes, $\Delta T = 100$.

The government multiplier is now $1/(1-0.8) = 5$. Any change in government spending is now multiplied 5 times over in the economy. If $\Delta G = 100$, then $\Delta Y = 5.100 = 500$.

The tax multiplier is $= -0.8/(1-0.8) = -4$. Any change in lump sum taxes is multiplied 4 times over in the economy. If $\Delta T = 100$, then $\Delta Y = -4 \cdot 100 = -400$. Note the minus sign implies an inverse relation between taxes and income. If lump-sum taxes are raised by 100, output or income Y falls by 4 times 100.

It is important to recognize that the effect of a lump-sum tax on the economy is different than the effect of, say, government spending. A $100 decrease in taxes generates only b or the MPC times the effect of income as a $100 increase in government spending. Suppose that the government makes a transfer to you of $100. In effect this is like a subsidy. With a MPC of 0.8, you spend the MPC times the lump sum amount (i.e., you spend 80% of the $100 and save the rest). It is therefore not the full $100 but $80 which is being turned over in the economy through the multiplier process.

What does the tax multiplier in the larger model look like? Suppose that we consider a model which includes the foreign sector, and a marginal tax rate. Carefully working out the algebra as we did above should yield a tax multiplier equal to $-b/(1 - b + bt + m)$. If we go a step further and include transfer payments and an income component for the investment function, the tax multiplier would be $\Delta Y/\Delta T = -b/(1 - b + bt + br + m-v)$.

Just to make sure you are following the analysis, try an example. Using equations (1) through (9) and using (3A) and (5A) instead of (3) and (5) respectively, confirm that the formula for the tax multiplier shown above is correct.

The Balanced Budget Multiplier

Now let's put the two together and see what happens when the government increases taxes and expenditures by equal amounts. For example our model shows us how an increase in government spending will ultimately lead to an increase in output or income in the economy. In contrast, an increase in taxes reduces the level of income or GDP in the economy. We also know that changes in government spending affect the federal budget deficit, where the federal budget deficit may be thought of as the difference between government spending (G) and tax revenue collected, T. Hence, $BD = G - T$, where BD = the budget deficit, G = government spending and T = tax revenue.

What impact does an increase in spending by the government have on the federal budget? The answer seems obvious enough. An increase in government spending leads to a deficit in the federal budget assuming it was previously balanced or worsens if it were already in a deficit. Upon careful reflection, however, we realize that an increase in government spending G will lead to an increase in output Y in the economy. But since tax revenue collected depends on the level of income in the economy, when Y increases so does tax revenue T. Is it possible that the increase in tax revenue offsets the increase in government spending, leaving the budget unchanged?

Consider the following case to illustrate the problem. Suppose that a government decides to finance an expenditure of $10 million by raising taxes to the tune of $10 million. In this case the federal budget will be unchanged since ΔG = $10 million = ΔT. An interesting question in this context is, what is the impact of an increase in spending of $10 million and a simultaneous increase in taxes of $10 million, on income or output Y in the economy?

Let us assume a simple economy in which the government multiplier is $\Delta Y/\Delta G = 1/(1-b)$. The tax multiplier which we derived earlier is simply $\Delta Y/\Delta T = -b/(1-b)$.

Suppose you are told that the marginal propensity to consume b in this economy is 0.75. Using these formulas, the increase in output Y from an increase in government spending G of $10 million is $\Delta Y/10 = 1/(1-0.75)$, or $\Delta Y/10 = 4$ and therefore ΔY = $40 million.

Now the increase in taxes will reduce output Y in the economy. To find out by how much we can use the tax multiplier. The change in taxes ΔT = $10 million. Hence, $\Delta Y/10 = -0.75/(1-0.75)$, or $\Delta Y/10 = -3$. $\Delta Y = -\$30$, which shows that output will fall by $30 million when taxes are increased by $10 million in this simple economy. The net change in output from a $10 million increase in both spending and taxes is $40 - $30 million = $10 million. Notice that output increases by exactly the same amount as the initial increase in government spending. This interesting observation has come to be known as the *balanced budget multiplier* result, which states that if government spending and taxes are raised by the same amount, output Y in the economy rises by exactly the same amount as the increase in government spending or taxes. If we add the government multiplier and the tax multiplier algebraically, they add up to 1:

$$\Delta Y/\Delta G + \Delta Y/\Delta T = 1/(1 - b) + -b/(1 - b) = (1 - b)/(1 - b) = 1,$$

i.e. $$\Delta Y/\Delta G + \Delta Y/\Delta T = 1.$$

The value of the balanced budget multiplier is therefore 1 for this special case of an economy with a lump sum tax, T.

Conclusion

Throughout this chapter you have been exposed to extensions of the basic Keynesian model. In all these cases we want to demonstrate that a slightly different specification of some of the variables gives us a variation on the basic reduced-form equation. As long as you are careful with the algebra, deriving new formulas with different specifications of the various variables should not present any problems. Ultimately algebra enhances our understanding of macroeconomics and makes the subject so much more fun.

Problems

1. Derive the full multiplier and the reduced-form equation for income in the economy if the government expenditures function and the export function both have independent and endogenous components. Let $G = G_0 + gY$ instead of $G = G_0$, and let $X = X_0 + xY$ instead of $X = X_0$.

2. Suppose that exports in the United States change by an amount ΔX. Show that the resultant change in imports, ΔM, can never be greater than the original change in exports ΔX (i.e., prove that M can never be greater than X. Hint: Use the multiplier formula and the definition or formula for the marginal propensity to import).

Answers to In-Text Questions

1. $514.3 billion.
2. (a) $\Delta Y/\Delta I = 1/(1 - b + bt + br + m - v) = 2$.
    (b) Increase by $100 million.

5

The International Locomotive Effect

In the last chapter we developed some algebraic extensions of the multiplier model. In this chapter we focus on international repercussions in the multiplier model. As countries have become more interrelated, international policy coordination has received more emphasis. Recent efforts for increased coordination of macroeconomic policy among countries date back to the adverse oil shocks of the 1970s.

Following the rise in prices of crude oil by OPEC in 1973-74, most of the oil-importing countries including the United States, Japan and Germany began experiencing rising unemployment rates. Each of the oil-importing countries adopted expansionary monetary and fiscal policies to counter the oil price hike by OPEC. The world money supply grew enormously. The combined expansionary policies created a demand shock that resulted in a surge of inflation in the industrialized countries of the world.

The experience of the second oil shock in 1978-79 similarly caused inflation. In response to that inflation the Federal Reserve introduced a tight monetary policy. This brought inflation under control by the mid-1980s, but led to a significant recession in the U.S. and a world-wide debt crisis in developing countries. The reason was that the higher interest rates in the United States resulted in a stronger dollar. The strong dollar led to a shrinking of U.S. exports and an increase in imports as the domestic economy continued to improve. The deterioration of the U.S. current account led to increasing pressure on Congress to impose tariffs and other such measures to protect the domestic industries. Had other countries coordinated their macroeconomic policies with the U.S. imposing similar restrictive monetary policies, it was felt that the adjustment process would have been smoother and the push for protective tariffs would have been less.

It is in this spirit that the leaders of the United States, United Kingdom, Japan, Germany and France met at the Plaza Hotel in New York City in 1985 and reached the Plaza Agreement, which called for countries to work more closely with each other on fiscal, monetary and exchange rate policies. The Plaza Agreement was followed by a summit meeting in Tokyo in May 1986 where the group was expanded to include Canada and Italy and is now formally called the Group of Seven or G-7. The Tokyo meeting was followed by the Louvre meeting in Paris in 1987. By this time, the G-7 countries had reached an agreement to monitor economic performance in each country and coordinate economic policies to achieve smoother adjustments to shocks hitting the world economy and sustained economic growth. Following the Louvre meeting, the G-7 agreed to meet every year to continue a dialogue for mutually beneficial domestic policies.

The Locomotive Effect

The need for coordination results from the fact that macroeconomic policies in one country have implications for other countries. When one country expands its fiscal or monetary policy it operates as a *locomotive* for other countries. In policy circles, this has come to be termed the *international locomotive effect*.

In the Keynesian model, this international effect can be seen by including the interrelationship among countries in the model. The math can get a little cumbersome, but the exercise is helpful to become familiar with the algebra of the simple Keynesian model. In this chapter we explore a model with such an interconnection. To keep it as simple as possible, our model of the world economy only includes two countries, the United States and Japan. Imports of the U.S. are nothing but exports of Japan and vice versa. Thus an increase in income or GDP in the U.S. will lead to an increase in U.S. imports, which as just stated are Japanese exports. An increase in the exports of Japan will lead to an increase in Japan's income or GDP and consequently an increase in the imports into Japan as well. Thus, there will be a *feedback* effect of policy in one country. The locomotive model quantifies this feedback effect and the mechanism may be described as follows:

$$\uparrow Y_{US} \;\rightarrow\; \uparrow M_{US} \;\rightarrow\; \uparrow X_{JAPAN} \;\rightarrow\; \uparrow Y_{JAPAN} \;\rightarrow\; \uparrow M_{JAPAN} \;\rightarrow\; \uparrow X_{US} \rightarrow \uparrow Y_{US} \;\; \text{and so on.}$$

The Locomotive Multiplier Model

For ease of understanding and for mathematical simplicity we drop the tax function for each of the two countries. We assume therefore that each country has a marginal propensity to consume and a marginal propensity to import, but no lump-sum or proportional taxes. The structural equations for the two countries are shown below. The superscripts *us* and *j* distinguish the equations for the United States and Japan respectively:

United States			Japan		
(1)	C^{us}	$= C_0^{us} + b^{us}\,Y^{us}$	C^j	$=$	$C_0^j + b^j Y^j$
(2)	I^{us}	$= I_0^{us}$	I^j	$=$	I_0^j
(3)	G^{us}	$= G_0^{us}$	G^j	$=$	G_0^j
(4)	X^{us}	$= X_0^{us}$	X^j	$=$	X_0^j
(5)	M^{us}	$= M_0^{us} + m^{us}\,Y^{us}$	M^j	$=$	$M_0^j + m^j Y^j$
(6)	Y^{us}	$= C^{us} + I^{us} + G^{us} + X^{us} - M^{us}$	Y^j	$=$	$C^j + I^j + G^j + X^j - M^j$

The equilibrium level of income for the U.S. is given by

$$Y = (C_0^{us} + I_0^{us} + G_0^{us} + X_0^{us} - M_0^{us})/(1 - b^{us} + m^{us}).$$

To simplify some of the algebra, let us use one term for the exogenous consumption, investment and government spending terms, i.e., let

$$E_0^{us} = C_0^{us} + I_0^{us} + G_0^{us}.$$

The above reduced-form equation for equilibrium output can now be written as

(7) $$Y^{us} = (E_0^{us} + X_0^{us} - M_0^{us})/(1 - b^{us} + m^{us}).$$

As we mentioned, in a two-country model of this type, exports of the U.S. are nothing but imports of Japan and vice versa. Therefore,

(8) $$X_0^{us} = M_0^j + m^j Y^j.$$

Substituting for Equation (8) in (7),

(9) $$Y^{us} = (E_0^{us} + M_0^j + m^j Y^j - M_0^{us})/(1 - b^{us} + m^{us})$$

Similarly the equilibrium level of income for Japan is

$$Y^j = (C_0^j + I_0^j + G_0^j + X_0^j - M_0^j)/(1 - b^j + m^j).$$

As we did with the reduced-form equilibrium equation for the U.S., let $E_0^j = C_0^j + I_0^j + G_0^j$; then

(10) $Y^j = (E_0^j + X_0^j - M_0^j)/(1 - b^j + m^j),$

and since Japan's exports are nothing but the imports of the U.S., $X_0^j = M_0^{us} + m^{us}Y^{us}$ can be substituted in equation (10) to yield

(11) $Y^j = (E_0^j + M_0^{us} + m^{us}Y^{us} - M_0^j)/(1 - b^j + m^j).$

The multiplier for the U.S. with the trade feedback can now be obtained by substituting equation (11) into equation (9)

$$Y^{us} = \{(E_0^{us} + M_0^j - M_0^{us}) + m^j[(E_0^j + M_0^{us} + m^{us}Y^{us} - M_0^j)/(1 - b^j + m^j)]\}/$$
$$(1 - b^{us} + m^{us}).$$

Simplifying,

$$Y^{us} = \{(E_0^{us} + M_0^j - M_0^{us})(1 - b^j + m^j) + m^j(E_0^j + M_0^{us} + m^{us}Y^{us} - M_0^j)\}/$$
$$[(1 - b^j + m^j)(1 - b^{us} + m^{us})].$$

Collecting all the Y^{us} terms together on the left-hand side,

$$Y^{us}(1 - b^j + m^j)(1 - b^{us} + m^{us}) - m^j m^{us} Y^{us} = (1 - b^j + m^j)(E_0^{us} + M_0^j - M_0^{us}) +$$
$$m^j(E_0^j + M_0^{us} - M_0^j).$$

Factoring out Y and collecting all exogenous terms on the right-hand side,

$$Y^{us}[(1 - b^j + m^j)(1 - b^{us} + m^{us}) - m^j m^{us}] = (1 - b^j + m^j)(E_0^{us} + M_0^j - M_0^{us}) +$$
$$m^j(E_0^j + M_0^{us} - M_0^j), \text{ or}$$

$$Y^{us} = [(1 - b^j + m^j)(E_0^{us} + M_0^j - M_0^{us}) + m^j(E_0^j + M_0^{us} - M_0^j)]/[(1 - b^j + m^j)$$
$$(1 - b^{us} + m^{us}) - m^j m^{us}].$$

Substituting back for E_0^{us} and E_0^j,

(12) $Y^{us} = [(1 - b^j + m^j)(C_0^{us} + I_0^{us} + G_0^{us} + M_0^j - M_0^{us}) + m^j(C_0^j + I_0^j + G_0^j + M_0^{us} - M_0^j)]/[(1 - b^j + m^j)(1 - b^{us} + m^{us}) - m^j m^{us}].$

The multiplier for a two-country model for any autonomous change can be easily written from equation (12). For example, to obtain the multiplier for a change in investment (ΔI) in the U.S., we are concerned only with the terms within the parentheses which are multiplied by I_0^{us} both in the numerator and denominator of equation (12). Hence,

(13) $\Delta Y^{us}/\Delta I^{us} = (1 - b^j + m^j)/ [(1 - b^j + m^j) (1 - b^{us} + m^{us}) - m^j m^{us}]$.

Equation (13), the multiplier with locomotive effects, makes sense. If we exclude the two-country effect, dropping Japan from our model, then both $b^j = 0$ and $m^j = 0$. Equation (13) now reduces to just $1/(1 - b^{us} + m^{us})$, the simple multiplier we calculated in Chapter 4. In fact, the multiplier of equation (13) is larger in magnitude. We can prove this mathematically, but the intuition is clear. With the locomotive effect in operation we have the interrelation not just of one country's propensities to consume and import but of both the countries on the exogenous changes in government spending or investment.

Are there any locomotive effects from an increase in investment in Japan on the United States economy? In other words, will an increase in investment by firms in Japan (I^j) have an effect on GDP (Y^{us}) in the United States? Equation (12) and our two-country multiplier suggests that the multiplier for a change in GDP in the U.S. resulting from the change in investment by Japanese firms (ΔI^j) is given by

(14) $\Delta Y^{us}/\Delta I^j = m^j/[(1 - b^j + m^j) (1 - b^{us} + m^{us}) - m^j m^{us}]$.

An Example

Let us look at a problem with actual numbers to illustrate the locomotive effect. Suppose that the marginal propensities to consume in the United States and Japan are 0.85 and 0.7 respectively. Let the propensities to import of the United States and Japan be 0.3 and 0.2 respectively. Suppose the Japanese government approves a stimulus package to spend $100 billion to move its economy out of a slump. How much is GDP likely to change by in (1) the United States and (2) in Japan?

A change in GDP in the U.S. because of a change in government spending G^j in Japan is given by $\Delta Y^{us}/\Delta G^j$ which is given by exactly the same formulas as equation (14). Hence,

$$\Delta Y^{us}/\Delta G^j = m^j/[(1 - b^j + m^j) (1 - b^{us} + m^{us}) - m^j m^{us}].$$

Substituting for ΔG^j, b^j, m^j, b^{us} and m^{us} in the above formula,

$$\Delta Y^{us}/100 = 0.2/[(1 - 0.7 + 0.2)(1 - 0.85 + 0.3) - 0.2 \cdot 0.3]) = 1.212,$$

$$\Delta Y^{us} = 100 \cdot 1.212 = \$121.2 \text{ billion.}$$

Hence the impact of a $100 billion increase in spending in Japan is to increase GDP in the United States by 1.212 times the initial change. The change in GDP in the United States is $121.2 billion.

What about the change in GDP in Japan from the same increase in government spending of $100 billion in Japan? The formula we require is $\Delta Y^j / \Delta G^j$. The change in GDP in Japan: $\Delta Y^j / \Delta G^j = (1 - b^{us} + m^{us}) / [(1 - b^j + m^j)(1 - b^{us} + m^{us}) - m^j m^{us}])$.

Note that the numerator of the formula above is different from equation (13) since we want the change in GDP in Japan for a change in government spending *in Japan*. Equation (13) on the other hand was the multiplier for the *change in GDP in the U.S. for a change in spending in the U.S.* If you derive the reduced-form formula for equilibrium income in Japan Y^j, you will obtain the above formula for the multiplier. If this is not apparent, you should confirm this by actually deriving the formula for Y^j before proceeding any further.

Substituting for G^j, b^j, m^j, b^{us} and m^{us} in $\Delta Y^j / \Delta G^j$,

$$\Delta Y^j / 100 \quad = \{(1 - 0.85 + 0.3)/[(1 - 0.7 + 0.2)(1 - 0.85 + 0.3) - 0.2 \cdot 0.3]\}$$
$$= 2.727.$$

$$\Delta Y^j = 2.727 \cdot 100 = \$272.7 \text{ billion.}$$

The numerical example shows that an increase in government spending in Japan not only increases GDP in Japan through the multiplier effect, but also increases GDP in the trading country, the United States in this case. The example highlights the locomotive effects in the international economy. It is not surprising that the G-7 countries have as their primary goal policies to promote rapid economic growth, since growth in one country implies the locomotion of growth in the other member countries as well. The intuition behind the multiplier and the mathematical derivation in the two-country case is the same as with other multipliers you have seen throughout your course and in Chapter 4 of this companion text. While the formula for the multiplier in the two-country case is a *little* more complicated than before, the derivation is based on the same algebraic principles that you learned in Chapter 4.

Exercise 1: Using the same propensities as the above example, calculate the following multipliers: (1) $\Delta Y^{us}/\Delta G^{us}$ (2) $\Delta Y^j/\Delta G^{us}$.

Conclusion

As you can see, the algebraic manipulation from these multiple-country multipliers becomes complicated. And that's just with two countries. Add 3 or 4 or 224 countries and you have a mess trying to solve the problems using this substitution method. There are, however, many ways to solve large systems of equations that are much neater — using vector analysis and determinants. We won't go into them here but will simply remind you that they exist and that if you are truly interested in coming up with numerical answers to complicated questions, learning more math is an absolute necessity.

Problems

1.
a. The Japanese Government introduced a spending packet to stimulate the Japanese economy in November 1993. The plan included $9.5 billion to be spent on improving Japanese infrastructure and another $9.5 billion to help small companies. Is this stimulus package likely to have an effect on the United States economy? Explain. Show what the respective multipliers are likely to be for a change in this government spending on GDP in both the United States and Japan.
b. Suppose that the Clinton administration is not satisfied with the above Japanese stimulus package and is able to persuade the Japanese government to incur a new round of government spending in 1995 to the tune of $100 billion. The savings rates in the United States and Japan are 0.15 and 0.3 respectively. The propensities to import for the United States and Japan are 0.3 and 0.2 respectively. If we consider the locomotive effects to be in force, what is the change in GDP in (1) the United States and (2) Japan?

2.
a. Compare and contrast the government multiplier without the locomotive effect with the government multiplier when the locomotive effect between two countries is considered, i.e., compare $\Delta Y/\Delta G$ with and without the locomotive effect.
b. Show mathematically that the multiplier with the locomotive effect considered is always larger than without the locomotive effect.
c. Can you offer an economic explanation for why this might be the case?

3. Introduce taxes into our two-country model. Let the tax functions for the United States and Japan be $T = T_0 + tY$ and $T^j = T_0^j + t^jY^j$, respectively. Prove that the multiplier for a change in government spending (ΔG) on the change in GDP (ΔY) in the United States is equal to $(1 - b^j + b^jt^j + m^j)/[(1 - b^j + b^jt^j + m^j)(1 - b + bt + m) - m^jm]$.

4. Once again consider the economies of the United States and Japan. The structural equations describing the two economies are

United States		Japan	
C	$=$ $100 + 0.8Y$	$C^j =$	$50 + 0.7Y^j$
I	$=$ 200	$I^j =$	100
G	$=$ 500	$G^j =$	200
M	$=$ $200 + 0.2Y$	$M^j =$	$20 + 0.1Y^j$

a. With the locomotive effect considered, calculate the equilibrium level of GDP in the United States.
b. Does the United States have a trade balance? If not, calculate the trade deficit or surplus.

Answers to In-Text Questions

1.   (1) $\Delta Y^{us}/\Delta G^{us} = 3.03$ (2) $\Delta Y^{j}/\Delta G^{us} = 1.81$.

6

The Geometry of the IS-LM Model

The Keynesian model presented in Chapters 4 and 5 until recently has remained the cornerstone of all macroeconomic models and has been extended in a variety of ways. The most well known of these extensions is the IS-LM model (Investment-Savings - Liquidity-Money model) which uses a geometric trick to translate three dimensions into two by looking at only equilibrium points.

In this chapter we present the IS-LM model developed by John Hicks in 1937. This IS-LM model is a graphical representation of simultaneous equilibrium in both the goods and money markets. It is a model with which we can consider the effect of changes in the money market on the goods market. In this IS-LM model the analysis of the real sector (the goods market) is captured by the IS (the Investment-Savings) curve, and the analysis of the financial sector (the money market) is captured by the LM (the Demand for Liquidity - Supply of Money) curve.

There are many ways to develop and interpret the IS-LM model. We should warn the reader that, because of recent changes in the interpretation of the Keynesian and the Classical models, we have chosen to develop it slightly differently from the standard method that is based on Modigliani's treatment of IS-LM in 1944. Specifically, in our presentation we distinguish between Keynesian and Classical views of the goods market (IS curve), rather than distinguishing Classical and Keynesian views of the money market (LM curve). We do so because as far back as the 1970s both Keynesians and Classicals denied that the position of the LM curve assigned to them correctly captured their view. By the by the 1990s, it is difficult to distinguish the monetary views of Classical and Keynesian economists, and the functioning of the money market has been dropped as the distinguishing feature between the two groups.

More recently macroeconomic models have focused on the dynamic adjustment process in the real sector as the main distinguishing feature between Keynesians and the Classicals. That is the approach presented in the textbook. Consequently the IS-LM model that we present here follows up on this distinguishing feature and makes the shape and interpretation of the IS curve the critical difference between the Keynesian and the Classical models. Thus in this chapter we present a composite view of the LM curve and distinguish between the Keynesian IS curve, which includes a multiplier effect, and the Classical IS curve which does not. We won't get into these differences in interpretations here since such discussions are best left for higher level courses. You should, however, be aware that there are other interpretations, and the IS-LM model is too simple to describe either the Keynesian or the Classical views adequately.

Deriving the IS Curve

The IS curve portrays combinations of interest rates and income levels in which the goods market is in equilibrium. Thus, to derive it we must take into account the effect of the interest rate on the level of equilibrium income in the economy. If you think back to Chapters 4 and 5 where we extended the basic Keynesian model, we treated the interest rate in the economy as a shift factor of aggregate expenditure or aggregate demand. The IS-LM analysis incorporates this interest rate shift factor directly into the analysis by considering (1) the investment decision and (2) the savings decision in the economy, and considering how those decisions lead to an equilibrium interest rate.

The Investment and Savings Decision

Both Keynesians and Classicals agree that economic decisions are made on the basis of comparing costs and benefits. As individuals we decide to buy a particular item if the benefits that accrue from it outweigh its cost. Similarly, we can expect that a firm will invest in a project if its benefits to the firm in the long run exceed its costs. The cost of a project depends to a large extent on the cost of borrowing funds which is highly dependent on the interest rate. If the interest rate in the economy falls, other things equal, a firm will increase its investment. If the interest rate rises, the firm is likely to postpone investment, especially if it expects that the interest rate will fall in the near future. This means that investment is a decreasing function of the interest rate. So,

$$I = f(i)$$

where $dI < 0.$

Both Keynesians and Classicals agree that the interest rate is not very important in making short-run consumption and savings decisions, so we will assume that the savings function is independent of the interest rate. Savings, in the Keynesian model, is dependent on income (via the consumption function). In the Classical model, it is not. Thus, the Keynesian savings function is

$$S = f(Y) = S_0 + sY.$$

and the long-run Classical savings function is

$$S = S_0.$$

Figure 6.1(a) provides a graphical representation of the savings and investment function in relation to the rate of interest. Notice that for both, the savings function (S) is vertical and the investment function (D) is downward sloping.

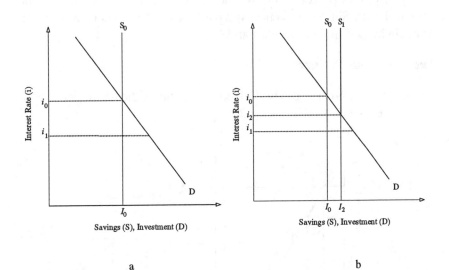

Figure 6.1 (a,b)

Where the Keynesian and Classical views of the investment/savings market differ is in the disequilibrium dynamics. Keynesians see a dynamic feedback effect occurring in the adjustment process that changes the equilibrium; Classicals do not. To see this, say that for some reason the interest rate falls from i_0 to i_1 even though the two curves do not change. This fall is shown in Figure 6.1(b). In the Classical case, equilibrium will be achieved in this market by a rise in the interest rate to bring savings and investment back into equilibrium at the initial level of interest and investment (i_0, I_0).

In the Keynesian case the dynamics are different. The increase in the investment caused by the fall in the interest rate will cause income to increase which will cause people to save more which will shift the savings curve out to, say, S_1. The new equilibrium will be at a higher level of investment, I_2, and a lower interest rate, i_2. Thus, even if the interest rate adjustment process is working somewhat, the old equilibrium will not be achieved since the savings function will have shifted. The new Keynesian equilibrium will be at a lower interest rate and a higher income level than before.

Actually the Classical specification is a bit more complicated since they do allow that, as a temporary phenomenon, savings might be a function of income, but the relationship between the two is considered to be much less responsive than in the Keynesian view. Moreover, in the Classical case the relationship is only a short-run phenomenon—something that will be eliminated as soon as the price level adjusts. In the Keynesian case it is much more pervasive.

We will now proceed to derive the IS curve in both the Keynesian and Classical case. Since the IS curve is a particularly Keynesian construct, let us begin by deriving the Keynesian IS curve.

The Keynesian IS Curve

The Keynesian IS curve can be derived by expanding the I-S diagram specified above. We do so in Figure 6.2.

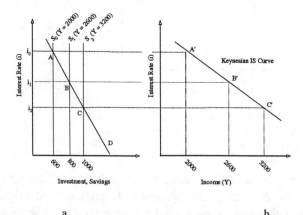

a   b

Figure 6.2 (a,b)

We know that the combination of interest rate i_0 and Y_0 (point A) is a point in which the goods market (the inverse of the investment/savings market) is in equilibrium. In Figure 6.2(b) we plot that point in a graph of equilibrium points with interest rate on the vertical axis and income on the horizontal axis (point A'). Now say, for some reason, the interest rate falls to i_1. This fall in the interest rate will increase investment which will increase income (by the multiplier effect) which will have a feedback effect on savings shifting the savings curve to S_1. Thus, we have a new equilibrium at i_1 and Y_1 (point B). We plot this new equilibrium point in Figure 6.2(b) (point B'). Now say that the interest rate falls again to i_2. This causes investment to increase and income to increase by a multiple of that amount which means that the savings curve shifts to S_2 and the new equilibrium is point C. We have a new combination of equilibrium interest rates and income levels, i_2, Y_2 (point C').

If we carry out the process, we will have all equilibrium interest rates and income levels for which the goods market will be in equilibrium. Connecting points A', B' and C', we can see that this combination of equilibrium interest rates and income levels at which the investment/savings market is in equilibrium will be a downward sloping curve. This curve is the Keynesian IS curve—the combination of interest rates and income levels at which the goods market will be in equilibrium given the Keynesian assumptions about savings and investment

Another way of showing the derivation of the Keynesian IS curve is to include the interest rate effect on investment in the simple Keynesian model. This is shown in Figure 6.3 below.

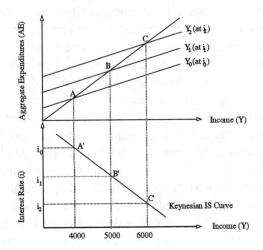

Figure 6.3

Lower interest rates will shift the aggregate expenditures curve up as shown in the graph resulting in higher equilibrium levels of income (points A, B and C). At each of the points, A, B, and C, aggregate production equals aggregate expenditures which means that investment equals savings. Plotting these points we get the same Keynesian IS curve as before. *The shape and slope of the Keynesian IS curve depend on the effect that interest rates have on investment and on the size of the multiplier.* If a small change in interest rates results in a large change in investment, the AE curve shifts up by a lot and the IS Curve will tend to be flatter than otherwise. Likewise, if the multiplier is large, the AE curve will be steep so that a for a given shift in the AE curve, the change in income resulting from a given change in interest will be large and again the IS will be flatter than otherwise.

The Classical IS Curve

As we stated above, the IS curve is a particularly Keynesian construction, and thus fitting the Classical view into it is difficult. Actually, we should say that the technical analysis is simple; it is the interpretation that is complicated. To get at what is considered the Classical view in the 1990s one needs to distinguish both a long-run and a short-run Classical IS curve. The long-run Classical IS curve is the easiest, so let us go through that first.

Given the assumption of the perfectly vertical and autonomous supply curve of savings, deriving this is easy. A fixed supply curve for savings means that equilibrium income in the economy can be at only one level—its natural rate—and that a fall in the interest rate must be pushed back to its equilibrium level if the investment/savings market is to be in equilibrium. Thus in the Classical long run there is only one interest rate—the natural rate—and one income level—the natural rate—at which the economy can be. The Classical IS curve reduces to a single point.

Classicals recognized that the long run takes a while to arrive, and they allowed that in the short run the economy could be in temporary disequilibrium. In this temporary disequilibrium there could be a variety of interest rates and income levels at which the economy would be in temporary equilibrium. It would not be a full equilibrium in the sense that all people are at their desired choices. Institutional constraints must exist that prevent everyone from making their desired choices. Let's consider how the Classical short-run IS curve can be derived from the investment/savings market. In Figure 6.4 we consider the same fall in the interest rate we considered in the previous analyses.

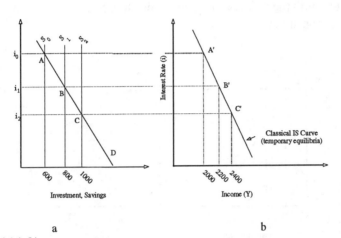

a

b

Figure 6.4 (a,b)

In the short-run Classical case, the desired savings curve does not shift out as it does in the Keynesian case, since savings is not a function of income. However, savings does increase temporarily and hence total output does shift (as measured by sales) as long as the price level does not rise instantaneously. This is what might be called *forced savings*—savings that result because people are fooled about what they will receive for supplying factors of production. Temporarily, real income will increase since people are fooled into working more than they want.

Thus the fall in interest rate to i_1 is associated with a temporary increase in income to Y_1. Similarly, a fall in interest to i_2 will be associated with an increase in income to Y_2, and so on. Thus in the short run a host of temporary equilibria are possible along the demand for investment curve. In Exhibit 6.4(b) we graph these various temporary equilibria, combining interest rates and income levels in which the goods market (assuming fixed prices) is in temporary equilibrium.

Notice that this IS curve is downward sloping as is the Keynesian IS curve. There are however two differences. First, given the same effect of interest rates on investment, its slope is steeper than the slope of the Keynesian IS curve. This is because it does not include a multiplier effect—the expansionary effect on income that an increase in investment has in the Keynesian model. In the Keynesian model, the short-run equilibrium incomes are read on the savings curve associated with each income level. An increase in investment causes income to increase by a multiple of the increase in investment. In the Classical model the income increase is just the level of income associated with the increase in investment. In Figure 6.5, we show the difference in the slope.

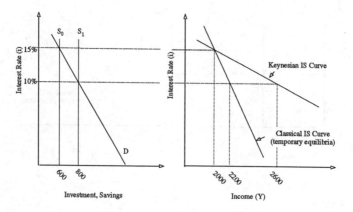

Figure 6.5

For example, say that the interest rate fell from 15% to 10%, causing investment to increase by 200 units. In the Keynesian model, a multiplier of magnitude, say 3, causes overall income Y to increase by 3 times the change in investment, i.e., $\Delta I \cdot 3 = \Delta Y$, or $3 \cdot 200 = 600$. In the Classical IS curve there is no such multiplier effect. While the decrease in interest rates does give rise to an increase in investment, and in output, of 200 units, the process stops right there. There is no multiple chain of income creation as in the Keynesian model. This necessarily means that in the Classical model, the long-run IS curve is steeper.

The second difference is that whereas the Keynesian case is a combination of permanent equilibria—the goods market can be in long-run equilibrium in the Keynesian model at various interest rates and income levels—the Classical IS curve is a temporary phenomenon dependent on prices being fixed and people being fooled that the prices are not fixed. If that is not the case and prices are flexible, the economy will be driven back to the Classical long-run equilibrium point—the natural rate of interest and the natural rate of income.

In the Classical model when the interest rate deviates from its natural rate, we have only a temporary goods market equilibrium. As the price level adjusts, in the long run, we return to the initial equilibrium output at the natural rate of interest. Thus in the Classical model, the long-run equilibrium is chosen by the system—it is a natural equilibrium and policy cannot change it. This is in sharp contrast to the Keynesian case in which there is no notion of the natural rate of interest or a natural rate of income. In the

Keynesian model, there are multiple equilibria along the IS curve and policy makers can choose among different equilibrium rates of interest and output at which the goods market is in equilibrium.

Points Off the IS Curve

While every point on the IS curve is a point at which the goods market is in equilibrium, clearly every point off the IS curve must be a disequilibrium point. Let us try and examine what happens at a disequilibrium point like B in Figure 6.6. At B, the interest rate is i' which is higher than the equilibrium interest rate of i^*. At the higher interest rate i' investment is low. Why? Because investment demand is inversely related to the interest rate. A lower level of investment implies a lower aggregate expenditure on goods and services than the actual level of output Y^* at equilibrium. Since aggregate expenditure, AE, is less than the aggregate supply or production of goods and services in the economy, there is an 'excess supply of goods' at point B. In general at all points above the IS curve we have disequilibrium and an excess supply of goods and all points below the IS curve exhibit an excess demand for goods.

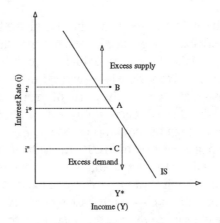

Figure 6.6

Factors That Shift the IS Curve

Both the Keynesian and Classical IS curves are drawn holding constant the shift factors that either increase or decrease aggregate expenditure, and therefore cause output or income Y to change. Thus we assume that all the autonomous factors that we considered in the model from which they are derived, such as autonomous investment, autonomous government spending, autonomous taxes or autonomous imports, are held constant when drawing the IS curve. Clearly, if any of these autonomous factors change, the IS curve will shift either to the right or to the left. Consider for example an increase in government spending, *G*.

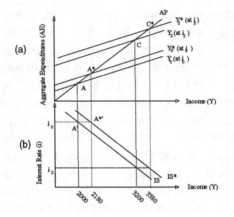

Figure 6.7

We can see the effect that increase will have on the Keynesian IS curve by following the effects through the Keynesian expenditure model. Say we have initially derived the IS curve in Exhibit 6.7(b) relevant to the AE/AP model in Exhibit 6.7(a). Now there is an increase in G of $60. This will shift each AE curve associated with a given rate of interest up, and the income level associated with that AE curve up by a multiple (say it is 3) of that amount. Thus rather than the equilibrium being i_0, Y_0 it will be i_0^*, Y_0^* which will be at an income level of $180 to the right of the IS curve for each interest rate. This will be true for all interest rates and income levels. Thus an increase in G of 60 will shift the IS curve to the right by an amount that is a multiple of the shift in G—in this case by 180. A decrease in autonomous spending will produce exactly the opposite effect.

The bottom line here is that all those factors that affected aggregate expenditure in the Keynesian model such as autonomous consumption, autonomous investment, autonomous taxes, and autonomous government spending, will cause a shift in the IS curve by a multiple of that shift.

In the Classical case the IS curve will similarly shift out or in, but there will be no multiplier effect. Moreover, the effect will be temporary, and the effect will be dependent on the assumption that prices are being held constant so that people are being fooled into increasing savings when they do not want to. As soon as people have correct expectations, the Classical economy will be driven back to the natural rate of income and output, and the new equilibrium will be different only if it affected both supply and demand forces.

Deriving the LM Curve

The LM curve represents those combinations of interest rates and income levels where the money or financial market is in equilibrium. The term LM comes from demand for liquidity (L) and supply of money (M). The LM curve is generally derived from the analysis of the supply and demand for money, and we shall follow that presentation here.

Demand for Money

Since money is a financial asset that pays no interest, it costs people to hold it in forgone interest. Why do they hold it? Because it is useful for making transactions. The higher the income in the economy the more money people want to hold. However, how much people and firms economize on holding money depends on the interest rate. The higher the interest rate, the less money people will want to hold. Thus, we can write the demand for money as follows

$$M_D = f(Y, i),$$

where $\qquad Y$ = income, and
$\qquad i$ = interest rate.

Figure 6.8 graphs this function.

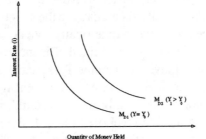

Figure 6.8

M_{D1} is the relevant demand curve for income level Y_0. As the income level in the economy increases the amount of money held by individuals would correspondingly increase. Thus, an increase in income would shift the money demand curve to the right. M_{D2} in Figure 6.8 shows the money demand at the higher income level.

Supply of Money and Equilibrium in the Money Market

To keep the analysis simple we will assume that the supply of money is unaffected by either the interest rate or income level in the economy. It is controlled by the central bank. Figure 6.9 shows this fixed supply of money and adds the demand for money from above. Equilibrium in the market for money occurs where the supply of money equals the demand for money.

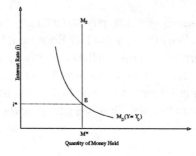

Figure 6.9

At the point E, the equilibrium interest rate is $i*$ and the quantity of money that equates the demand and supply is $M*$. Given a supply and demand for money, there are a number of combinations of interest rates and income levels where the money market is in equilibrium. By transferring these points to a graph of equilibrium space with interest rates on the vertical axis and income on the horizontal axis we can use the supply and demand information to derive the LM curve geometrically. We do so in Figure 6.10.

The supply of money is assumed fixed. The money demand curve relevant for three different levels of income Y_0, Y_1 and Y_2, is drawn in Figure 6.10(a). Initially, the economy is in equilibrium at income level Y_0 and interest rate i_0. We graph this equilibrium A in equilibrium space in Figure 6.10(b). Now say the income level rises to Y_1. If the money market is to remain in equilibrium the interest rate must rise to i_1. Thus a second point on the LM curve will be point B. By continuing this process and connecting these combinations of income and interest rates which keep the money market in equilibrium, we get a LM curve. Notice that it is an upward sloping curve. For the money market to remain in equilibrium, when income rises the interest rate must rise.

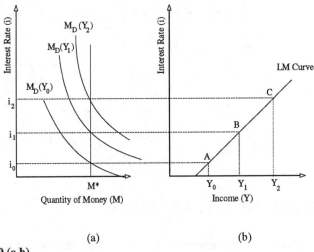

(a)   (b)

Figure 6.10 (a,b)

Points Off the LM Curve

Let's consider what happens at points off the LM curve. We know that any point off the LM curve must be a point of disequilibrium where either there is an excess demand or an excess supply of money. Let us examine two disequilibrium points B and C in Figure 6.11. At B, the interest rate is i' which is higher than the equilibrium interest rate of i^*. At this higher interest rate i' money demand is low. Recollect that there is an inverse relation between the demand for money and the interest rate. Money demand is low compared to the supply of money and we have an excess supply of money. Similarly, at point C below the LM curve, interest rates are low and therefore the demand for money is high and we have an excess demand for money. In general, at all points above the LM curve we have an excess supply of money and at all points below the LM curve there is an excess demand for money.

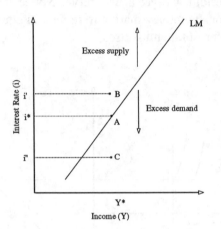

Figure 6.11

Factors That Shift the LM Curve

As with the IS curve, we are interested in knowing what factors would shift
the LM curve down to the right or up to the left. We know that the Federal
Reserve can control the supply of money by using three main instruments:
the reserve requirement, the discount rate and open market operations.
Suppose that the Fed expands the money supply shifting the money supply
out from M_{S0} to M_{S1}.

This is depicted in our money market graph by a right-ward shift of the
vertical money supply curve. What does this mean for the LM curve? Suppose that we were on the curve LM_0 in Figure 6.12, and the Fed conducted
an open market purchase of bonds. At each level of interest, the additional
money can support a higher level of income. The entire LM curve shifts
down and to the right. Hence an increase in money supply shifts the LM
curve from LM_0 to the right to LM_1. Likewise, a decrease in money supply
would shift the LM curve to the left of LM_0.

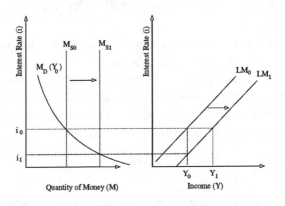

Figure 6.12

Combining the IS and LM Curves

We are now ready to put the IS curve and the LM curve together to determine aggregate equilibrium. We do this in Figure 6.13.

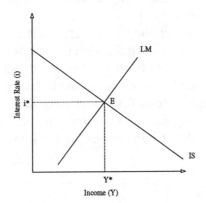

Figure 6.13

Aggregate equilibrium occurs where both the goods market and the money market are in equilibrium. Since the LM curve includes all points at which the money market is in equilibrium, and the IS curve includes all points at which the goods market is in equilibrium, aggregate equilibrium will be where the IS and LM curves intersect—point E in Figure 6.13.

Fiscal Policy and Monetary Policy in the IS-LM Model

The IS-LM model provides a way for us to examine equilibrium in both the goods and money market. In this section we look at the short-run effects of both fiscal and monetary policy. Since our discussion of the IS curve focused on the difference between the Classical and Keynesian interpretation of the IS curve, we make that the central distinction here in analyzing the effects of monetary and fiscal policy.

Monetary Policy

Monetary policy refers to the use of monetary policy instruments by the Federal Reserve to alter the money supply in the economy. As we stated above, an increase in money supply causes the LM curve to shift down or to the right as shown in Figure 6.14. Figure 6.14 assumes that the IS curve is relatively flat, the Keynesian interpretation. As the LM curve shifts, the interest rate in the economy falls which causes investment to rise. Again since this is the Keynesian IS curve, the multiplier effect of the change in investment kicks in, resulting in an increase in the overall level of income or GDP in the economy.

In the Classical model, the effect of expansionary monetary policy on income in the economy is small since the IS curve is steeper. So the fall in interest rates increases investment with no multiplier effect. Figure 6.15 shows that the resultant increase in income from expansionary monetary policy is smaller than in Figure 6.14. Our Classical and Keynesian interpretations notwithstanding, the upshot of monetary policy is clear. The more elastic or flatter the IS curve the more effective is monetary policy.

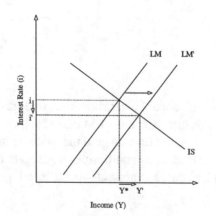

Figure 6.14

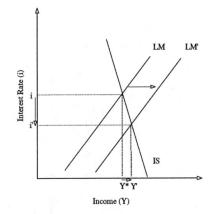

Figure 6.15

Exercise 1: Show the effects of contractionary monetary policy on interest rates and output with both a flat and a steep IS curve.

Fiscal Policy

Government spending G, and Taxes T, are the two fiscal policy instruments used to stabilize the economy. Expansionary fiscal policy aimed at stimulating employment or growth in the economy can be achieved by either increasing spending or decreasing taxes or some combination of the two. We can use the IS-LM model to look at the effects of fiscal policy. Figures 6.16 and 6.17 refer to the expansionary effects of fiscal policy with steep and flat IS curves respectively. With an upward sloping LM curve, we can see the effect on income from expansionary policy. Where does the effect on income seem to be larger? This is rather ambiguous. It seems from our pictures below that the effect of expansionary fiscal policy in the Classical (steep IS) is not much different from the Keynesian case (flat IS). But what if we make our LM curve more responsive to interest rates meaning the LM curve is now relatively flat? With a more elastic LM curve we can clearly see that the effect of expansionary policy on income is larger with the Keynesian IS curve than with the Classical IS curve. This is shown in Figures 6.18 and 6.19 below. We can conclude that the flatter the IS curve and the flatter the LM curve the more effective is fiscal policy.

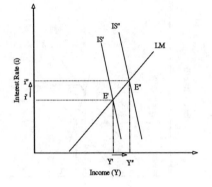

Figure 6.16

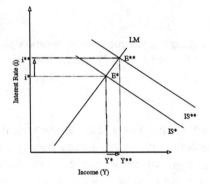

Figure 6.17

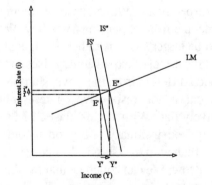

Figure 6.18

Exercise 2: With a relatively flat LM curve, show the effect of an increase in taxes on equilibrium interest rates and output for both a steep and a flat IS curve.

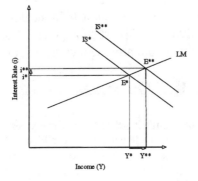

Figure 6.19

Conclusion

Having discussed how fiscal policy and monetary policy can be used to stabilize the economy from shocks such as unemployment and inflation, we should state that the two are not mutually exclusive. The government and the Federal Reserve often use both fiscal and monetary policy simultaneously to achieve some desired target level of interest rate and income in the economy. In the process of introducing this model, our focus in this chapter has been to make clear the distinction between the Keynesian and the Classical interpretations. The IS-LM model is therefore a useful tool to analyze the short-term effects of policy in the economy under both the Classical and Keynesian scenarios. It gives us a good insight into the working of the macroeconomy and provides us with a logical way to think about the effects of certain policy decisions on our economy.

Problems

1. The LM curve we derived was based on the assumption that the supply of money was perfectly inelastic. Derive or show what the LM curve would look like if the supply of money was relatively elastic.

2.
a. Suppose that the economy of Belarus has begun to 'overheat.' Show how you would use (i) monetary policy and (ii) fiscal policy to stabilize the economy of Belarus.

b. Which policy seems to be more effective in your opinion? Explain your reasoning.

c. Does the interpretation of the IS curve (Classical or Keynesian) have any bearing on the effectiveness of a particular policy? Use the IS-LM model to demonstrate your answer and provide a verbal explanation.

Answers to In-Text Questions

1. This can be shown by a shift left in the LM curve in Figures 6.14 and 6.15 respectively.
2. This can be shown by a shift left in the IS curve in Figures 6.18 and 6.19 respectively.

7

The Algebra of the IS-LM Model

In Chapter 6 we presented the IS-LM model geometrically. In this chapter we present the IS-LM model algebraically. The derivation presented here follows the geometric derivation of the last chapter. The IS curve is derived from the market for goods and services. The LM curve is derived from the financial market. Then the two are combined to get a general equilibrium. We start by showing the derivation of the Keynesian IS curve.

The Keynesian Goods Market Equilibrium (The IS Curve)

In considering the goods market we keep the analysis simple by assuming only linear relationships among variables. The equations specifying the Keynesian goods market are the following:

(1) $\quad C = C_0 + bY_d$, where $1 > b > 0$;
(2) $\quad Y_d = Y - T$;
(3) $\quad T = T_0 + tY$, where $1 > t > 0$;
(4) $\quad I = I_0 - ci$, where $1 > c > 0$;
(5) $\quad G = G_0$;
(6) $\quad Y = C + I + G$.

All variables are as defined in previous chapters with the addition of c, the interest rate sensitivity parameter measuring the change in investment for a given change in the interest rate. Goods market equilibrium is derived by combining these equations. Accordingly, substitute equations (1), (2), (3), (4), and (5) in (6). This yields

$$Y = C_0 + b (Y - T_0 - tY) + I_0 - ci + G_0 .$$

Distributing b gives

$$Y = C_0 + bY - bT_0 - btY + I_0 - ci + G_0 .$$

Bringing the ci term to the left-hand side and taking the Y term to the right side,

$$ci = C_0 + bY - bT_0 - btY + I_0 + G_0 - Y.$$

Factoring out the Y term on the right-hand side yields

$$ci = C_0 + I_0 + G_0 - bT_0 - Y(1 - b + bt).$$

Dividing both sides by c,

(7) $\qquad i = (C_0 + I_0 + G_0 - bT_0)/c - [(1 - b + bt)/c]Y.$

This equation tells us that the equilibrium interest rate is a function of income. Equation (7) specifies the IS curve, with combinations of (i, Y) yielding equilibrium in the market for goods and services. We can write the IS curve as a function of income Y, i.e., with Y on the left-hand side, but the geometric derivation of the IS curve in the previous chapter had the interest rate i on the y-axis and income Y on the x-axis. Isolating i on the left-hand side lets us show you how this equation is the same IS curve derived geo-metrically.

Note that the term $[(C_0 + I_0 + G_0 - bT_0)/c]$ is the y-intercept, which is positive, and $-(1 - b + bt)/c$ is the slope of the IS curve, which is negative. We know this is the slope because the slope of the IS curve is exactly $\partial i/\partial Y = -(1 - b + bt)/c < 0$. If the interest rate had no effect on investment $(c = 0)$ the IS curve would become a vertical line because the slope term $-[(1 - b + bt)/c]Y$ and the intercept term $(C_0 + I_0 + G_0 - bT_0)/c$ go to infinity.

Shifts of the IS curve result from shifts in any exogenous component of the intercept term (C_0, I_0, G_0, T_0). To show what happens to equilibrium income as the IS curve shifts, first we isolate Y on the left. We can rewrite the IS curve as

$$[(1 - b + bt)/c]Y = [(C_0 + I_0 + G_0 - bT_0)/c)] - i, \text{ or}$$

$$Y = [c/(1 - b + bt)] [(C_0 + I_0 + G_0 - bT_0)/c) - i].$$

The IS curve will shift with changes to exogenous consumption, invest-ment, government spending, and taxes. We consider each in turn. To find what happens to income Y as, say, consumption C_0 changes (i.e., what hap-pens to the IS curve with a change in exogenous consumption), take the first derivative of Y with respect to C_0 in the above equation:

$$\partial Y/\partial C_0 = 1/(1 - b + bt) > 0.$$

Since $\partial Y/\partial C_0 > 0$, an increase in C_0 shifts the IS curve to the right.

Similarly, to find out how Y changes in response to a change in exogenous investment, we take the first derivate with respect to I_0:

$$\partial Y/\partial I_0 = 1/(1 - b + bt) > 0.$$

Since $\partial Y/\partial I_0 > 0$, an increase in I_0 shifts the IS curve to the right.

Again, to find out how Y changes in response to a change in government spending, we take the first derivate with respect to G:

$$\partial Y/\partial G_0 = 1/(1 - b + bt) > 0.$$

Since $\partial Y/\partial G_0 > 0$, an increase in G_0 shifts the IS curve to the right.

Finally we do the same for taxes:

$$\partial Y/\partial T_0 = -b/(1 - b + bt) < 0.$$

Since $\partial Y/\partial T_0 < 0$, an increase in T_0 shifts the IS curve to the left.

Notice that the derivative of Y with respect to G_0 is just the government spending multiplier derived in your textbook. Since $0 < (1 - b + bt) < 1$, the shift in the IS cuve is greater than any autonomous changes in C_0, I_0 or G_0. Since $0 < b < 1$, the tax multiplier is smaller than the consumption, government spending and investment multiplier. Also note that $\partial Y/\partial C_0 > 0$, $\partial Y/\partial I_0 > 0$ and $\partial Y/\partial G_0 > 0$ but $\partial Y/\partial T_0 < 0$. This tells us that while increases in C_0, I_0 and G_0 will lead to increases in Y, an increase in T_0 will lead to a fall in Y.

Exercise 1: Derive the expression for the multiplier for changes in autonomous consumption. What tax rate between 0 and 1 would you choose to minimize the impact of changes in autonomous consumption on the economy? Explain the economic intuition.

The Classical Goods Market Equilibrium (The IS Curve)

The modern Classical analysis of the goods market is simple. We keep the analysis straightforward by once again assuming only linear relationships as we did with the Keynesian IS curve. With no multiplier effects, consumption is simply autonomous (i.e., there is no marginal propensity to consume so that the bY_d term drops out of the consumption function). Since the Y_d term drops out so does equation (3) $Y_d = Y - T$. Taxes in this model do not affect income since we assume that consumption is entirely exogenous. Investment is a function of the interest rate. The structural equations in this case are

$$\text{(8)} \qquad\qquad C = C_0;$$

$$\text{(9)} \qquad\qquad I = I_0 - ci;$$

$$\text{(10)} \qquad\qquad G = G_0.$$

Again, we derive the reduced-form equation by substituting equations (8), (9) and (10) in equation (6) to yield

$$Y = C_0 + I_0 - ci + G_0.$$

Subtracting Y and adding ci to both sides,

$$ci = C_0 + I_0 + G_0 - Y.$$

Again, we want to isolate i to the left:

$$\text{(11)} \qquad\qquad i = (C_0 + I_0 + G_0)/c - (1/c)Y.$$

The term $(C_0 + I_0 + G_0)/c$ is the intercept and $-(1/c)$ is the slope of the IS curve. The slope can be derived mathematically by taking the derivative of i with respect to Y: $\partial i / \partial Y = -(1/c) < 0$.

As with the Keynesian model, note that if the interest rate had no effect on investment and therefore on income in the goods market, the IS curve would become a vertical line.

The difference between the Keynesian and Classical IS curve can be summarized so far by comparing equations (7) and (11). The key difference is the slopes. The Keynesian slope has a numerator of $(1 - b + bt)$ while that of the Classical IS curve is 1. Since $(1 - b + bt) < 1$ the slope of the Keynesian IS curve is less than the slope of the Classical IS curve.

Shifts of the Classical IS curve can once again be interpreted easily as we did in the Keynesian case by isolating Y on the left and seeing how changes in the exogenous components of the intercept term affect Y. We can rewrite the Classical IS curve as

$$(1/c)Y = (C_0 + I_0 + G_0)/c - i, \text{ or}$$

$$Y = c[(C_0 + I_0 + G_0)/c - i].$$

To see how exogenous consumption affects income, we take the derivative of Y with respect to C_0 in the above equation:

$$\partial Y/\partial C_0 = 1 > 0.$$

Since $\partial Y/\partial C_0 = 1 > 0$, the IS curve shifts to the right when C_0 increases. Similarly for exogenous investment,

$$\partial Y/\partial I_0 = 1 > 0.$$

Since $\partial Y/\partial I_0 = 1 > 0$, the IS curve shifts to the right when I_0 increases. Finally for government spending,

$$\partial Y/\partial G_0 = 1 > 0.$$

Since $\partial Y/\partial G_0 = 1 > 0$, the IS curve shifts to the right when G_0 increases.

The direction of the shifts is the same as with the Keynesian model, but since the partial derivatives with respect to C_0, G_0 and I_0 equal one, the multipliers are one. The shifts will equal the changes in the exogenous components. There is no multiplier effect with the Classical IS curve. The change in income is likely to be small or negligible.

The Money Market Equilibrium (The LM Curve)

There are a number of distinctions that have been made between the Keynesian and the Classical specifications of the LM curve. To keep the analysis simple, however, we will not make them here. The LM curve can be determined algebraically where the money market is in equilibrium. Thus the LM curve can be obtained by equating the demand for money with the supply of money. The demand for money is comprised of the transactions, precautionary and speculative demands for money. Transactions and precautionary demands for money depend primarily on income Y, while the speculative demand for money is negatively related to the interest rate:

Transactions demand $L_t \quad = \quad f(Y)$

$$\text{Precautionary demand } L_p = f(Y)$$
$$\text{Speculative demand } L_s = f(i)$$

For simplicity let us assume the money demand function is linear. Let that part of money demand which depends on income be equal to $j + kY$ (i.e., transactions demand (L_t) + precautionary demand $(L_p) = j + kY$). Let the speculative demand for money which is negatively related to interest be $L_s = -hi$.

The money demand equation may now be written as

$$M_d = L_t + L_p + L_s, \text{ or}$$

$$M_d = j + kY - hi ,$$

where j = a constant term independent of income or interest
        k = the income sensitivity parameter
        h = the interest sensitivity parameter, and
        $1 > j, k, h > 0$.

Money supply is assumed to be exogenously determined by the Federal Reserve. Hence money supply, M_s, is a given constant.

To find equilibrium in the money market set $M_s = M_d$. Thus,

$$M_s = j + kY - hi.$$

To show that this is the LM curve derived in the previous chapter, we need to isolate i on the left-hand side. First, subtract M_s and add hi to both sides:

$$hi = j - M_s + kY.$$

Next, we divide through by h:

$$i = (j - M_s)/h + (k/h)Y.$$

This is the LM curve which yields combinations of (i,Y) in which the money market is in equilibrium. Note once again that $(j - M_s)/h$ is the intercept which is positive if $j > M_s$ or negative if $j < M_s$. The term (k/h) is the slope of the LM curve, which is positive. Mathematically we can show that this is the slope by taking the first derivative of i with respect to Y: $\partial i / \partial Y = (k/h)$.

As was the case with the IS curve, changes in exogenous components of the intercept term (here only M_s) will shift the LM curve. A slight rearrangement of the LM curve can enable us to understand how shifts in the LM curve affect income (Y). Accordingly, we must isolate Y:

$$Y = (h/k)[i - (j - M_s)/h].$$

To find how an exogenous change in money supply (all other things held constant) affects the LM curve, we need to find the first derivative of Y with respect to money supply M_s. We find that

$$\partial Y/\partial M_s = (1/k) > 0.$$

Since $\partial Y/\partial M_s > 0$, the LM curve shifts to the right when M_s increases.

The Complete Classical and Keynesian Algebraic Fixed-Price Model

To obtain a complete IS-LM model or a reduced-form equation which gives us equilibrium in both the goods and the money market, we need to combine the IS and the LM curves that we have just derived. We have two equations in two unknowns, i and Y, so we can easily find the interest rate and the level of output that equilibrates both the goods and the money market.

Keynesian IS Curve: $i = (C_0 + I_0 + G_0 - bT_0)/c) - [(1 - b + bt)/c]Y.$

Classical IS curve: $i = (C_0 + I_0 + G_0)/c - (1/c)Y.$

LM curve: $i = (j - M_s)/h + (k/h)Y.$

The Keynesian Fixed Price Model

Substitute the LM curve, or substitute for i in the IS curve:

$$(j - M_s)/h + (k/h)Y = [(C_0 + I_0 + G_0 - bT_0)/c)] - [(1 - b + bt)/c]Y.$$

Now, solve for Y by multiplying both sides by c:

$$c[(j - M_s)/h + (k/h)]Y = (C_0 + I_0 + G_0 - bT_0) - (1 - b + bt)Y.$$

Bring the Y terms together on the left-hand side:

$$Y[(1 - b + bt)+ (kc/h)] = (C_0 + I_0 + G_0 - bT_0) + (c/h) (M_s - j), \text{ or}$$

$$Y = [(C_0 + I_0 + G_0 - bT_0) + (c/h) (M_s - j)]/[(1 - b + bt)+ (kc/h)].$$

This is the equilibrium level of income Y where the IS and LM curves intersect. We can demonstrate that expansionary fiscal and monetary policy will increase the level of income or output Y by taking the first derivative Y with respect to G_0 and M_s in the above equation:

$$\partial Y/\partial G_0 = 1/[(1 - b + bt)+ (kc/h)].$$

$\partial Y/\partial G_0 > 0$ since $(1 - b + bt) > 0$ and k, c and h are all positive. Expansionary fiscal policy increases income. $\partial Y/\partial G_0$ is the multiplier under the IS-LM framework. The only difference from the government multiplier is the additional term kc/h in the denominator, which reduces the value of the multiplier. An increase in government spending G_0 will increase income Y, but not as much as would expansionary fiscal policy holding the interest rate constant.

Similarly, expansionary monetary policy can be captured by the derivative of Y with respect to M_s:

$$\partial Y/\partial M_s = (c/h)/[(1 - b + bt)+ (kc/h)],$$

which is also greater than 0. Thus expansionary monetary policy also leads to an increase in income Y.

Exercise 2: Analyze the impact of a change in government spending where money demand is infinitely sensitive to interest rates ($h \to \infty$). Compare this to the government spending multiplier associated with equation (7). Explain the economic intuition.

The Classical Fixed Price Model

Once again substitute the LM curve, or substitute for i in the Classical IS curve and solve for Y.

$$(j - M_s)/h + (k/h)Y = (C_0 + I_0 + G_0)/c - (1/c)Y.$$

Now, solve for Y by multiplying both sides by c:

$$c[(j - M_s)/h + (k/h)]Y = (C_0 + I_0 + G_0) - Y.$$

Bring the Y terms together on the left-hand side:

$$Y[1 + (kc/h)] = (C_0 + I_0 + G_0) + (c/h)(M_{s.} - j), \text{ or}$$

$$Y = [(C_0 + I_0 + G_0) + (c/h)(M_s - j)]/[1 + (kc/h)].$$

This is the equilibrium level of income Y where the Classical IS and LM curves intersect. It is similar to the equilibrium level of income using the Keynesian IS curve, except now the denominator is slightly different. Once again the effect of expansionary fiscal and monetary policy can be shown by taking the first derivative of Y with respect to G_0 and M_s as follows:

$$\partial Y/\partial G_0 = 1/[1 + (kc/h)].$$

$\partial Y/\partial G_0 > 0$, since k, c and h are all positive. Expansionary fiscal policy increases income. $\partial Y/\partial G_0$ is the multiplier under the Classical IS-LM framework.

Compare this with the multiplier in the Keynesian case: $\partial Y/\partial G_0 = 1/[(1 - b + bt) + (kc/h)]$. Which is larger? It should be obvious to you that $1/[(1 - b + bt) + (kc/h)]$ is larger than $1/[1 + (kc/h)]$. The Keynesian multiplier is larger than the Classical multiplier.

Suppose that the marginal propensity to consume $b = 0.8$, the marginal tax rate $t = 0.2$, and the ratio $(kc/h) = 0.5$. Then the multiplier in the Keynesian case is $1/[(1 - b + bt) + (kc/h)] = 1/[1 - 0.8 + 0.8 \cdot 0.2 + (0.5)] = 1/0.86 = 1.16$. The multiplier in the Classical case is $1/[1 + (kc/h)] = 1/[1 + (0.5)] = 1/1.5 = 0.67$.

Expansionary monetary policy in the Classical case is obtained from the derivative of Y with respect to M_s:

$$\partial Y/\partial M_s = (c/h)/[1 + (kc/h)] > 0.$$

We can conclude that expansionary monetary policy also leads to an increase in income Y but the increase in Y is much smaller than in the Keynesian case, because, again, $(c/h)/[1 + (kc/h)] < (c/h)/[(1 - b + bt) + (kc/h)]$.

Conclusion

Let us reiterate the difference between the Classical and the Keynesian models of the economy that these specifications assume. The Keynesian case allows for *multiplier effects* of changes in fiscal or monetary policy. When exogenous spending or the money supply changes, equilibrium income changes by more than that shift. The Classical economists postulated no such multiplier effects. Equilibrium income would change only by the amount of the shift. Our derivation of the two types of IS curves and the algebraic fixed-price model convey emphatically this important difference.

In addition, the Classical economists considered money demand to be insensitive to changes in interest rates. Consider once again the money demand curve:

$$M_d = j + kY - hi.$$

If we take this insensitivity assumption in the Classical case literally, then in our money demand equation, mathematically $h = 0$, so that the Classical money demand curve may now be written simply as

$$M_d = j + kY.$$

Setting $M_s = M_d$ and rearranging,

$$kY = M_s - j, \text{ or}$$

$$Y = (M_s - j)/k.$$

The above equation suggests that there is only one level of equilibrium income that the economy can reach irrespective of the interest rate in the economy. The LM curve in this scenario is vertical or perfectly inelastic. Any change in fiscal policy will raise interest rates but will have no impact on Y, which is just another way of saying that there are no multiplier effects in the Classical model.

Problems

1. Suppose that the consumption function is a function of both income Y and the interest rate i in the economy (i.e. $C = C_0 + bY_d - di$). Algebraically derive the IS curve.

2. Show that the LM curve becomes more elastic when the money supply is not an exogenous constant M_s, but has an endogenous element as well. (For example, money supply $= M_s + z\,i$. Money supply is positively related to the interest rate in the economy.)

3. Derive the IS curve in an open economy model with trade. Assume exports are exogenous, $X = X_0$, and imports are a function of Y, given by $M = M_0 + mY$. Derive the reduced-form equation or the equilibrium value of income Y in both the goods and money markets.

Answers to In-Text Questions

1. $\partial Y / \partial C_0 = 1/(1 - b + bt)$. To minimize the impact of changes in C_0 on the economy, t should be 1. When $t = 1$, the multiplier will be 1. This makes economic sense because in this case any increases in income will be taxed away and cannot be multiplied through the economy.

2. The government spending multiplier, $\partial Y / \partial G = 1/[(1 - b + bt) + (kc/h)]$, when h $\rightarrow \infty$ is just $1/(1 - b + bt)$. This is the same multiplier associated with equation (7). When money demand is infinitely sensitive to interest rates, the interest rate will not change. This is equivalent to the assumption of a constant interest rate in equation (7). In both cases there is no crowding out of investment associated with increases in government spending.

8

The Multiplier-Accelerator Model

The Keynesian multiplier model that we examined in Chapter 4 is a highly simplified model of the economy. This simple model does not include the time dimension of the adjustment to equilibrium and many of the intricate relationships among the various variables which can change the nature of the adjustment process. One such relationship is between investment and output. Firms invest to increase productive capacity and replace worn out capital. A firm will want to increase productive capacity if it expects to sell more in the future, i.e., if it expects income to rise. Investment thus depends upon the change in income. This modified model is called the *investment-accelerator model* of the economy. In Chapter 4 we included investment in the model as a function of income rather than as a function of the change in income. Including investment was relatively simple; the multiplier was adjusted by the marginal propensity to invest. Otherwise the model changed very little.

In the first part of this chapter, we show you how making investment a function of the change in income, a more realistic formulation, complicates the math enormously. And this is one of the simplest modifications of the multiplier model. In the second part of this chapter, we use the investment accelerator model as a backdrop to discuss some more complicated math which has recently been discussed a lot in mathematics—chaos theory, complexity, and nonlinear dynamics. It is in the higher level math from which future changes in the macroeconomic model will come.

The investment-accelerator model itself dates back to the 1930s when the Keynesian textbook was being developed in large part at a seminar held at Harvard by Alvin Hansen and John Williams. At a meeting of the seminar, Hansen pondered out loud about what might happen to investment as income or output increased. He said that it did not seem reasonable that investment was an exogenous constant as in the simple Keynesian model, but that firms would further increase investment as output grew. Hansen felt that this idea of a link between investment and output could be integrated into a model, but he wasn't sure how.

One of the students in the seminar took that idea and worked out a fully developed mathematical model and brought it back to Hansen. He called the relationship between investment and output the accelerator and the model is called the multiplier-accelerator model. The student, Paul Samuelson, won the Nobel Prize in economics in 1970 for this work and other additional insightful contributions to the field of economics.

The Link Between Investment and Output

In Chapter 4, we suggested that rather than considering investment to be just an exogenous constant, we could let investment depend on the level of output Y in the economy. The investment function was written as $I = I_0 + vY$. With consumption in the economy defined as $C = C_0 + bY$, the reduced-form equation for equilibrium can easily be derived by substituting for C and I in the equation $Y = C + I$. Thus,

$$Y = C_0 + bY + I_0 + vY.$$

Bringing the Y terms together on the left and solving for Y yields

$$Y = [1/(1 - b - v)](C_0 + I_0).$$

Note that the equilibrium level of output Y in this case will depend on both the marginal propensity to consume, b, and the marginal propensity to invest, v.

But what happens if the level of investment, I, does not depend on the level of output, but instead, depends on the change in the level of output Y? What such a specification says is that when output rises or accelerates, firms will want to increase investment so that they will have the facilities to meet the higher demand that will be associated with this higher output. Alternatively, when the change in output is small or negative firms will wish to hold investment steady or even disinvest by allowing their stocks of inventories to be depleted.

Thus investment in the accelerator model is given by

$$I = I_0 + v\Delta Y.$$

To keep the analysis as simple as possible we will assume there are discrete time periods, so that ΔY may be written as the difference between output in period t and period $t-1$. ΔY in this model is the rate of change in output. Thus investment depends on the rate at which firms produce output or goods and services in the economy (i.e., ΔY is the acceleration in the production of goods and services). Now you can see from where the name accelerator model emerges.

Therefore,

(1) $$I_t = I_0 + v\,(Y_t - Y_{t-1})$$

where v = a coefficient or parameter which relates investment to the change in income.

Before we begin dealing with the math, it is helpful to think about the implications of the relationship in equation (1). Investment by firms is undertaken depending on the expected profitability of the particular investment project. Clearly higher and higher levels of output will lead to a greater demand for investment.

The Multiplier-Accelerator and Keynesian Model Together

Let us illustrate the multiplier-accelerator principle with a simple model. Consider, for example,

(2) $$C_t = C_0 + bY_t,$$

(3) $$I_t = I_0 + v(Y_t - Y_{t-1}).$$

The consumption function is the familiar one except that it has a time dimension. The investment function may be interpreted as saying that the level of a firm's investment during the current period, t, depends on the rate of change of output during the period t and the previous time period, t-1.

At equilibrium we know that

(4) $$Y_t = C_t + I_t.$$

Substituting equations (2) and (3) into (4) we get

$$Y_t = C_0 + bY_t + I_0 + v(Y_t - Y_{t-1}).$$

Collecting terms and solving for Y_t we get

(5) $Y_t = (C_0 - vY_{t-1} + I_0)/(1 - b - v).$

Note that equation (5) is very similar to the reduced-form equations we derived in Chapter 4. Output Y_t depends not only on the parameter values of C_0, b and v, but also on the level of output in the period $t-1$. Equation (5) is called a *first-order difference equation*. If we knew the parameter values for C_0, b and v, we could solve this system of equations. As you will see, this small change makes a big difference to the solution.

Actually solving this difference equation is a bit beyond the math required for this book. But we can give you a sense of the solution by solving it for specific values. So, let us now try and solve a difference equation system in which we assign values to the different parameters. We'll follow the same presentation that Paul Samuelson used when he first developed the model.

Consumption during the current period t depends on income Y from the last period $t-1$. Samuelson also assumed in this example that investment, I, was conditional on the level of output from the previous two periods, $t-1$ and $t-2$. Our consumption and investment functions may now be written as

(6) $C_t = C_0 + bY_{t-1}$,

(7) $I_t = I_0 + v/2\ (Y_{t-1} - Y_{t-2}).$

Again, using the equilibrium defined in (4) we get

(8) $Y_t = C_0 + bY_{t-1} + I_0 + v/2\ (Y_{t-1} - Y_{t-2}).$

Suppose we assign particular values to a, b, v, and I_0. Let $C_0 = 75$, $b = 0.5$, $v = 2$, and $I_0 = 50$. Equation (8) becomes

$$Y_t = 75 + 0.5\ Y_{t-1} + (Y_{t-1} - Y_{t-2}) + 50 \text{ or}$$

(9) $Y_t = 75 + 1.5\ Y_{t-1} - Y_{t-2} + 50.$

Once you are given some initial values for output for two periods and autonomous investment, solving this equation for the output in the following period is a trivial exercise. We illustrate solutions to equation (9) for different values for parameters b and v.

Case 1

Suppose that the equilibrium levels of output in period 0 and period 1, Y_0 and Y_1, equal 250. We can now find the level of output Y_2 in period 2 using equation (9):

$$Y_2 = 75 + 1.5Y_1 - Y_0 + 50 = 75 + 1.5(250) - (250) + 50 = 250.$$

Similarly we find the level of output in period 3:

$$Y_3 = 75 + 1.5Y_2 - Y_1 + 50 = 75 + 1.5(250) - (250) + 50 = 250.$$

If you solve for subsequent values of output Y_4, Y_5, Y_6 and so on you will get a steady constant value of 250. In other words Y_4, Y_5, $Y_6,$ .... are all equal to 250, given Y_0 and Y_1 were both 250.

Suppose that we give the initial system a little push so that $Y_0 = 250$, but in period two, $\Delta I = 64$ so that

$$Y_1 = Y_0 + \Delta I = 250 + 64 = 314.$$

I_0 returns to its original value of 50 thereafter. Then

$$Y_2 = 75 + 1.5Y_1 - Y_0 + 50 = 75 + 1.5\,(314) - (250) + 50 = 346.$$

We can find the value of Y_3 by substituting the values for Y_2 and Y_1 in equation (9) where $Y_1 = 314$ and $Y_2 = 346$. Hence,

$$Y_3 = 75 + 1.5\,Y_2 - Y_1 + 50 = 75 + 1.5(346) - (314) + 50 = 330.$$

If we have the value for Y_3, we can solve for Y_4. The values for output Y through periods 1 to 10 are shown in the table below.

Table 1
Solution for Difference Equation $Y_t = 75 + 1.5 \, Y_{t-1} - Y_{t-2} + 50$

$b = 0.5$, $v = 2$,	$Y_0 = 250$ $Y_1 = 250$	$b = 0.5$, $v = 2$,	$Y_0 = 250$, $Y_1 = 314$
Period	Output Y_t	Period	Output Y_t
2	250	2	346
3	250	3	330
4	250	4	274
5	250	5	206
6	250	6	160
7	250	7	159
8	250	8	204
9	250	9	271
10	250	10	328

The shock to the model results in fluctuations in income which are depicted in Figure 8.1.

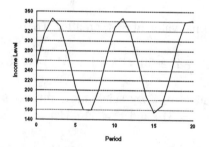

Figure 8.1

Notice what happens to the value of output Y in subsequent periods. It decreases until period 7 but then starts going up again. If you carry out this exercise beyond period 10, you will find that output oscillates. You may like to verify that $Y_{11} = 346.3$ and that the system oscillates once again reaching 341.9 in period 20.

Exercise 1: Suppose that we reduce the parameter value b from 0.5 to 0.25 while v remains the same. First examine the case when Y is constant at 250. Then shock the system with an increase in autonomous investment of 64 in the first period. In all other periods, I_0 is still 50. Solve the model for income for 10 periods. Observe your results carefully. What happened to the oscillations? What would you guess would happen to the oscillations if b were higher than 0.5?

Case 2

If either *b* or *v* are increased from their initial values, the oscillations become larger and larger. Let us verify this for *v* by increasing the value of the marginal propensity to invest, *v*, from 2 to 4. We leave the marginal propensity to consume, *b*, unchanged. With parameter values $b = 0.5$ and $v = 4$, the investment function will be altered. At equilibrium,

$$Y_t = 75 + 0.5Y_{t-1} + 4/2 \ (Y_{t-1} - Y_{t-2}) + 50, \text{ or}$$

$$Y_t = 75 + 2.5Y_{t-1} - 2Y_{t-2} + 50.$$

The solution to the model is shown in column 1 of Table 2.

Table 2
Solution for Difference Equation $Y_t = 75 + 2.5Y_{t-1} - 2Y_{t-2} + 50$

$b = 0.5$, $v = 4$,	$Y_0 = 250$ $Y_1 = 250$	$b = 0.5$, $v = 4$,	$Y_0 = 250$, $Y_1 = 314$
Period	Output Y_t	Period	Output Y_t
2	250	2	410
3	250	3	522
4	250	4	610
5	250	5	606
6	250	6	420
7	250	7	-37
8	250	8	-808
9	250	9	-1820
10	250	10	-2809

In column two the solution to this model with a one-time shock in period one of increased exogenous investment of 64 is shown. When the propensity to invest is increased from 2 to 4, with initial values for output held constant at 250, the equilibrium level of output remains at 250. However, when we give the system a little push, increasing autonomous investment in period 1 by 64, the oscillations in output in the following periods become larger and larger. Output reaches its first high of 610 in period 4 but then falls all the way to -3259 in period 11 (not shown above) before it starts climbing up again. You may want to calculate the solution for periods 11 through 20 yourself. The oscillations are depicted in Figure 8.2.

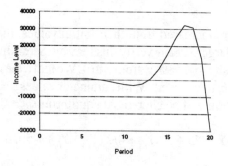

Figure 8.2

As you can see, the model is highly sensitive to the combination of parameter values. The combination of parameter values which produce various
characteristic oscillations are summarized in the Figure below and based on
the work of Paul Samuelson. It presents possible values of v and b, sepa-
rating combinations that result in similar model behavior.

For combinations within regions I and II, a small a one-time shock to the
system will result in damped oscillations and and the model will converge
to its original level of income. A constant increase (decrease) in exogenous
spending will result in a convergence to a new higher (lower) level of income. That new level is determined by the size of the multiplier and the size
of the shock. One-time shocks in a system with parameters in region III will
result in explosive oscillations around the original level of income. A constant increase (decrease) will result in explosive oscillations around new
higher (lower) level of income, again determined by the size of the shock
and the multiplier. Finally, combinations in region IV will result in a chaotic system exploding to infinity.

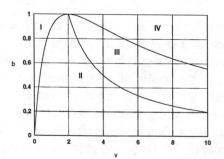

Figure 8.3

Implications of the Multiplier-Accelerator Principle

The above solution to the difference equation is quite straight forward. But this simple version of the accelerator model has some broad implications. What the accelerator principle seems to be saying is that a change in the rate of growth of output (ΔY_t) has an impact on the level of investment I_t. Depending on the fluctuations and oscillations in output Y, investment may be expected to fluctuate quite a lot. This has important implications for the role of investment on the business cycle in the economy. Further, recollect from Chapter 4 that changes in investment have an amplified effect on output through the operation of the *multiplier* principle. Our simple accelerator theory of investment along with the multiplier principle gives us a simple way to think about how business cycles with peaks and troughs, or alternatively periods of booms followed by recessions, are generated in the economy.

Chaos, Complexity and Nonlinear Dynamics in Macroeconomics

The above investment accelerator model is one of the simplest dynamic models one can design. If you think about the economy, you will see that the dynamic interrelationships will likely be much more complicated. For example, rational individuals will likely try to figure out whether cycles repeat themselves and predict future cycles based on past cycles. In doing so, they will likely look for turning points which themselves are functions of past cycles and thus will base decisions on changes in changes in variables and on more complicated combinations of changes over various time periods. As one takes these into account, the *switch points*—points at which the characteristics of the systemic movements change and at some point become chaotic—make the system appear random while they are in fact determined by underlying mathematical relationships.

More and more economists are coming to the conclusion that the switch points of many of the variables we are interested in are essentially chaotic. There is no way to correctly theoretically predict such variables in such a case. The best we can do is to use judgment with vector autoregression.

But if economists with all their mathematical tools cannot predict a variable, how can we expect individuals to do so correctly? Instead, we would expect them to develop simple rules of thumb. This foundation for macroeconomics as a field separate from microeconomics and microfoundations can be found in the chaos of real-world time series.

Problems

1. Consider the following system of equations: $C_t = C_0 + bY_t$, $I_t = I_0 + v(Y_t - Y_{t-1})$, and $G_t = g(Y_t - Y_{t-1} - Y_{t-2})$ where G_t is government spending in period t. Derive an expression for the level of output in period t.

2. Suppose that $C_t = 200 + 0.25Y_{t-1}$ and $I_t = 50 + 0.5(Y_{t-1} - Y_{t-2})$.
a. Derive the resulting difference equation based on this system of equations.
b. Suppose that $Y_0 = Y_1 = 100$. Obtain the values for output Y through the next ten periods. i.e. values of output from Y_2 through Y_{11}.
c. Let output $Y_0 = 100$, but now give this initial value a push so that $Y_1 = 50 + Y_0$. Obtain, as before, output for the next ten time periods. Compare the two systems before and after the push. Are there any discernible differences between the two?

Answers to In-Text Questions

1. Equilibrium income is $Y_t = 75 + 0.25Y_{t-1} + (Y_{t-1} - Y_{t-2}) + 50$, or $Y_t = 75 + 1.25 Y_{t-1} - Y_{t-2} + 50$. The solution for 10 periods is summarized in the following table.

Solution for Difference Equation $Y_t = 75 + 1.25 Y_{t-1} - Y_{t-2} + 50$

$b = 0.25$, $v = 2$,	$Y_0 = 250$ $Y_1 = 250$	$b = 0.25$, $v = 2$,	$Y_0 = 250$ $Y_1 = 314$
Period	Output Y_t	Period	Output Y_t
2	187.50	2	267.50
3	109.38	3	145.38
4	74.22	4	39.23
5	108.40	5	28.66
6	186.28	6	121.60
7	249.45	7	248.34
8	250.52	8	313.83
9	188.71	9	268.95
10	110.36	10	147.36

When the marginal propensity to consume b is lowered, we still get oscillations in output Y but the oscillations are somewhat dampened compared to Case 1 with $b = 0.5$. If b were higher, the oscillations would be higher. At $b = 1$, the system explodes.

9

Interest Rates, Present Value and Future Value

Interest rates are directly related to relative prices over time. For example, a good may have a price of $1 in time period x and a price of $1.10 in time period $x+1$. The *own rate of interest* of any good in general is

$$(P_2 - P_1)/P_1 \text{, or}$$

$$P_2/P_1 - 1.$$

The own rate of interest for this good, is $1.10/1.00 - 1 = 0.1$.

In principles of economics we generally talk about the *rate of interest* as the rate of interest for money—the relative price of money—which stands for generalized purchasing power over time. When the price level of goods is changing we must make a distinction. To say that the real interest rate is positive is to say that the relative prices of goods (the average of all goods) in terms of generalized purchasing power are decreasing. Often the prices of all goods are not decreasing; they are rising, but if the nominal interest rate is higher than the inflation rate, the real rate of interest will be positive. Otherwise, it is negative.

Financial markets allow individuals and firms to make trades of generalized purchasing power over time. The interest rate specifies the terms of those trades. Lenders forgo current consumption in exchange for a promise to pay back the principal, or original loan amount, plus some agreed upon sum that represents interest payments from borrowers. Interest rates are important to the study of macroeconomic theory for they play a role in the decisions by firms to invest and in decisions by individuals to save.

In this chapter we develop present value and future value formulas which allow us to change flows of income over time into a single stock at a point in time. Since interest rates express relative prices over time, and hence the relative weights that income should be valued at relative to other periods, they play a central role in present and future value analyses.

Future Value

Let's start with the concept of *future value*—the value in the future of a certain sum today. If you were to put $1 in the bank today, and your bank paid 10% interest, how much would your bank account be worth in one year? It would be worth the same $1 initial investment plus 0.10 in interest or $1.10. Remembering this, would you rather be given $1 today or $1 in one year? With a positive interest rate, you would prefer the $1 today so that you could have $1.10 in one year instead of just the $1. Interest rates tell us the relationship of the value of a dollar today compared to the value of a dollar in the future.

Consider how much a sum C will be worth in one year given an interest rate i. It will be worth C plus the interest earned on C, or Ci. The future value, FV, of C in one year is

$$FV(C) = C + Ci \ .$$

Factoring out the C, this can be rewritten as

$$FV(C) = C(1+ i).$$

This is the future value of C, or FV in one year.

We can extend this to two years. The value C would be worth C (initial investment) plus Ci (interest the first year) plus $(Ci + C)i$ (interest the second year):

$$FV(C) = (C + Ci) + (Ci + C)i$$

Factoring out C gives

$$FV = C[(1+ i) + (1 + i)i].$$

Factoring out $(1+ i)$ gives

$$FV = C(1 + i)[(1 + i)] = C(1 + i)^2.$$

This can be extended to n years. $(1 + i)$ in this case will be factored out n-1 times to get

$$FV = C(1+ i)^n.$$

An Example

A numerical example should make this clear. Suppose that you had $100 to save for one year and the interest rate was 10%. In one year you will receive $100 plus the 10% interest on the initial $100 saved, 0.1(100) = $10. The future value, FV, is

$$100 + .1(100) = \$110.$$

Suppose that you reinvested this $110 at 10% interest for another year. At the end of two years you would have

$$\$110 \, (1 + 0.1) = \$121,$$

which can be written as

$$\$100 \, (1 + 0.1)(1 + 0.1) = 121, \text{ or } \$100 \, (1 + 0.1)^2 = \$121.$$

Once again reinvesting your $121 for an additional year, you would receive at the end of the third year,

$$\$121 \, (1 + 0.1) = \$100 \, (1 + 0.1)^3 = \$133.10.$$

The future value of $100 at the end of *n* years at 10% interest rate is

$$FV = 100 \, (1 + 0.1)^n.$$

Exercise 1: Calculate the future value of $200 at 20% for 10 years.

Present Value

Now that we have answered the question of the future value of savings today, we can reverse the question and ask the present value of a future sum. That is, what payment today would make you indifferent between it and $1 one year from now? This sum that you would be willing to accept today is called the *present value* of the future payment. In the above example, we found that $100 saved today at 10% interest was worth $110 in one year. Clearly, you would be indifferent between receiving $110 in one year and $100 today. They have the same value. The formula for future value can be manipulated to calculate present value. Recall,

$$FV = C(1+i)^n.$$

FV is the sum in the future and *C* is a sum in the present. Therefore, *C* is the same as present value. First substituting *PV* for *C*, and solving this for *PV*, we get

$$PV = FV/(1 + i)^n.$$

To minimize confusion let's substitute *F* for *FV* to represent a certain sum in the future. Rewriting the formula for present value we get

$$PV = F/(1 + i)^n.$$

Present value is often referred to as the present *discounted* value. That is because the future value is *discounted* by the interest rate *i*.

Two simple rules emerge from the present value equation:

1. Present value declines as the interest rate rises. This is clear because *i* appears in the denominator, meaning *PV* and *i* are inversely related.
2. Present value falls the later the payment is made. Intuitively this is clear, because as *n* increases $(1 + i)$ increases, and $(1 + i)$ is in the denominator.

Exercise 2: Calculate the present value of a future promised payment of $2645 at 15% 2 years from today. What would happen to the present value if the interest rate rises to 20%? Does this make economic sense?

Present Value and Bonds and Other Assets

What is the relationship between the present discounted value and the price of a zero coupon bond? Zero coupon bonds promise to pay a certain amount in the future. There are no interest payments. So we can directly apply the formula for present value to calculate how much an individual would be willing to pay for a given zero coupon bond. Suppose the bond promises to pay you $1000 in two years and the market interest rate is 8%. Using our present value formula,

$$PV_B = \$1000/(1 + 0.08)^2 = \$857.34,$$

we find that the bond is worth $857.34 today. This gives us an indication of how much the bond should sell for, or its price.

The present value formula is not only useful in calculating the price of bonds but also in evaluating any financial assets in the economy. All financial assets can be translated into promises to pay given amounts in the future. In particular, the present value formula can be used to determine the rate of return on a financial asset. Say you know the future value and the present value of an asset. Here, i can be interpreted as the rate of return on that asset. Solving for the present value formula when $n = 1$ for i we get

$$i = (FV - PV)/PV.$$

Consider the following example. You are a financial analyst and make the investment decisions for a modest mutual fund. If your fund increased in value from $17.1 million to $19.323 million over the last year what is the rate of return? Substituting $17.1 million for PV and $19.323 for FV we get

$$i = (19.323-17.1)/17.1 = 13\%.$$

A Fixed Mortgage Payment

Having understood the notion of the present value of a single promised future amount, we can now extend this concept to the present value of a series of future values. Recollect how we calculated the present value of an asset that yields a future amount of $1 at interest rate i: $PV = 1/(1 + i)$. For example if you were to receive $100 one year from a one-year U.S. Treasury Bill and the interest rate is 8%, its present value is

$$PV_{TI} = 100/(1 + .08) = \$92.59.$$

Let's assume you were also to receive $200 from another U.S. Treasury Bill, but this time the interest rate is 10% and the sum is received in two years. The present value of this would be

$$PV_{T2} = 200/(1+.10)^2 = \$165.29.$$

Since present value is expressed in dollar amounts, we can calculate the present value of these two assets combined as

$$PV_{TI+T2} = PV_{TI} + PV_{T2}, \text{ or}$$

$$100/(1+.08) + 200/(1+.10)^2 = \$257.88.$$

The general form of the present value of future streams of income can be expressed as

$$PV = C_1/(1 + i_1) + C_2/(1 + i_2)^2 + C_3/(1 + i_3)^3 + \dots + C_n/(1 + i_n)^n,$$

where C_n represents the payment in year n.

An example of such a stream of income payments is a simple fixed rate mortgage on a house. The borrower of a sum of money from, say, a bank pays back a fixed sum every year, say, C_1, C_2, C_3, etc. To determine the interest rate implicit in the arrangement, we once again use the present value formula. The present value of such a fixed mortgage cash flow is just

$$PV = C_1/(1 + i_1) + C_2/(1 + i_2)^2 + C_3/(1 + i_3)^3 + \dots + C_n/(1 + i_n)^n.$$

Suppose that you borrow \$1000 from the bank which has a fixed rate payment of \$100 every year for 20 years. We want to determine the implicit rate of interest the bank is charging. First we write the present value formula for this case:

$$1000 = 100/(1 + i) + 100/(1 + i)^2 + 100/(1 + i)^3 + \dots + 100/(1 + i)^{20}.$$

Solving this equation for i we get $i = 7.76\%$. Calculating the interest rate can be quite difficult. In fact, the authors used an amortization spreadsheet to calculate the interest rate. Banks and real estate agents have tables which are quite handy in telling the prospective borrower what the interest rate and yearly payments are likely to be on a fixed mortgage loan.

Coupon Bonds

If the future amounts are all equal as in the case of the fixed mortgage payment, we call this an annuity. Coupon bonds are examples of an annuity. Here the holder of the bond invests or buys a bond which promises him a fixed coupon payment every year until the bond matures plus the face or par value of the bond on maturity. Suppose that you buy a bond for \$2000, which promises to pay you a sum of \$200 every year for the next twenty years plus the face value at the end of twenty years. We find the implicit interest rate by setting the present value of the bond equal to all the future discounted coupon payments:

$$\$2000 = 200/(1 + i) + 200/(1 + i)^2 + 200/(1 + i)^3 + \ldots + 200/(1 + i)^{20} + 2000/(1 + i)^{20}.$$

In general the present value of a coupon bond is given by

$$PV = C/(1 + i) + C/(1 + i)^2 + C/(1 + i)^3 + \ldots + C/(1 + i)^n + F/(1 + i)^n.$$

where PV = Present Value or the price of the coupon bond,
        C = the coupon payment made each year
        i = the interest rate
        n = the number of years to maturity of the coupon bond.
        F = the face value of the bond.

Again the calculations of such formulas are quite messy. Tables exist to help in such calculations.

Perpetuities

While the examples of financial instruments we considered above have a finite maturity date, some financial instruments promise a coupon payment forever. An annuity which has no maturity period and promises a coupon payment forever is called a perpetuity. Although perpetuities are rare they did exist during the 18th and 19th centuries in England. The price of the perpetuity is given by the formula

$$PV = P_c = C/(1 + i) + C/(1 + i)^2 + C/(1 + i)^3 + \ldots$$

where P_c = the price of the perpetuity,
        C = the fixed annual coupon payment,
        i = the interest rate.

It is easy to calculate the present value of (or rate of return to) such a perpetuity using some simple algebra. The series goes on for an infinite number of years, but luckily the series converges to a value. Mathematicians have found that such a series as above, called a *geometric series*, converges to C/i.

Let's first present the algebra of infinite series. The sum $r + ra + ra^2 + ra^3 + ... + ra^n$ is the general form of a geometric series. The formula for the solution to this general geometric series is

$$(r + ra + ra^2 + ra^3 + ... + ra^n) = r/(1 - a) .$$

The proof of this solution this is rather simple. Suppose that we define S as

(1) $\qquad\qquad S = (r + ra + ra^2 + ra^3 + ... + ra^n).$

Multiplying equation (1) by a yields

(2) $\qquad\qquad Sa = (ra + ra^2 + ra^3 + ... + ra^n).$

Subtracting equation (2) from (1),

$S - Sa = (r + ra + ra^2 + ra^3 + ... + ra^n) - (ar + ra^2 + ra^3 + ... + ra^n),$ or

$S - Sa = r(1 + a + a^2 + a^3 + ... + a^n - a - a^2 - a^3 - ... - a^n).$

On the right-hand side, all terms with a's cancel one another out leaving

$$S (1 - a) = r, \text{ or}$$

$$S = r/(1 - a).$$

Recall, $S = (r + ra + ra^2 + ra^3 + ... + ra^n)$. Our equation for a perpetuity is the same geometric series where $a = 1/(1 + i)$ and $r = C/(1 + i)$. Substituting these values into the equation $S = r/(1 - a)$, we get

$$PV = [C/(1 + i)]/[1 - 1/(1 + i)].$$

Simplifying, we get

$$PV = C/i.$$

Consider a perpetuity which you buy for $1000 and promises to pay you $100 forever (until you die). We can calculate the implicit interest rate by equating the price of the perpetuity with the future stream of discounted coupon payments:

$$\$1000 = 100/(1 + i) + 100/(1 + i)^2 + 100/(1 + i)^3 + ... + 100/(1 + i)^n.$$

We then use the simplified perpetuity formula to find

$$1000 = 100/i.$$

Solving for i we find that $i = 10\%$.

Although perpetuities are rare, the formula for a perpetuity is useful, because it reminds us of the inverse relation between the interest rate and the present value of a bond which we saw held true with the fixed mortgage payment and the coupon bond as well.

Some Practical Examples of the Present Value Concept

Saving for Your Retirement

Most of you have probably not started thinking about saving for your retirement years. Suppose that you are now 20 years old and wish to retire by the age of 50. Suppose you decide to start saving $1000 every year until you turn 50. The first $1000 that you save today will have 30 years to accumulate interest and can be written as $1000(1 + i)^{30}$. Similarly the second $1000 that you save when you turn 21 will accumulate compound interest for 29 years and is worth $1000(1 + i)^{29}$ at retirement.

The total that you accumulate in savings by the time you are 50 is

$$1000 (1 + i)^{30} + 1000 (1 + i)^{29} + 1000 (1 + i)^{28} + 1000 (1 + i)^{27} + ... + 1000(1 + i)^0.$$

This total sum is the future value of your savings. If you knew the interest rate i you could calculate the value your savings at retirement. This is of course difficult and cumbersome, but you can use a future value (or compounding) table to calculate your future savings.

Calculating the Rate of Return From an Investment

Suppose that you are asked to pay $\$P$ today and told that you will receive $\$F$ every year for n years. How do you decide whether investing in this asset for $\$P$ is a good idea? Our discussion of present values should give you the answer. Calculate the present value of this stream of payments $\$F$ for n years and compare it with the price $\$P$. Now the present value of this annuity is

$$F/(1 + i) + F/(1 + i)^2 + F/(1 + i)^3 + ...+ F/(1 + i)^n.$$

If the present value of the future stream of income at some interest rate i is greater than P, then it is worth investing in this asset.

Consider the following example. Suppose that you buy a stereo system for $1000 to rent out for two years at $600 for each year, thus making a $200 profit. Makes sense. But have you done the right thing? The answer to this question depends on the rate of return implicit in the transaction. Once again setting up the present value equation,

$$1000 = 600/(1 + i) + 600/(1 + i)^2.$$

There is more than one way to find out the rate of return from the above equation. In fact, since it is a quadratic, there is more than one solution. Some calculators can be programmed to yield the answer. Similarly you can set up a simple computer program in a spread sheet to find the answer. We could of course plug in values for i and see which works best by a process of trial and error. We do just that.

At $i = 13\%$, the present value of $600/(1 + i)$ $+ 600/(1 + i)^2 = \$1000.86$
At $i = 14\%$, the present value of $600/(1 + i)$ $+ 600/(1 + i)^2 = \$988.00$

Thus if interest rates were 13% you just break even. At 14% your present value of this annuity is less than the price of $1000 you paid for the stereo and it would not be a good idea to invest in the stereo system. Instead you should invest the money in the bank at 14% and at the end of two years you would have earned $1000(1 + 0.14)^2 = \$1299.60$, instead of earning $600 the first year, investing it at 14% for one year and earning $600 the second year for a total of $1284. The rate of return on this investment is between 13 and 14 percent.

An alternate way to find the exact return is to use the quadratic formula $x = [-b \pm (b^2 - 4ac)^{1/2}]/2a$. In this example, $x = 1 + i$, $a = 1000$, $b = -600$, and $c = -600$. Solving for i, we get 13.07% or -153%. Since a negative return in this example makes no economic sense, we discard this solution leaving $i = 13.07\%$.

Interest Rates, Asset Markets and the Economy

Interest rates play a central role in macroeconomics. While both Keynesians and Classicals agree about the math of present value and future value, they disagree about the market in which the interest rate is determined. The Classical school believed that interest rates in the economy are determined by the demand for and supply of loanable funds in the loanable funds market. They believed in a smoothly operating financial sector. On the other hand, Keynesians believed that interest rates were determined by the demand and supply for money in the money market. They believed that financial markets are not always efficient and the interest rate cannot be determined by real factors alone. These alternative theories of interest rate determination are discussed in your textbook.

The importance of these differences can only be understood by understanding the math of present value and future value. That's why the formulas presented and discussed in this chapter are part of every economist's tool kit.

Problems

1.
a. What is the present value of a security which promises to pay you $1000 at the end of the first year, $1500 at the end of the second year and $2000 at the end of the third year? Assume the interest rate is 10%.
b. Suppose that this annuity promises to pay $2500 at the end of the fourth year in addition to the income payments in (a) above. You bought the security for $5000. Have you made a sound investment? Why or why not?
c. Calculate the rate of return for this four-year security which would make you indifferent between buying this security or holding this sum of money in the bank at this real return or interest rate.

2.
a. Suppose that a benefactor to your college wishes to establish an endowed chair in your economics department. If his aim is to ensure that the chair receives a salary of $100,000 per year and the interest rate in the economy is currently 8%, what is the amount of money he should donate to the college today?
b. The benefactor realizes that he has not considered growth in salaries over time. If he wishes to ensure that the chair gets a 5% rise in his salary of $100,000 every year, what should his total contribution to the college be today?
(*HINT:* Write down the present value of the total cash flow and account for the 5% rise in the salary.)

Answers to In-Text Questions

1. $1238.35.
2. (a) $2000; (b) It would fall to $1836.81. This makes sense because if the interest rate were higher then I would be able to invest a lower amount to arrive at the same $2000 two years from now.

10

The Exchange Rate, Balance of Trade and the J-Curve

Equilibrium in the foreign exchange market is determined where the demand and supply for the currency intersect. If the demand for a currency is derived from the demand for exports and the supply for a currency is derived from the demand for imports, it makes sense that a country's balance of trade is reflected by the relation between the supply and demand for its currency. A negative trade balance is reflected by an excess supply of currency and a positive trade balance is reflected by excess demand for currency. If the exchange rate were e_1, (the price of dollars in terms of foreign exchange) there would be an excess supply of dollars and a negative trade balance as shown in Figure 10.1.

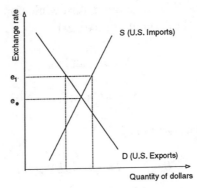

Figure 10.1

A fall in the exchange rate in this case would be expected to reduce the U.S. trade deficit. As discussed in your textbook, however, in the short run more often a depreciation in a country's exchange rate worsens a county's trade balance. As time goes on, however, the balance of trade improves. This phenomenon was introduced to you in the textbook as the *J-curve phenomenon* and is shown in Figure 10.2. In this chapter, we relate that discussion to the supply and demand for currencies and present the J-curve effect more formally showing that the J-curve effect is simply standard micro analysis applied to exports and imports.

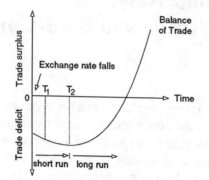

Figure 10.2

Trade Balance

The algebra of the Keynesian and IS-LM model presented in the textbook assumed that exports, X, were autonomous, while imports, M, of a country depended on the level of output or income Y.

$$X = X_0, \text{ and}$$

$$M = M_0 + mY.$$

The trade balance was written as

$$TB = X - M = (X_0 - M_0) - mY.$$

Everything was in real terms and prices didn't matter.

If both countries had fixed price levels and fixed exchange rates, that assumption was reasonable, but when the exchange rate changes, the prices of goods in one currency change relative to prices in the other and the assumption is no longer reasonable.

The Exchange Rate

We first introduce the exchange rate and its determination before examining its effect on the goods and services market. An *exchange rate* is the price of one country's currency measured in another country's currency. Formally, the exchange rate, e, is shown as

e = price of domestic currency in terms of a foreign currency.

i.e. e = foreign currency/domestic currency.

Our analysis here focuses on the real exchange rate, an exchange rate adjusted for changes in relative price levels. Here, to keep the math simple, we assume that the price levels in both countries are fixed so that the change in the nominal exchange rate equals the change in the real exchange rate.

Exchange Rates and the Demand and Supply of Imports and Exports

Introducing exchange rates into our discussion enables us to write the export demand function as

$$Q_x = f(Y^*, e),$$

where Y^* is foreign income and e is the real exchange rate. A fall in the exchange rate, e, implies that domestic goods are less expensive compared to foreign goods. Consequently the quantity demanded of exports will rise. The partial derivative of exports with respect to the exchange rate is

$$\partial Q_x/\partial e < 0.$$

Similarly the import function may now be written as

$$Q_m = (Y, e).$$

A fall in the exchange rate, which implies that domestic goods are less expensive compared to foreign goods, results in a fall in the quantity of imports demanded:

$$\partial Q_m/\partial e > 0.$$

A fall in the exchange rate would lead to an increase in the quantity of exports demanded and a decrease in the quantity of imports demanded for the domestic economy. This is simply the standard microeconomic law of demand. Suppose for example that the exchange rate between the dollar and the pound falls from £0.6/$ to £0.5/$. The dollar has fallen in value or depreciated. At this lower exchange rate British citizens tend to buy more U.S. exports since every pound can buy more U.S. goods. On the other hand U.S. citizens will import less from Great Britain since each dollar buys fewer pounds. How much more British citizens and how much less U.S. citizens will buy depends on the respective demand elasticities. In the short run, the demand is inelastic, but becomes more elastic in the long run.

As you may recollect from your microeconomics class, *elasticity* is defined as the responsiveness of quantity demanded to the percentage change in the price of the good or service. The law of demand states that as the price of a good rises, the quantity demanded falls, *ceteris paribus*. The price elasticity of demand for example, E_d, is defined as

E_d = % change in quantity demanded/ % change in price.

If a 10% rise in price results in a larger than 10% fall in quantity demanded, demand would be *elastic*. If a 10% rise in price results in a less than 10% rise in quantity demanded, demand would be *inelastic*. Finally, if the percentage change in price leads to the same percentage change in quantity demanded demand would be *unit elastic*.

To see what effect the change in exchange rates has on the dollar value of the trade balance, we first write the trade balance as

$$TB = P_x Q_x - (P_m/e)Q_m,$$

where P_x = Price of export goods in dollars,
         Q_x = Quantity of export goods,
         P_m = Price of import goods in foreign currency,
         Q_m = Quantity of import goods
         e = Price of the dollar in terms of the foreign currency.

If the exchange rate e falls, (a depreciation of the domestic currency), the dollar price of imports, P_m/e, rises and the foreign currency price of exports, $P_x e$, falls. In response Q_x rises and Q_m falls. What happens to the supply and demand for currencies depends on the relative amounts of those changes.

Demand and Supply of a Currency

The demand and supply of a country's currency in part originates from the
desire to buy and sell goods since those goods must be purchased in the
appropriate currency. Demand for imports creates a supply of a currency
and demand for exports creates a demand for currency. To keep the analysis
simple, we assume away all other elements of the supply and demand for
currencies (the most important of which are the interest rate and the level of
income in the two countries). This approach was the approach used by early
Classical economists in their analysis of exchange rates. Given these assumptions,

$$\text{Supply of a currency} = (P_m/e)Q_m.$$

$$\text{Demand for a currency} = P_x Q_x.$$

As you can see, the demand and supply for currencies is not simply the
demand for exports and imports, but the demand for exports and imports
valued in the domestic currency. When a country's exchange rate rises, it
may demand more imports, but the price it pays for those imports will have
fallen, and how much foreign currency it will need to pay for those imports
depends on the amount of that fall relative to the rise in the quantity of
imports demanded. The shape of the demand for and supply of a currency,
therefore, depends upon the change in the prices of exports and imports and
the change in demand for exports and imports both brought about by the
change in the exchange rate.

Supply of Currency

The slope of the supply of dollars is determined by the money needed for
imports. As the exchange rate falls, the price of imports in the domestic
currency rises and the quantity of imports demanded will tend to fall. The
price changes by the same percentage change in the exchange rate while the
change in quantity demanded depends upon the elasticity of demand for
imports. If demand is unit elastic, the percentage rise in price caused by a
depreciation in the domestic currency will be exactly offset by an equal
percentage decline in quantity of imports demanded. The supply of the
currency, $(P_m/e)Q_m$, will remain the same and the supply curve for currency
will be vertical. This is shown as S_0 in Figure 10.3.

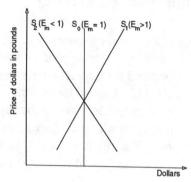

Figure 10.3

If the demand elasticity for imports were greater than one, the percentage increase in the quantity of imports demanded will be greater than the percentage decline in the dollar price of imports and the supply of domestic currency, $(P_m/e)Q_m$, will rise. The supply of currency will be upward sloping such as S_1. If the demand elasticity for imports were less than one, the percentage increase in the quantity of imports demanded will be less than the percentage decline in price and the supply of domestic currency, $(P_m/e)Q_m$, will decline. The supply of currency will be backward bending such as S_2.

Demand for Currency

The demand for a currency is similarly determined by the demand elasticity of exports. Recall the demand for currency is $P_x Q_x$. In this case P_x is already valued in the domestic currency and remains fixed. Because only the change in quantity demanded, Q_x, matters, the shape of the demand for currency can be described exactly by the elasticity of demand for exports. If the elasticity of demand for exports is zero, Q_x remains unchanged as e changes and the demand for currency will be vertical. This is shown as D_0 in Figure 10.4. If the elasticity of demand for exports is greater than zero, the demand curve for domestic currency is downward sloping and as the elasticity of demand for exports rises, the demand for currency becomes flatter.

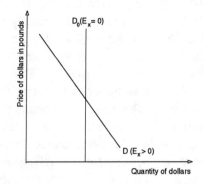

Figure 10.4

The Supply and Demand for Currencies in the Real World

In Figure 10.5 we put together a supply and demand curve for dollars in a currency market. The vertical axis measures the pound price of dollars (i.e. pounds per dollar). Let's now use this graph to see how a J-curve can come about.

In the real world, the quantity of exports and imports demanded responds slowly. The elasticity of demand for imports in the short run is less than one (close to zero—backward bending supply curve), and the elasticity of demand for exports is significantly less than one (close to zero—downward sloping but steep demand curve). Such supply and demand curves are depicted in Figure 10.5.

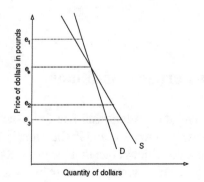

Figure 10.5

Let's say that we start at exchange rate e_1. Demand is greater than supply of dollars. In this case, you would normally expect a rise in the exchange rate. However, given the slope of the curves that we have assumed, that rise would worsen the situation; excess demand would rise. Alternatively, say you're at exchange rate e_3. The supply of dollars is greater than demand. Here one would expect a fall in the exchange rate. But given the shape of the curves, again such a fall would worsen the situation; excess supply would rise. Thus while there is an equilibrium at e_e, it is an unstable equilibrium. It is just this phenomenon that gives rise to the J-curve. If the exchange rate begins at e_2 and falls to e_3 (a depreciation of dollars in this case) the excess supply of currency (i.e. the trade deficit) will widen instead of diminish as expected.

In the long run, the supply and demand curves for a country's currency generally have normal shapes. That is, they become much more elastic so that a falling exchange rate equilibrates the demand and supply for a country's currency and net exports become zero as in Figure 10.6. That is why in the J-curve analysis it's assumed that a depreciation of the currency will eventually improve the trade deficit.

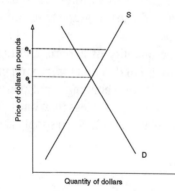

Figure 10.6

The Marshall-Lerner Conditions

The precise statement of the relationship between the value of a country's currency and its trade balance is found in the *Marshall-Lerner conditions*. The Marshall-Lerner conditions state that the more elastic are the demands for exports and imports of a country, the more likely it is that a depreciation in the domestic currency will improve the trade balance.

Let us start by assuming that there is a perfect balance of trade. The total value of exports is equal to the total value of imports.

(1) $TB = P_x Q_x - (P_m/e)Q_m = 0,$

where all variables are defined as before. In other words,

(2) $P_x Q_x = (P_m/e)Q_m.$

Expressing equation (1) as a function of exports and imports,

(3) $TB = P_x Q_x (Y^*, e) - (P_m/e)Q_m (Y, e), = 0.$

where Y = domestic income and
        Y^* = foreign income.

We are interested in knowing how the trade balance, *TB*, changes in response to a change in the exchange rate. In terms of calculus this is the partial derivative of TB with respect to e, $(\partial TB/\partial e)$ or the derivative of equation (3) with respect to the exchange rate.

To find $\partial TB/\partial e$ we use the chain rule of calculus for the term $[(P_m/e)Q_m (Y, e)]$,

(4) $\partial TB/\partial e = P_x \partial Q_x /\partial e - (P_m/e)\partial Q_m /\partial e + (P_m/e^2)Q_m = 0$

The elasticity of demand for exports is defined as the ratio of the percentage change in exports to the percentage change in the prices of exports. Since the exchange rate e is nothing but a price of the foreign currency in terms of the domestic currency, the *price elasticity of demand for exports*, N_x, may be written as

$$N_x = (\partial Q_x /Q_x)/(\partial e/e) = (e/Q_x)(\partial Q_x /\partial e).$$

Similarly the elasticity of demand for imports is defined as the ratio of the percentage change in imports to the percentage change in the price of imports. The *price elasticity of demand for imports*, N_m, may be written as

$$N_m = (\partial Q_m /Q_m)/(\partial e/e) = (e/Q_m)(\partial Q_m /\partial e).$$

We want to introduce these elasticities of exports and imports into our partial derivative. By multiplying equation (4) by $[e/(P_x Q_x)]$, the first term will be the elasticity of exports N_x, defined above:

(5) $\quad [e/(P_x Q_x)](\partial TB/\partial e) = (e/Q_x)\partial Q_x /\partial e - [P_m/(P_x Q_x)](\partial Q_m /\partial e) +$
$\quad\quad [P_m/(eP_x Q_x)]Q_m = 0$

As we know from equation (2) $P_x Q_x = (P_m Q_m)/e$, equation (5) can be simplified to

(6) $\quad [e/(P_x Q_x)](\partial TB/\partial e) = (e/Q_x)\partial Q_x /\partial e - (e/Q_m)(\partial Q_m /\partial e) + 1 = 0.$

Using the definitions of N_x and N_m above, we can rewrite equation (6) then as

(8) $\quad\quad\quad\quad [e/(P_x Q_x)]\partial TB/\partial e = N_x - N_m + 1 \text{ or}$

(9) $\quad\quad\quad\quad \partial TB/\partial e = (N_x - N_m + 1)(P_x Q_x /e)$

For a depreciation, a decrease in e, to improve the balance of trade, $\partial TB/\partial e < 0$. Therefore,

(10) $\quad\quad\quad\quad (N_x - N_m + 1)(P_x Q_x /e) < 0.$

The terms $(P_x Q_x /e)$ and $(N_x - N_m + 1)$ must have opposite signs.

We know that since the exchange rate e, the price of exports P_x, and the quantity of exports Q_x are positive, $(P_x Q_x /e)$ is positive. That means $(N_x - N_m + 1) < 0$; this is the Marshall-Lerner condition. With algebraic manipulation this can also be expressed as

(11) $\quad\quad\quad\quad (N_m - N_x) > 1.$

Since the price elasticity of demand for exports, $(e/Q_x)(\partial Q_x /\partial e)$, is negative, (i.e. $\partial Q_x /\partial e < 0$), the negative sign in the second term along with the negative sign on N_x make the entire term positive and equation (11) can be rewritten as

(12) $\quad\quad\quad\quad (N_m + N_x) > 1.$

The Marshall-Lerner conditions state that for a depreciation to improve the trade balance the sum of the export and import elasticities of demand must be greater than 1. It is not necessary for the individual export and import elasticities to be elastic (larger than 1). It is sufficient that the *sum* of the elasticities be greater than one.

The Marshall-Lerner Conditions and the Demand and Supply of Currency

Given our assumption that exports and imports are the only determinant of the supply and demand for currencies, the Marshall-Lerner conditions are directly related to the supply and demand for a currency. For a depreciation in the dollar to improve the trade balance, the supply and demand curves for dollars must have their normal shapes. This will occur only when the elasticity of demand for exports or imports is greater than one or their sum is greater than one.

What this condition implies is best seen by relating the elasticities to the supply and demand for currencies. When $N_m = 1$, the supply of the currency is perfectly inelastic. When $N_M < 1$, the supply of the currency is backward bending. When $N_x > 1$ the supply of the currency is normally shaped. The demand for a currency is either perfectly vertical, $N_x = 0$, or downward sloping ($N_x > 0$).

To make the analysis simple, let's assume that $N_x = 0$, making the demand for the country's currency perfectly inelastic as in Figure 10.7.

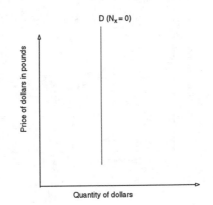

Figure 10.7

Substituting $N_x = 0$ into the Marshall-Lerner conditions gives

$$N_m + 0 > 1, \text{ or}$$

$$N_m > 1.$$

This is equivalent to saying that the supply curve must be upward sloping as in Figure 10.8 rather than backward bending as in Figure 10.9. As you can see when $N_m > 1$, the supply curve is upward sloping and a depreciation of the domestic currency improves the trade balance.

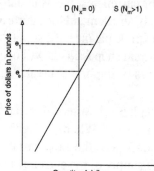

Figure 10.8

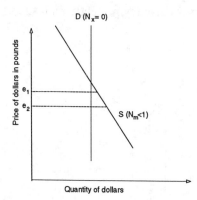

Figure 10.9

It also allows the supply curve to be somewhat backward bending if the demand curve is highly elastic as in Figure 10.10.

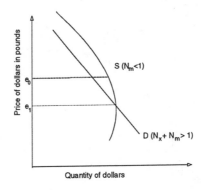

Figure 10.10

Conclusion

Exchange rate analysis in the real world is far more complicated than presented here. It is affected by the demand and supply of currencies as assets, as opposed to payment for goods. This asset demand for currencies is most directly affected by relative interest rates and expectations of changes in exchange rates as well as expectations of changes in interest rates. This asset demand swamps the payments demand for currency which is why in the text when we discussed determination of exchange rates we focused on interest rate issues.

Nonetheless, as a logical exercise, it is useful to go through the Marshall Lerner conditions and the microfoundations of the J-curve. Doing so, sharpens your intuitive understanding of the forces underlying the analysis and why the exchange rate market is so complicated and volatile.

Problems

1.
a. Derive the Marshall-Lerner condition for the case where trade is not initially balanced $P_x Q_x \neq P_m Q_m / e$, (i.e., you cannot use equation (2) and substitute into equation (6)). (Hint: Define some constant $C = P_m Q_m / (e P_x Q_x)$ and proceed with the algebra.)
b. Interpret the results.

2. Illustrate the foreign exchange market when the elasticity of imports is less than one and the elasticity of exports is zero ($N_m < 1$ and $N_x = 0$). Show how a depreciation could lead to a worsening of the trade balance.

Part III
Microeconomics

11

Supply and Demand

Supply and demand are the building blocks of much of economics. In this chapter we translate the ideas of supply and demand presented in the textbook into algebraic terms and show how you can come up with numerical answers to supply and demand questions. We begin with demand.

Demand is a schedule of amounts of a good or a service that a buyer is willing and able to consume at different prices in a given time period, other things being held constant (*ceteris paribus*).

A demand function for a good x can be specified as follows,

$$Q_{dx} = f(P_x, Y, P_z, \text{tastes, other factors})$$

where P_x = price of good x,
         Y = income,
         P_z = price of other goods.

The *law of demand* states that as the own price of a good falls, a buyer will buy more of that good, *ceteris paribus*. As the textbook discusses, the law of demand means that the demand curve is downward sloping. Changes in other factors such as income and the prices of other goods are called shift factors and shift the entire demand schedule.

Supply is a schedule of amounts of a good or a service that a seller is willing and able to supply at different prices in a given time period, other things being held constant.

A supply function for a good x can be specified as follows:

$$Q_{sx} = f(P_x, P_i, \text{technology, other factors})$$

where P_x = price of good x,
         P_i = price of inputs.

The *law of supply* states that as the own price of a good rises a seller will sell more of the good, *ceteris paribus*. Hence a supply curve is upward sloping.

Changes in other factors such as technology and the price of inputs are called shift factors and shift the entire supply schedule.

Market demand and market supply curves are derived by the horizontal aggregation of individual demand and supply curves respectively:

$$Q_{Dx} = \Sigma Q_{dx} = f(P_x, Y, P_z, \text{tastes}, \text{other factors});$$

$$Q_{Sx} = \Sigma Q_{sx} = f(P_x, P_i, \text{technology}, \text{other factors}).$$

The market supply and demand schedules are assumed to have slopes similar to the individual demand and supply schedules. The market supply curve is assumed to be a positive function of price and the market demand curve is assumed to be a negative function of price.

Market Equilibrium

Mathematically, linear demand and supply functions can be expressed as follows:

Demand: $Q_D = A - BP,$

where $A \geq 0$ and $B > 0$.

Supply: $Q_S = -C + DP,$

where $C \geq 0$ and $D > 0$.

A competitive market is in equilibrium when quantity demand equals quantity supplied. That is,

$$Q_D = Q_S.$$

The demand function has the expected negative slope, $-B$, and a positive intercept A; the supply curve has the expected positive slope, D, and a negative intercept, $-C$, because no products will be supplied at a price less than zero.

To determine the equilibrium price and quantity in this market, we solve the above equations simultaneously. Setting $Q_D = Q_S$ we have

$$A - BP = -C + DP.$$

Solving for P^*, equilibrium price, we get

$$P^* = (A+C)/(B+D).$$

P^* or the equilibrium market clearing price is a *determinate* value, that is a value that is defined or calculable. It is dependent on the parameters of the demand and supply functions: A, B, C, D. We do know that since these parameters are positive, P^* has to be greater than zero.

To find the equilibrium value, Q^*, substitute the value of P^* into either of the two equations. Doing this we find that

$$Q^* = (AD-BC)/(B+D).$$

An Example

Let the demand and supply equations for soybeans in the U.S. be expressed as follows:

$$Q_D = 200 - P,$$

$$Q_S = -50 + P.$$

where　P is the price in cents/lb, and
　　　　Q is the quantity of soybeans in millions of pounds.

To get the competitive market equilibrium price and quantity, set $Q_D = Q_S$, and solve the resulting equation for P^*:

$$200 - P = P-50$$

Substitute P^* in either the demand or supply curves to find Q^*. Doing this we find $P^* = 125$ and $Q^* = 75$.

In an unregulated market, if there is an imbalance in the market between supply and demand, market forces automatically correct for the imbalance, thus bringing about equilibrium.

A Nonlinear Supply and Demand Model

The previous demand and supply functions were linear. The assumption of linearity is more for analytical simplicity than a true representation of the real world. Both supply and demand functions can be nonlinear, and the process of determining the equilibrium can be carried out in the same way as before.

An Example

Let the demand function be a nonlinear quadratic equation, $Q_D = 8 - P^2$, and the supply equation continue to be a linear function, $Q_S = 3P - 2$. The equilibrium condition remains the same: $Q_D = Q_S$.

As under the linear case, we can reduce the system of two equations into one equation and one unknown:

$$8 - P^2 = 3P - 2, \text{ or}$$

$$P^2 + 3P - 10 = 0$$

Recall from the algebra chapter that this is a quadratic equation in P and in general will have two solutions. We can rewrite the above expression as

$$P^2 + 5P - 2P - 10 = 0.$$

$P + 5$ and $P + 2$ can be factored out to get

$$(P-2)\,(P+5) = 0.$$

Thus the equilibrium price is $P = 2$ or $P = -5$. Since negative prices are ruled out, the equilibrium price is $P^* = 2$. Substituting back into the supply or demand equation we find that $Q^* = 4$.

Another Example

Let's consider another example, but now specify both supply and demand functions to be nonlinear. Let the demand function, supply function and equilibrium condition be

$$Q_D = 111 - P^2,$$

$$Q_S = P^2 - 51,$$

$$Q_D = Q_S.$$

Setting the demand and supply functions equal to one another we get

$$111 - P^2 = P^2 - 51.$$

Solving for P^*, we find $P^* = \pm 9$. We can rule out $P^* = -9$. Now solving for Q^*, we find equilibrium in this market is at $P^* = 9$ and $Q^* = 30$.

Exercise 1: The total demand for wheat in the U.S. is given by $Q_D = 1750 - 130P$. Domestic supply, $Q_S = 1000 + 170P$. Calculate the equilibrium price and quantity. Price is measured in dollars per ton while quantity is in thousands of tons.

Intervention in the Free Market

In the competitive market that we have just discussed, the invisible hand or the price mechanism coordinates the actions of buyers and sellers bringing about equilibrium. But very often governments are unhappy with the resulting markets and they intervene to either raise or lower prices. The government could impose a *price floor* by artificially legislating a price higher than the competitive market price. Examples of this are the minimum wage legislation and agricultural price support programs. Alternatively the government could impose a *price ceiling* by legislating a price much lower than the competitive market price. Usually, the effect of a price floor is a surplus or excess supply in the market, while that of a price ceiling is a shortage or excess demand, which also could result in a black market.

An Example

Let's consider a market for fish. Let Q be tons of fish and P be price per ton of fish in dollars. Let the market demand and market supply in the fish market be specified by

$$Q_D = 300 - 2.5\,P,$$

$$Q_S = -20 + 1.5\,P.$$

Competitive market equilibrium is defined as

$$Q_D = Q_S.$$

Competitive Market Equilibrium

As before, we can solve for the competitive equilibrium price and quantity by setting supply equal to demand, and then solving for P^* and Q^*:

$$300 - 2.5\,P = -20 + 1.5\,P.$$

Here we find that $P^* = 80$ and $Q^* = 100$. This equilibrium is shown in Figure 11.1.

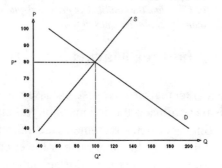

Figure 11.1

Price Floor

Suppose the fishing industry persuades Congress to save the family fishing industry by mandating a price floor (the opposite of a legally mandated price ceiling) at $100 per ton of fish. This is shown in Figure 11.2

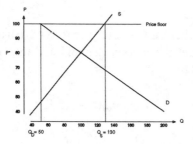

Figure 11.2

At this legally mandated price, the new level of quantity demanded is $Q_D = 300 - 2.5 \cdot 100 = 50$ and the new level of quantity supplied is $Q_S = -20 + 1.5 \cdot 100 = 130$. Since $Q_S > Q_D$, there is an excess supply of fish (80 tons) in the market.

Price Ceiling

Suppose Congress responds to numerous public outcries of high fish prices and mandates a price ceiling of $50. This is shown in Figure 11.3.

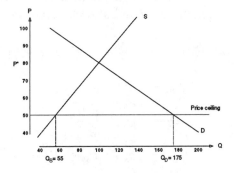

Figure 11.3

At the new price ceiling level, quantity demanded, $Q_D = 300 - 125 = 175$, while quantity supplied is $Q_S = -20 + 75 = 55$. Since $Q_D > Q_S$, excess demand or a shortage of fish emerges (120 tons).

Exercise 2: In the above example with a price ceiling of $50 per ton, what can you say about a black-market price that may emerge?

Multi-Market Equilibrium

So far, we have specified demand and supply as a function of its own price. But, prices of other products will also affect demand and supply of a given good. For every product, there are usually many substitutes and complementary products. Let's say the price of chicken rises. The quantity of chicken demanded would be expected to fall. Consumers, however, would substitute toward say, pork; even though the absolute price of pork has not fallen the quantity of pork demanded at each price has risen. Thus, when we specify the demand function for a product, it should not only capture the effects of changes in the own price but also changes in most related products. Such an interdependency is also true of the supply function. Changes in the price of steel will have an impact on changes in the prices of automobiles. Once we allow such interdependencies to exist, we need to look again at the notion of market equilibrium and how equilibrium values of prices and quantities are determined.

Intuitively, when there is a single commodity in an isolated market, the equilibrium condition stipulates that $Q_D = Q_S$ or the excess demand for that commodity must be zero. If there is more than one market, upon reflection it should become clear that excess demand for each and every commodity should also be zero in equilibrium. If that were not the case, then changes in the market not in equilibrium would also cause change in other related markets.

Let us look at the example of a multi-market model with two markets.

(1) $Q_{D1} = A_0 + A_1 P_1 + A_2 P_2$

(2) $Q_{S1} = B_0 + B_1 P_1 + B_2 P_2$

(3) $ED_1 = Q_{D1} - Q_{S1} = 0$

(4) $Q_{D2} = a_0 + a_1 P_1 + a_2 P_2$

(5) $Q_{S2} = b_0 + b_1 P_1 + b_2 P_2$

(6) $ED_2 = Q_{D2} - Q_{S2} = 0$

where Q_{Di} and Q_{Si} specify demand and supply for good i and P_i denotes price of good i. ED_i signifies excess demand. Notice that the quantity demanded and supplied depends on its own price as well as the price of the good in the second market.

Although this system looks a lot more complex than our simple one-market case, the principle behind solving it remains the same. Use the equilibrium conditions in each market to create two equations with two unknowns. Substitute (1) and (2) into (3); (4) and (5) into (6) thus reducing the system into the following expressions for the two markets respectively:

(7) $A_0 + A_1 P_1 + A_2 P_2 = B_0 + B_1 P_1 + B_2 P_2.$

(8) $a_0 + a_1 P_1 + a_2 P_2 = b_0 + b_1 P_1 + b_2 P_2.$

Collecting terms in each of (7) and (8) we get

(9) $(A_0 - B_0) + (A_1 - B_1) P_1 + (A_2 - B_2) P_2 = 0$

(10) $(a_0 - b_0) + (a_1 - b_1) P_1 + (a_2 - b_2) P_2 = 0$

We can simplify equations (9) and (10) by rewriting them as

(11) $g_0 + g_1 P_1 + g_2 P_2 = 0,$

where $g_i = (A_i - B_i)$ for $i = 0, 1, 2,$ and

(12) $$h_0 + h_1 P_1 + h_2 P_2 = 0,$$

where $h_i = (a_i - b_i)$ for $i = 0, 1, 2.$

Using (11) to solve for P_1 and then substituting into the other equation and solving for P_2 gives

(13) $$P_2 = (g_0 h_1 - g_1 h_0)/(g_1 h_2 - g_2 h_1).$$

Doing the same for P_2 and P_1 respectively we find that

(14) $$P_1 = (g_2 h_0 - g_0 h_2)/(g_1 h_2 - g_2 h_1).$$

These expressions can make economic sense if some restrictions are imposed on the parameters . Firstly, the denominators cannot be zero ($g_1 h_2 \neq g_2 h_1$). Secondly, to ensure positive price, the numerators should be the same sign as the denominators. Once P_1^* and P_2^* are found, Q_1^* and Q_2^* can be found from equations (1)-(6).,

An Example

Consider demand and supply the following two markets:

(1a) $$Q_{D1} = 20 - 2P_1 + 3P_2,$$

(2a) $$Q_{S1} = 5 + 4P_1 + 4P_2,$$

(3a) $$Q_{D2} = 20 - 6P_1 + 4P_2,$$

(4a) $$Q_{S2} = 10 + 2P_1 + 3P_2.$$

We know that $ED_1 = Q_{D1} - Q_{S1} = 0$ and $ED_2 = Q_{D2} - Q_{S2} = 0$. Thus using equations (1a) and (2a) and (3a) and (4a), we get

(5a) $$20 - 2P_1 + 3P_2 - 5 - 4P_1 - 4P_2 = 0,$$

(6a) $$20 - 6P_1 + 4P_2 - 10 - 2P_1 - 3P_2 = 0.$$

Simplifying equations (5a) and (6a),

(7a) $$15 - 6P_1 - P_2 = 0,$$

(8a) $$10 - 8P_1 + P_2 = 0.$$

Solving (7a) and (8a) simultaneously, we get $P_1* = \$1.78$ and $P_2* = \$4.32$.

Conclusion

The interdependencies can become much more complicated but the above discussion of a two-market interdependency will give you a good sense of the importance of these market interdependencies, and why shift factors need to be taken into account whenever markets are analyzed.

Problems

1. The Rent Control Authority of Chicago has found that total market demand for apartments is $Q_D = 400 - 25P$. The Authority also noted that supply is given by $Q_S = 200 + 25P$. Price is measured in hundreds of dollars and quantity is measured in thousands of apartments.

a. What is the free-market equilibrium price and quantity for apartments?
b. Suppose the Authority decides to impose a rent control of $300, how many people will be unable to find an apartment at that price?

Answers to In-Text Questions

1. $P* = \$2.50$, $Q* = 1425$ thousands of tons.
2. At the ceiling price of $50 per ton, 55 tons are supplied. The black-market price is found by substituting the tonnage demanded at $50 into the demand equation to find how much consumers would be willing to pay. It is $98/ton.

12

The Mathematics of Elasticity

In the textbook we introduced you to the concept of *elasticity*, which measures the degree of responsiveness in one variable to the change in another variable. There, we focused on the price elasticity of supply and demand; here we develop the concept of *income elasticity* and *cross-price elasticity* in more depth. Before we do that, however, let's review the concept of price elasticity of demand.

Price Elasticity of Demand

Price elasticity of demand is the percentage change in the quantity demanded of a good in response to a percentage change in the price of that good. It can be specified mathematically as

$$E_d = \% \text{ change in } Q / \% \text{ change in } P, \text{ or also,}$$

$$E_d = (\Delta Q/Q)/(\Delta P/P).$$

For normal goods, price and quantity move in opposite directions. Hence the elasticity is characterized by a negative sign. However, economists ignore the minus sign and remember that it's negative, using the absolute value of elasticity. So, $(E_d = 3)$ is more elastic than $(E_d = 2)$ even though mathematically -3 < -2. Using the absolute value avoids this confusion.

The terminology associated with elasticity can be summarized as follows:

When $E_d = \infty$, the price elasticity of demand is said to be *perfectly elastic*.
When $1 < E_d < \infty$, the price elasticity of demand is said to be *elastic*.
When $E_d = 1$, the price elasticity of demand is said to be *unitary elastic*.
When $0 < E_d < 1$, the price elasticity of demand is said to be *inelastic*.
When $E_d = 0$, the price elasticity of demand is said to be *perfectly inelastic*.

An Example

Say the demand for a product is given by $Q_D = 10 - P$. This demand curve is shown in Figure 12.1. Let's assume market price, P, is \$6. If price increases by 5%, we want to determine the resulting decline in quantity demanded and also the elasticity of demand.

First, we determine the quantity demanded at $P = \$6$. Substituting into $Q_D = 10 - P$. We find that at $P = \$6$, $Q_D = 4$. A 5% increase implies a new price of \$6.30, at which point quantity demanded is 3.7. Quantity demanded fell by 7.5%. We can calculate price elasticity of demand to be $-7.5/5 = -1.5$ or just 1.5.

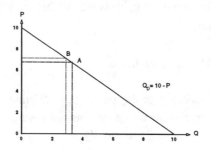

Figure 12.1

Notice that we measured elasticity from A to B. Now, let's measure elasticity of demand from B to A. Now the price *declines* by 4.7% and the quantity demanded rises by 8.1%. Here, the elasticity of demand is 8.1/-4.7 or 1.72. This is larger than the elasticity of demand calculated before. If the points were further apart, the difference would be even greater. This is because the elasticity of demand changes along a linear demand function.

To avoid the problem presented in the previous example, economists have developed two measures of calculating the price elasticity of demand: *arc elasticity* and *point elasticity*.

Arc Elasticity

As demonstrated in the previous example, when considering discrete price changes, the magnitude of the change in elasticity depends on whether we are going up the demand curve or down it. *Arc elasticity* is the average of the elasticities in each direction and defines the elasticity of a section of a demand curve. It can be mathematically written as

$$[(Q_2 - Q_1)/(Q_2 + Q_1)]/[(P_2 - P_1)/(P_2 + P_1)].$$

In the previous example, the price elasticity of arc AB would be $(1.5+1.72)/2 = 1.61$.

An Example In 1989, the price of unleaded regular gasoline was $1.20 per gallon and the quantity of gasoline consumed was 6.8 million barrels per day. By 1993, the price of unleaded regular gasoline fell to $0.94 per gallon and consumption rose to 7.3 million barrels per day. Assuming all other things remained constant, we want to determine the arc elasticity of demand with respect to the price for gasoline.

Using the formula given we calculate the arc elasticity to be

$$[(7.3-6.8)/(7.3 + 6.8)]/[(0.94 - 1.2)/(0.94 + 1.2)] = -0.03 / 0.12 = -0.29.$$

Price elasticity of demand for gasoline is inelastic since its absolute value is less than one.

Point Elasticity

When considering infinitesimally small changes in price and quantity (i.e. dP and dQ), we use a different concept of elasticity. *Point elasticity* measures elasticity at a point in contrast to within a range of points. Point elasticity can be written mathematically as

$$E_d = (dq/q)/ (dp/p).$$

We can rewrite this as $(dq/dp)/(q/p)$, where dq/dp is the inverse of the slope of the demand curve. Since dq/dp represents the marginal quantity demanded and q/p represents the average quantity demanded of the given demand function, price elasticity can also be expressed as

$$E_d = \text{marginal quantity demanded/ average quantity demanded.}$$

Example One Let the demand curve be of the general form,

$$Q_d = A - BP.$$

The slope is

$$dQ/dP = -B.$$

Recalling the definition for the price elasticity of demand, $(dQ/Q)/(dP/P)$ or $(dQ/dP)\cdot(P/Q)$, we can find the elasticity of a point on the demand curve at point G (P_G, Q_G) by substituting in for the values of P and Q at that point on the demand curve:

$$E_d = -B(P_G/Q_G).$$

Example Two Find the general form of E_d for the demand function, $Q_d = 10 - 20P + 10P^2$.

First recall that $E_d = dQ/dP/(Q/P)$. Taking the first derivative of Q_d with respect to P we get

$$dQ/dP = -20 + 20P.$$

Calculating the denominator of the equation for elasticity, Q/P, we get

$$[(10/P) - 20 + 10P].$$

Combining these two parts of the elasticity formula we get

$$E_d = (-20 + 20P)/(10/P - 20 + 10P).$$

Simplifying we get

$$E_d = 2P/(P - 1).$$

Here, elasticity is a function of price. We can find the point elasticity at any price level.

Example Three Let the market demand for soybeans be given as $P = 200 - Q_d$. Calculate the point elasticity of demand when the price of soybeans is $75/ton. At this price, is the demand for soybeans elastic or inelastic?

First, we write the demand curve as

$$Q_d = 200 - P.$$

Secondly, calculate quantity demanded at $P = \$75$ to be $Q_d = 125$. We then take the first derivative to get

$$dQ_d/dP = -1.$$

We can now calculate the point elasticity of demand by first recalling the formula for elasticity:

$$(dQ/dP)(P/Q).$$

Substituting the values calculated above, we get

$$E_d = -1 \cdot (75/125) = -0.6.$$

Demand at this point is inelastic.

Example Four Let's now find the elasticity of demand specified by

$$Q_D = P^{-3}.$$

First, take the natural log of both sides:

$$\ln Q_D = -3\ln P.$$

Recalling that $d\ln x = (1/x)\, dx$, and that dx/x is the percent change in x, we want to find dQ/Q and dP/P to find the point elasticity. We can do this by taking the derivative of Q_D to get

$$dQ/Q = -3dP/P.$$

Rearranging terms, we get

$$(dQ/Q)/(dP/P) = -3.$$

This is precisely the definition of elasticity. Notice that the elasticity is -3 which is the exponent of the demand equation. Economists frequently use this log form of demand so that elasticity is clearly evident from the equation without further calculation.

Exercise 1: If the demand curve is of the form Q = 100/P, what is the elasticity at P = 10?

Income Elasticity of Demand

As discussed in the text, the *income elasticity* of demand is defined as a proportional change in quantity demanded of a good resulting from changes in income. The analysis is similar to price elasticity but this time, we are measuring the change in quantity demanded given a change in income. The income elasticity of demand can be positive, negative or zero.

Income elasticity is defined as

$$E_y = (\Delta Q/Q)/(\Delta Y/Y), \text{ where } Y \text{ is income.}$$

The following summarizes the terminology related to income elasticity:

If $1 < E_Y < \infty$ demand is *income elastic*. In this case, as income rises, the percent increase in quantity demanded will be greater than the percent change in income. This commodity is known as a *luxury good*. An example might be steak.

If $0 < E_Y < 1$ demand is also *income elastic*. Here, the percent rise in quantity demanded is less than the percent increase in income. These goods are termed *necessities*. An example would be staple food items.

If $E_Y < 0$, the quantity demanded falls as income rises. These goods are called *inferior goods*. An example would be shoe repair. As income rises, quantity of shoe repair demanded falls; people just replace worn shoes instead of having old ones fixed.

Example One

The Census Bureau reports that in 1988 when the average income for a household was $36,000 the total consumption of microwave ovens was 80 million units. In 1993, the average income rose to $40,000 and the quantity of microwaves sold increased to 86 million units. To see if microwaves are a necessity or a luxury, we calculate the income elasticity of demand:

$$
\begin{aligned}
E_Y &= \% \text{ change in } Q/\% \text{ change in } Y, \\
&= [(6{,}000{,}000/80{,}000{,}000)/(4{,}000/36{,}000)], \\
&= 0.075/0.111 = 1.67.
\end{aligned}
$$

Since E_Y is greater than one, microwaves are termed luxury goods.

Example Two

After the Iraqi invasion of Kuwait in 1990, a bunch of economists got together to figure out what impact the invasion would have on gasoline prices in the U.S. As a first step, they figured the demand for gasoline in this country for a representative household to be of the form

$$Q_D = (mY)/P,$$

where Q_D = demand for gasoline,
    P = price of gas,
    Y = average household income, and
    m = a constant greater than zero.

First we want to calculate the income elasticity of demand for gasoline in the U.S. and then interpret the solution.
    Again recall the definition of the income elasticity of demand:

$$E_Y = (dQ/Q)/(dY/Y), \text{ or}$$

$$E_Y = (dQ/dY)(Y/Q).$$

Substituting the values in this case, we get

$$E_Y = (m/P)(Y/Q_D).$$

But from the equation for demand we know that $Q_D = mY/P$, so

$$E_Y = (m/P)(Y/[mY/P]) = (m/P)(P/m) = 1.$$

Income elasticity of demand is unitary. For every one percent increase in income, quantity of gasoline demanded also rises by one percent.

Exercise 2: Is it true that on the average over all goods, income elasticity is unitary? Prove your answer.

Cross Price Elasticity of Demand

Cross price elasticity of demand captures the proportionate change in the quantity demanded of good x when the price of good z changes. This is an important real-word economic concept given interdependent markets and how quantity demanded of a commodity in one market is affected by changes in the price of other goods in other markets.

Mathematically, the cross price elasticity can be written as

$$E_{xz} = (\Delta Q_x/Q_x)/(\Delta P_z/P_z).$$

This is the percent change in the quantity of good x in response to a percent change in the price of good z.

Let's consider a few examples. Suppose the price of gasoline rose. Consumers of gasoline would respond by purchasing less gasoline by either driving less or using other methods of transportation. Either way, the quantity demanded of cars would fall. The cross price elasticity of demand would be negative. Gasoline and cars are complements.

Alternatively, suppose the price of tea rose. The quantity of tea demanded would be expected to fall. In response, consumers of tea might substitute another hot beverage—perhaps coffee. In this case, the quantity of coffee demanded would rise in response to a rise in the price of tea. The cross price elasticity of demand would be positive; tea and coffee are substitutes.

Lastly suppose the price of toothpaste rose. Would you suppose there would be any change in the quantity of hand-grenades demanded? Most likely not. These products are unrelated and the cross price elasticity of demand would be zero.

In summary,

If $E_{xz} < 0$, goods x and z are called *complements*.
If $E_{xz} > 0$, goods x and z are called *substitutes*.
If $E_{xz} = 0$ goods x and z are unrelated.

An Example

Suppose Shea Motors and Foster Motors both sell cars in the town of Middlebury. Last year when the price of a typical Foster Motors car rose from \$12,000 to \$15,000, car sales at Shea Motors rose from 1000 to 1300. What is the cross price elasticity of demand and what is the relationship between the two types of cars?

Recall, $E_{xz} = $ (% change in quantity demanded of good x)/(% change in price of good z). We calculate the percent changes in price and quantity demanded respectively:

$$\% \text{ change in } P_z = [(15{,}000 - 12{,}000)/12{,}000]*100 = 25$$
$$\% \text{ change in } Q_x = [(1300 - 1000)/1000]*100 = 30.$$

Thus $E_{xz} = 30/25 = 1.2 > 0$. Cars at Foster Motors and at Shea Motors are substitutes.

General Demand Function and Demand Elasticities

Having looked at the individual measures of elasticity, we can relate the measures to a general linear demand function. Recall that the quantity demanded of a good x is not only a function of own price (P_x), but also of income (Y), and price of other goods (P_z).

Thus, quantity demanded for good x can be written as

$$Q_x = A_0 + BP_x + CY + DP_z.$$

In this own price elasticity of demand,

$$E_d = (dQ_x/dP_x)/(P_x/Q_x) = B(P_x/Q_x).$$

Following the law of demand, $B < 0$, so we know $E_d < 0$.

Income elasticity of demand is

$$E_Y = (dQ_x/dY)/(Y/Q_x) = C(Y/Q_x).$$

Since both Y, and Q_x are nonnegative, the sign of the income elasticity of demand is the same as the sign of C.

Cross price elasticity of demand can be written as

$$E_{xz} = (dQ_x/dP_z)/(P_z/Q_x) = D(P_z/Q_x).$$

Both P_z and Q_x are nonnegative amounts; again the sign of the cross price elasticity of demand is the same as the sign of D. If $D > 0$, then $E_{xz} > 0$ and the goods are substitutes. If $D < 0$, $E_{xz} < 0$ and the goods are complements.

Price Elasticity of Supply

So far, we have discussed elasticity only in terms of demand. The price elasticity concept can also be applied to supply. The *price elasticity of supply* is the proportional change in the quantity supplied of a good to a change in the price of the good. Mathematically, this can be written as

$$E_s = \% \text{ change in } Q / \% \text{ change in } P.$$

$$= (\Delta Q/Q)/(\Delta P/P).$$

Again, this measures the responsiveness of the quantity supplied to a change in the price of that good. The supply curve for a typical good is upward sloping, so the price elasticity of supply is positive.

Just as with demand curves, price elasticity changes along almost all supply curves. The only case where the price elasticity of supply is constant is when supply is a linear function of price, and the supply curve goes through the origin. The price elasticity of supply can be measured as point elasticities or arc elasticities.

For example, suppose the supply function for CDs is given as

$$Q_S = 2P - 10.$$

Assume the market price of CDs was originally $20 and then rose by 10%. What is the price elasticity? At price of $20, 30 CDs are supplied. When price rises to $22, the quantity supplied rises to 34. The increase in quantity supplied is 13%, so the price elasticity is $13/10 = 1.3$.

In the case of the CDs, the percent increase in Q_S was greater than the percent change in P. From $P = \$20$ to $P = \$22$, supply is *elastic* ($E_s > 1$). If the percent change in the quantity supplied had been less than the percent increase in price, supply would have been *inelastic*. We only summarize three other cases. All are found in your textbook.

If ($E_s = 1$), then supply is of *unitary elasticity*; the percent increase in quantity supplied exactly equals the percent increase in price.

If ($E_s = 0$), then supply is *perfectly inelastic*; there is no change in the quantity supplied in response to a change in price.

If ($E_s = \infty$), supply is *infinitely elastic*; the change in quantity supplied is infinite in response to a change in price.

Geometric Tricks for Estimating the Elasticity of Supply

In the textbook it is suggested that if the supply curve (or a line tangent to it) intersects the vertical axis, supply is elastic (at that point). If it goes through the origin, it is of unitary elasticity (at that point) and if it intersects the horizontal axis, it is inelastic (at that point). Here we present the proof of this proposition.

Consider the definition of the elasticity of supply:

$$(\Delta Q/Q)/(\Delta P/P).$$

This can be written as

$$(\Delta Q/\Delta P)(P/Q).$$

Which is equivalent to

$$(1/\text{Slope})(P/Q).$$

Look now at a linear supply curve with unit elasticity, S_0 in Figure 12.2. Its slope is given by P/Q, but

$$(1/\text{slope})(P/Q) = [1/(P/Q)](P/Q) = (Q/P)(P/Q) = 1,$$

so with unit elasticity, the two terms cancel, regardless of the value of the slope.

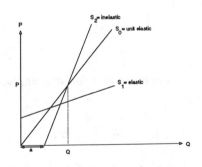

Figure 12.2

The same argument holds for a supply curve intersecting the horizontal axis. Its slope is given by $P/(Q-a)$ where a is the quantity sold at zero price $(a > 0)$. Calculating E_s we have

$$E_s = 1/[P/(Q-a)](P/Q) = [(Q-a)/P](P/Q) = (Q-a)/Q = 1 - a/Q.$$

Since a is positive,

$$E_s = 1 - (a/Q) < 1.$$

In other words, all points on such a supply curve are inelastic. For the proof of the proposition that all points on a linear supply curve intersecting the vertical axis are elastic, see the exercises.

Conclusion

A thorough understanding of demand and supply functions is critical to the basic knowledge of economics. The laws of demand and supply while simplifying the real world to a great extent by focusing on only the key variable, price, are a powerful explanation of the operation of many markets. While these laws indicate the direction of change in quantity demanded of a commodity to changes in price, the measure of price elasticity is important in assessing the magnitude of change. Other measures of elasticity capture the effect of other important variables such as income, price of other goods, price of inputs on demand and /or supply.

Problems

1. The market demand curve for rides in the local amusement park in a small community is given by

$$Q = 4000 - 20P,$$

where P is the fare per ride in cents and Q is the number of rides each day.

a. If the price is 75 cents per ride how much revenue will the park collect each day?
b. What is the price elasticity of demand (at the given price) for rides?

c. If the park needs more revenue, should it raise its price or lower it? Explain briefly the relationship between the price elasticity of demand and total revenue.

d. How would your answer to the above two parts change if the initial fare charged had been 100 cents instead of 75 cents per ride?

2. Recall the demand function for oil presented in this chapter:

$$Q_d = kY/P,$$

where k is some constant greater than zero.

What is the value of the own price elasticity of demand? What shape would the demand curve be to satisfy this value of elasticity?

3. Prove why a linear supply that intersects the vertical axis is elastic.

4. For a linear demand curve, $P = f(Q)$, prove that the price elasticity of demand is equal to the lower segment of the demand curve divided by the upper segment of the demand curve at any given price.

Answers to In-Text Questions

1. Elasticity at $P = 10$ is -1.

2. Yes. Suppose the consumer spends her income on two goods, x and z. The budget equation is $Y = P_x x + P_z z$. Thus $dY = P_x dx + P_z dz$, with prices and income remaining unchanged. Dividing by dY, $1 = P_x (dx/dy) + P_z (dz/dy)$. Multiplying and dividing the first parenthetic term by x/Y and the second parenthetic term by z/y, respectively, we get $1 = [(xP_x/y)(dx/dy)(y/x)] + [(zP_z/y)(dz/dy)(y/z)]$. This can be rewritten as $1 = S_x E_{xy} + S_z E_{zy}$, where S_x and S_z are the share of income spent on x and z respectively. E_{xy} and E_{zy} are the respective income elasticities. Thus the weighted average of income elasticities of demand over all goods must equal 1.

13

Theory of Choice and Consumer Behavior

The theory of consumer choice details what lies behind an individual's demand curve. Consumers are driven by their preferences, or likes and dislikes, and given a fixed income and prices of commodities, buy goods and services in the market place to achieve the highest level of satisfaction. In the textbook, the consumer's choice was considered using cardinal utility, and given diminishing marginal utility, the consumer would be in equilibrium when the marginal utility of x, MU_x is equated to its market price, P_x:

$$MU_x = P_x.$$

Why? Because, if the marginal utility of the good is greater than the price, the consumer can increase his welfare by purchasing more x. But in so doing, the law of diminishing marginal utility kicks in and additional units bring less satisfaction. The consumer will continue to buy more x until the increased satisfaction of the additional good equals the price in equilibrium. Similarly, if the marginal utility is less than the price, the consumer can increase his total welfare by reducing the quantity purchased.

If a consumer buys many commodities, the condition for the equilibrium of the consumer is the equality of the ratios of the marginal utilities of the individual commodities to their prices:

$$MU_1/P_1 = MU_2/P_2 = ... = MU_n/P_n.$$

An Example

Consider Pete's consumption of pizza (P) and Ben & Jerry's Ice Cream (B). The market price of pizza, P_P, is $1.50 per slice and the price of ice cream, P_B, is $2.50 per pint. Suppose Pete is currently purchasing 10 slices of pizza and 8 pints of ice cream over a month. Assume that his marginal utility from pizza, MU_P is 6 and marginal utility from Ben & Jerry's ice cream, $MU_B =$

14. Has Pete selected a bundle of goods that maximizes his utility? If not, how might he alter his purchases to increase his utility?

To maximize utility, the ratio of marginal utility of pizza and ice cream should be equal to the ratio of price of the two goods; i.e., 6/14 should be equal to 1.5/2.5. It isn't. Since prices are taken as given, consumption must be altered. Pete can be better off by cutting back on pizzas (thus increasing MU_P) and increasing consumption of ice cream (which will lower MU_B).

The indifference curve approach was outlined in the appendix of the textbook. Using the indifference curve approach we did not have to assume utility was measurable. All we had to assume was that the consumer can rank his preferences (order the various basket of goods) according to the satisfaction of each basket. He need not know precisely the amount of satisfaction. Thus only an ordinal measurement of utility was required.

We also didn't have to assume diminishing marginal utility. All we had to assume was diminishing marginal rate of substitution. That is, preferences ranked in terms of indifference curves were assumed to be convex (bowed inwards) to the origin. This implies that as one goes down an indifference curve, one has to give more and more successive units of the good being measured on the vertical axis to get one more unit of the good being measured on the horizontal axis to maintain total satisfaction along with consistency and transitivity of choice.

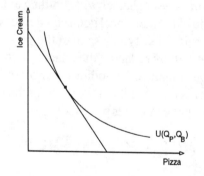

Figure 13.1

Figure 13.1 shows the equilibrium of a consumer using the indifference curve approach. In this chapter we will be more precise about the indifference curve approach and show how it relates to the generalized theory of choice. We start by specifying the marginal rate of substitution algebraically.

Marginal Rate of Commodity Substitution

Suppose that a consumer's purchases are limited to two commodities, x_1 and x_2 and that he derives a particular level of satisfaction, U_1 from consuming these goods. Thus his utility function is

$$U = f(x_1, x_2).$$

As the consumer moves from one point to another on an indifference curve, what is the change in total utility if consumption of both goods changes simultaneously?

Mathematically, total differentiation measures the change in a function allowing all variables to change. We first totally differentiate the utility function:

$$dU = (\partial U/\partial x_1) \, dx_1 + (\partial U/\partial x_2) \, dx_2$$

Since all points along an indifference curve give the same satisfaction, $dU = 0$.

$$(\partial U/\partial x_1) \, dx_1 + (\partial U/\partial x_2) \, dx_2 = 0.$$

This equation specifies an indifference curve. We can solve it to find the slope of an indifference curve, dx_2/dx_1:

$$dx_2/dx_1 = -(\partial U/\partial x_1)/(\partial U/\partial x_2).$$

The terms $(\partial U/\partial x_1)$ and $(\partial U/\partial x_2)$ are the marginal utilities associated with the respective commodity. Thus the slope of an indifference curve is

$$dx_2/dx_1 = -MUx_1/MUx_2 = -(marginal\ rate\ of\ substitution).$$

Exercise 1: For the following utility functions, find MU_x, MU_y, *and dU. Take care to group terms and simplify your expressions into manageable answers. (a)* $U(x,y) = x^{1/3} \, y^{2/3}$ *and (b)* $U(x,y) = 3x^2 + xy^2$.

Indifference Curves of Economic Bads

From the textbook you know the shape of indifference curves for economic *goods*, goods which adhere to the *prefer-more-to-less* principle. What is the shape of an indifference curve of an economic *bad*, one which adheres to a *prefer-less-to-more* principle?

Residential waste is such an example. Individuals are willing to accept more waste if compensated with other goods. Here, the marginal utility associated with the commodity is negative, so the slope of the indifference curve becomes

$$dx_2/dx_1 = -(-\partial U/\partial x_1)/(\partial U/\partial x_2),$$

which is positive. The indifference curve for an economic bad is shown in Figure 13.2. Utility increases from right to left since less of the economic bad is preferable to more.

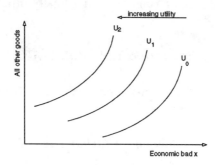

Figure 13.2

An Example

Consider Eve's choice between apples and bananas. Eve's preferences between apples and bananas is given by the following utility function $U = (Q_a + 2)(Q_b + 1)$. We want to show the slope of Eve's indifference curves for goods Q_a and Q_b is negative and that the curves are convex to the origin. That is, the absolute value of the slope of the indifference curve decreases as Q_b increases.

For the indifference curve to be downward sloping, dQ_b/dQ_a must be negative. So we must prove that $dQ_b/dQ_a < 0$. Here we assume that indifference curves are drawn by putting quantity of bananas on the vertical axis. Along any indifference curve, utility is constant. Consider where utility is U_0:

$$U_0 = (Q_a + 2)(Q_b + 1).$$

To find dQ_b/dQ_a we first solve this for Q_b:

$$Q_b + 1 = U_o/(Q_a + 2).$$
$$Q_b = [U_o/(Q_a + 2)] - 1.$$

Next take the first derivative of Q_b with respect to Q_a:

$$dQ_b/dQ_a = - U_o/(Q_a+2)^2 < 0.$$

Since $dQ_b/dQ_a < 0$, the indifference curve is downward sloping.

Now let's prove that the indifference curves are convex to the origin. This is true if the marginal rate of substitution declines as Q_a rises.

$$MRS = -dQ_b/dQ_a = -[-U_o/(Q_a+2)^2] > 0.$$

To find the change in *MRS* with respect to Q_a, we take the first derivative of *MRS*:

$$dMRS/dQ_a = d/dQ_a (-dQ_b/dQ_a).$$

For $dMRS/dQ_a < 0$, $d^2Q_b/dQ_a^2 > 0$. From above you know that

$$dQ_b/dQ_a = - U_o/(Q_a + 2)^2.$$

Applying the quotient rule,

$$d^2Q_b/dQ_a^2 = - [- 2U_o/(Q_a + 2)^3] > 0.$$

Hence $dMRS/dQ_a < 0$, implying that Eve's indifference curves are strictly convex to the origin.

An Example of Utility Maximization

Suppose a consumer in a two-good world has linear indifference curves where the $MU_z = 2$ and the $MU_x = 1$. We also know that $P_x = P_z = 1$ and income = 100. How much of each good will the consumer consume?

The indifference curves, in this case, have a constant slope of -1/2, (MU_x/ MU_z), which implies that the marginal rate of substitution is also a constant 1/2. The indifference curves are shown in Figure 13.3. The consumer wants to equate the marginal rate of substitution with the ratio of the prices of the two goods. Therefore, he will choose combinations of x and z where $P_x/P_z = MU_x/MU_z$, or $1/1 = 1/2$. But wait, this will never happen! Since the consumer, on the margin, prefers z over x, and the price of the two goods are the same, he will only consume z.

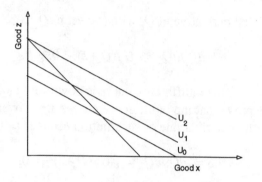

Figure 13.3

What if the prices change to $P_x = 1$ and $P_z = 2$? Again, the consumer will want to choose levels of z and x such that $P_x/P_z = MU_x/MU_z$, or $1/2 = 1/2$. There are an infinite number of optimal combinations of x and z.

Now that we've specified the algebraic foundation for the indifference curve, let's turn to the full algebraic specification of the analysis.

Consumer's Problem - Maximization of Utility

The consumer's problem is to maximize utility subject to a budget or an income constraint. It is assumed that the prices of the goods consumed and income are given. The only way for the consumer to maximize utility is to alter the consumption bundle. Algebraically, the consumer's problem is to

$$\text{maximize } U = f(x_1, x_2)$$

$$\text{subject to } P_1 x_1 + P_2 x_2 = Y.$$

The Lagrange method can be used to find the optimal values of x_1, x_2 for which utility of the consumer is maximized. First we set up a new function, L, reformulating the consumer problem to

$$\text{maximize } L = f(x_1, x_2) + \lambda(Y - P_1x_1 - P_2x_2).$$

Here the consumer maximizes the function with respect to x_1, x_2 and λ, where λ is called the Lagrange multiplier. Recall that in order to maximize the L function, the first-order conditions require that you partially differentiate L with respect to x_1, x_2 and λ, and set them equal to 0.

Let us assume that the utility function takes on a specific functional form, $U = x_1x_2$. Thus here the consumer's problem is to

$$\text{maximize } L = x_1x_2 + \lambda(Y - P_1x_1 - P_2x_2).$$

The first order conditions require that:

(1) $\partial L / \partial x_1 = x_2 - \lambda P_1 = 0;$
(2) $\partial L / \partial x_2 = x_1 - \lambda P_2 = 0;$
(3) $\partial L / \partial \lambda = (Y - P_1x_1 - P_2x_2) = 0.$

Setting equations (1) and (2) equal to zero, we get

(4) $x_2/P_1 = \lambda = x_1/P_2.$

But note that $MUx_1 = \partial U/\partial x_1 = x_2$ (in this case) and $MUx_2 = \partial U/\partial x_2 = x_1$. Thus we can rewrite (4) as

$$MUx_1/P_1 = MUx_2/P_2 \text{ , or}$$

(I) $MUx_1/MUx_2 = P_1/P_2$

This is our condition for consumer equilibrium—where the budget line is tangent to the highest achievable indifference curve.

We are also interested in finding the optimal values of $x_1{}^*, x_2{}^*$ and U^*. Using (4) it is clear that cross multiplication results in $x_2P_2 = x_1P_1$ or

(5) $x_2 = (x_1P_1)/P_2 \, .$

We can rewrite equation (3) as

(6) $P_1x_1 + P_2x_2 = Y$

to get two equations, (5) and (6), and two unknowns. Substituting (5) into (6) we get

$$P_1 x_1 + P_2 \, (x_1 P_1 / P_2) = Y \, .$$

Solving for x_1 we find that

(II) $x_1{}^* = Y/2 \, P_1 .$

Likewise using (II) and (5) to solve for $x_2{}^*$ we get

(III) $x_2{}^* = Y/2 P_2 .$

If we knew Y, P_1, P_2, we can solve out for the physical amounts of $x_1{}^*, x_2{}^*$ and subsequently U^*.

The key things to note from this consumer optimization problem are that at equilibrium, MRS = price ratio (I) and from (II) and (III) the law of demand holds—$x_1{}^*$ is inversely related to P_1 and $x_2{}^*$ is inversely related to P_2.

We called λ the Lagrange multiplier, but what does it tell us? If you look at the consumer's reformulated problem, then $\partial L / \partial Y = \lambda$, which means that it is a measure of the marginal utility of income—how a one-unit change in a consumer's income affects his utility.

Exercise 2: Jane Doe enjoys bowling (B) and playing tennis (T) weekly and derives pleasure according to a utility function $U = (BT)^{1/2}$. She has $40 a week to spend on the two sports and the price for an afternoon of tennis or an evening at the bowling alley is $5 each. How should she pursue her sporting interests to maximize utility?

Price Changes and Consumer Welfare

What happens to a consumer's welfare when the prices of goods consumed changes? In a market economy prices changes more often than do income levels of consumers. But these price changes affect a consumer's welfare by increasing or decreasing the purchasing power of the consumer's income, and the consumer is constantly forced to make changes in the consumption bundle to maximize utility and still stay within the budget constraint.

Any time the price of a good changes it triggers of two effects, called the substitution effect and income effect. *Substitution effect* is the change in consumption of a good that is associated with a change in its price, holding the level of satisfaction constant, i.e., the consumer is on the same indifference curve (Hicksian definition). If we are dealing with a price fall, it is the amount by which you *substitute* the now cheaper product for the more expensive product to maintain your utility. The *income effect* is the change in consumption brought about only by the fact that real income has fallen.

The Hicksian compensating and Slutsky compensating variation are two ways to find how a change in price affects consumer's welfare. The Hicksian compensation holds utility constant while the Slutsky compensation holds income constant.

Hicksian Compensating Variation

The Hicksian compensating variation is that amount of money that you would need to give to the individual to compensate her for the rise in relative prices so that she returns to the original utility curve (is as well off as before). The rise in the price of good x rotates the budget line inward to $P_2 x$. Now the consumer can no longer be on the utility curve U_1; instead she maximizes utility at $U_2 < U_1$. The Hicksian compensation is that amount of income that must be given to the individual that will shift the new budget line to the right just enough so that it is once again tangent to the original utility curve U_1. Assuming the price of all other goods is $1, the compensation is exactly C in Figure 13.4.

The change in quantity of X demanded from bundle a to bundle c in Figure 13.4 represents the response to the change in relative prices where income is adjusted to keep utility constant. It is the substitution effect. The income effect is shown by the change in quantity of X demanded between bundles c and b.

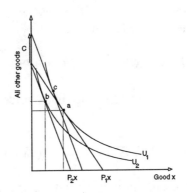

Figure 13.4

168   The Honors Companion

Slutsky Compensating Variation

The Slutsky compensating variation is how much money you would need to give to the individual so that he/she is able to purchase the *original bundle* (hold real income constant) when faced with the new higher prices. This variation is depicted in Figure 13.5. The consumer is compensated sufficiently to attain original bundle a. Again, the compensation is shown by the vertical distance C. As you can see from the figure below, the consumer with the compensation is now on a higher utility curve U_3 than the original utility curve U_2. The substitution effect is shown by the movement from a to c and the income effect is the movement from b to c.

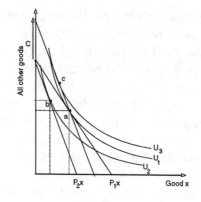

Figure 13.5

An equation that separates the effect of a price change on quantity demanded into substitution and income effects is called the *Slutsky equation*, named after Eugene Slutsky, who first put forward this expression. It is the change in X due to a change in P_x, dX/dP_x, decomposed into the substitution effect and the income effect:

$$dX/dP_x = \partial X/\partial P_x|_{U=U^*} + (\partial X/\partial Y)(\partial Y/\partial P_x).$$

Since the change in income due a change in the price of X, $(\partial Y/\partial P_x)$, is just $-X$, this can be simplified to

$$dX/dP_x = \partial X/\partial P_x|_{U=U^*} - X(\partial X/\partial Y).$$

The first term is the *substitution effect* and the second term is the *income effect* discussed in your textbook.

Important Results From the Slutsky Equation

For normal goods, the substitution effect is always negative and income effect is positive, implying that the whole expression is negative thus validating the law of demand.

For a *normal good* the substitution and income effects reinforce each other (as price goes down you buy more and vice versa). For an *inferior good*, the substitution and income effects oppose each other, but the substitution effect is greater than the income effect (as price goes down, you still buy more, but not as much as if the good were normal). For a *Giffen good* the substitution and income effects oppose each other, but the income effect is *less than* the substitution effect (as price goes down, you buy less). The demand curve for a Giffen good is upward sloping.

An Example

To solidify your understanding of these concepts let's go through an example. Suppose the utility function is given by $U = xz$, $P_x = \$10$, $P_z = \$20$, and income, Y, = \$200. What would the Hicksian substitution and income effects be for a 50% fall in the price of good x, *ceteris paribus*?

First we want to determined the utility maximizing combination of x and z. The consumer chooses that mix of x and z so the marginal rate of substitution equals the ratio of their prices. We first calculate the *MRS*:

$$MRS = MU_x/MU_z .$$

$$MU_x = \partial U/\partial x = z,$$

$$MU_z = \partial U/\partial z = x,$$

Combining these we find that

$$MRS = z/x.$$

In equilibrium, *MRS* = ratio of price, P_x/P_z. Thus,

$$z/x = 10/20.$$

Solving for z,

(1) $$z = 0.5 \, x.$$

Now we know the ratio of goods desired. We next construct the consumer's budget constraint:

$$P_x x + P_z z = Y.$$

In this case,

(2) $200 = 10x + 20z.$

We will solve (1) and (2) simultaneously by the substitution method. Substituting z from (1) into (2) the budget equation can be rewritten as

$$200 = 10x + 10x.$$

Solving for x,

$$x = 10.$$

Substituting x into (1) we find that the initial utility maximizing bundle is $x^* = 10$ and $z^* = 5$. Utility is maximized at $(5 \cdot 10) = 50$.

Now, let the price of good x fall by 50% to $5, *ceteris paribus*. Following a similar exercise as before we find the new optimal bundle is $x^* = 20$ and $z^* = 5$. (We leave the exercise of getting to this solution to you). The utility is now maximized at 100 utils. Utility has risen by 50 utils.

Hicksian Substitution and Income Effects

Now let's decompose this increase in utility into substitution and income effects. At initial prices of $P_x = \$10$, $P_z = \$20$, $U^* = (50)$. Here, we want to return to the original utility curve, but now maximize given the new prices.

Thus we want to choose a bundle so that

(3) $(xz) = (50),$

and marginal rate of substitution = new price ratio:

(4) $z/x = 5/20.$

Solving (4) for x,

$$x = 4z,$$

and substituting in the utility function we get

$$(4z)(z) = 50.$$

Solving for z we find that $z = (50/4)^{1/2} = 3.54$. Substituting this value of z into (4) we get

$$x = 14.16.$$

The total price effect measured in terms of x is the new bundle less the original bundle, $20 - 10 = 10$ units of x. This can be separated into the substitution effect: the bundle at the new prices keeping utility constant less the original bundle, $14.16 - 10 = 4.16$ units of x; and the income effect: the new bundle less the bundle at the new prices keeping utility constant: $20 - 14.16 = 5.84$ units of x.

Conclusion

The chapter analyzed how a rational consumer makes choices from competing commodity bundles available to her in order to maximize utility. In particular we explored the traditional cardinal utility approach and the more popular ordinal or indifference curve approach. From the calculus chapter, you learned that an economic agent's goal is to maximize some pre-specified objective function, and since we live in a world of scarce resources, the norm is usually constrained optimization as opposed to unconstrained optimization. In this chapter you were exposed to the first application of the widely utilized Lagrangean method to solve a typical consumer's maximization problem. The theory of choice and consumer behavior provides a critical link to understanding how and why consumers behave they way do and why the empirically observable law of demand holds true.

Problems

1. For the following utility function, $U = (x+y)/2x^2$, find MU_x, MU_y, and dU; and check whether the utility function exhibits diminishing marginal utility with respect to each good, x and y.

2. Use the Lagrangean method to solve the following consumer's optimization problem:

$$\text{Maximize } U(x, z) = x^{1/2} z$$
$$\text{subject to } P_x x + P_z z = Y.$$

where x and z refer to quantities of two goods (food and clothing) consumed. Also derive the demand functions for x and z and show that this consumer spends 2/3 of his income on good z and 1/3 of income on good x.

3.

a. Many developing countries resort to rationing essential commodities for their citizens. Assume that a consumer in Russia typically consumes two goods, bread and meat. Given the price of bread (P_B) and the price of meat (P_m) and a given monthly income of Y, what is the generic equation of the consumer's budget constraint?

b. Assume that in equilibrium, the consumer is consuming Q_{Bo} and Q_{mo} amounts of bread and meat respectively. Suppose that the government imposed rationing of Q_{B1} amount of bread (and $Q_{B1} < Q_{Bo}$) and of course the consumer has to exhaust the income.

Can you explain to the Russian President that rationing is not an optimal policy in that it hurts the consumer's welfare, despite a possible increase in the consumption of the non-rationed good?

Answers to In-Text Questions

1.

a. $MU_x = \partial U(x,y)/\partial x = (1/3)x^{-2/3} y^{2/3}$,
 $MU_y = \partial U(x,y)/\partial y = (2/3)x^{1/3} y^{-1/3}$,
 Total Utility $= MU_x dx + MU_y dY = [(1/3)x^{-2/3} y^{2/3}] dx + [(2/3)x^{1/3}y^{-1/3}]dy$

b. $MU_x = \partial U(x,y)/\partial x = 6x + y^2$
 $MU_y = \partial U(x,y)/\partial y = 2xy$
 Total Utility $= MU_x dx + MU_y dY = (6x + y^2) dx + (2xy)dy$.

2. To maximize satisfaction, Jane Doe should play tennis 4 hours and bowl 4 hours each week.

14

Production

The theory of production plays a dual role in price theory. First, it provides a basis for analyzing the relationship between costs and outputs. Second, it provides a basis for the theory of a firm's demand for factors of production. The analysis of production presented in the textbook is one most susceptible to both geometric and algebraic treatment. It is important to go through both.

Production involves the transformation of inputs into outputs. The production function that describes this process of transformation is

$$\text{Total product } (TP) \text{ or output } (Q) = f(x_1, x_2, x_3....x_n),$$

where x_n are inputs such as labor, capital, land.

The Standard Firm's Goal

In introductory economics it is assumed that the firm's production goal is to use the lowest cost combination of inputs to produce a given level of output. Two factors must be kept in mind before we go on to analyze the theory of production formally: First, a production function must be specified within a particular period of time, and second, the function is constrained by available technology and institutions. The second factor just says that we are analyzing a production decision in the short run (a period of time when at least one input is fixed). We do, however, briefly consider the mathematical specification of the long-run (when all inputs are variable) production function.

The Geometry of Production

Let's consider the production decision facing an entrepreneur who has to utilize factors of production to maximize output subject to a cost outlay. This analysis can be considered geometrically if we limit ourselves to two inputs. Actually, limiting ourselves to two inputs still leaves us with three dimensions—one output dimension and two input dimensions. We can reduce that to two dimensions by using the dimensional-reduction trick we introduced you to in the geometry chapter—hold one dimension constant and look at the remaining two dimensions. Thus, we follow the same procedure that we followed with indifference curves: we hold one dimension, the output dimension, constant and consider the different possible combination of inputs that can produce a specified level of output. We can translate such a curve into input space by asking what combination of inputs will give us a specified level of output. Such a curve is called an *isoquant*. Each isoquant is a two-dimensional cut of a three-dimensional figure. The collection of all isoquants corresponding to a given production function is called an *isoquant map*. An entire isoquant map conveys the same information as does a production function.

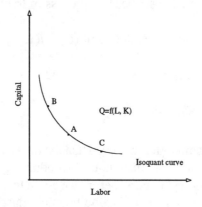

Figure 14.1

The isoquant shown in Figure 14.1 shows the combination of inputs that will produce a given level of output. Given the way we have drawn it, as you move down the isoquant you are substituting labor for capital to maintain constant output. The terms of that tradeoff are given by the slope of the isoquant which is defined by dK/dL. At a particular point, its slope is equal to the slope of a line drawn tangent to the curve at that point. If the slope is minus 1 as it is at point A, when we give up one unit of capital we must add one unit of labor to produce the same level of output. If the slope is minus 2 as it is at point B we must replace 2 units of capital with 1 unit of labor. At point C, the slope is minus 1/2; we must replace 1 unit of capital with 2 units of labor. The curvature of the isoquant tells us the degree of diminishing returns. The isoquant becomes more curved as marginal return diminishes more quickly. When the isoquant is a straight line there are no diminishing marginal returns; the slope of the curve does not change.

The rate at which one input can be substituted for another is called the *marginal rate of technical substitution* (MRTS). It refers to the rate at which the firm must substitute one factor for the other factor in order to maintain the same level of output.

Let's put this relationship algebraically. Since by definition output remains the same along an isoquant, the loss in physical production from a small reduction in capital must be offset by a gain in physical output from a small increase in labor. Hence,

$$- dK * MP_K = dL * MP_L,$$

where MP_L and MP_K are the marginal products of labor and capital respectively. This implies, that $dK/dL = - MP_L/MP_K$ or the absolute value of the slope of the isoquant (dK/dL) is equal to the ratio of the marginal productivities of the two inputs, which is equal to the marginal rate of technical substitution (MRTS) of labor for capital. Whenever there is diminishing marginal productivity, as we continue to substitute more and more labor for capital (i.e., move down an isoquant), the MRTS diminishes.

Exercise 1: To see that you understand the MRTS, draw the isoquants for these two cases: (a) inputs to production are perfect substitutes; (b) inputs to production are perfect complements. In each case, what is the MRTS between the two inputs?

The Isocost Line

The constraint in our production decision was that we only had a certain amount of money to spend. This is called the *total cost constraint* and is given by the equation,

$$TC = wL + rK,$$

where w is the average wage of labor (L), and
        r is the average rent to capital (K).

The constraint can be given geometric representation as a straight line with intercepts, TC/r on the vertical axis, and TC/w on the horizontal axis. This line is called the *isocost line*. All points on one isocost line are combinations of L and K that keep total cost constant. To derive this line geometrically, first ask how much capital a firm could buy if all its available budget were spent on capital. This would be *TC* divided by the cost of each unit, *r*, or *TC/r*. This is point K on Figure 14.2. Similarly, if the firm spent *TC* all on labor, it would buy *TC/w* units, point L. Connecting these two points gives us combinations of *L* and *K* that keep *TC* constant. Note that the slope of the isocost line is -*w/r*. We find the slope by solving *TC= wL + rK* for *K:*

$$K= TC/r - w/rL.$$

Next, differentiate *K* with respect to *L*.

$$dK/dL = - w/r.$$

We see that the slope is -*w/r* and the y-intercept is *TC/r*. The negative sign for the slope is usually omitted in discussions, but it is understood. Each isocost is associated with a certain total cost. If total cost were to rise, the isocost would shift to the right as shown in Figure 14.2. With TC', the firm can buy more of both labor and capital.

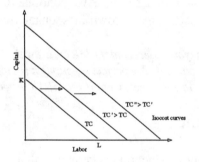

Figure 14.2

Determining Equilibrium

Point A in Figure 14.3 represents the equilibrium, a point at which the firm is using its factors of production optimally, minimizing costs and achieving the prescribed level of production. Let's see how this is true. Given the isoquant Q_0, determined by the MRTS and the desired level of output, Q_0, what combination of labor and capital will minimize total cost? That combination is shown by point *A*. Consider alternative points B and *C*. To produce at point B, total cost would have to be TC' > TC; the firm could lower total costs and produce the same output by producing at point A.

Point C is on the isocost curve TC, but is on a lower isoquant; the desired level of production is not met.

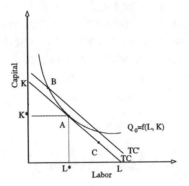

Figure 14.3

At point A, the slopes of the isocost and isoquant curves are equal; that is, $w/r = MP_L/MP_K$. In addition, the isocost curve is tangent to the isoquant curve.

Let's now consider a change in the relative cost of inputs. What is the optimal combination of inputs and level of output? In this case, we are given a budget constraint and we must maximize output. Assume capital becomes more expensive (r rises). The slope of the isocost curve (w/r) falls. This is shown in Figure 14.4 by a rotation of isocost curve LK to LK'. The amount of labor a firm can buy if it spends its entire budget on labor remains unchanged, but it cannot purchase as much labor ($K' < K$). Given the budget constraint LK', and the isoquant map, the firm will optimize production at B with output level $Q_1 < Q_0$. The firm can no longer produce at A because input costs have risen but its level of expenditures has not. At point B, $w/r = MP_L/MP_K$ and LK' is tangent to isoquant curve Q_1.

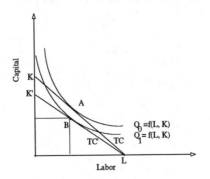

Figure 14.4

The Law of Diminishing Marginal Productivity

Production in the short run is generally assumed to be characterized by the *law of diminishing marginal productivity*. In other words, as more and more of a variable factor, such as labor is added to a fixed factor, the additional productivity of all labor eventually will diminish. If total product is a function of labor alone, the production function is represented by the general form

$$TP = f(L).$$

This function tells us the highest level of output than can be produced with a labor, L.

We won't discuss the production function much since you saw it in your textbook. Let's specify, however, some terminology mathematically: If total product, TP or Q is a function of labor, then the *marginal productivity* of labor is defined as follows:

$$MP_L = dTP/dL.$$

Similarly the *average product* of labor is defined as

$$AP_L = TP/L.$$

Let's consider a specific production function:

$$Q = 30L^2 - L^3.$$

This short-run production function is shown in Figure 14.5.

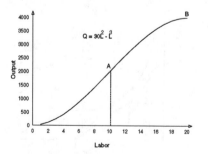

Figure 14.5

Using the terminology of production you can see that from 0 to A, as more workers are added, total product is increasing at an increasing rate (increasing marginal productivity of labor); from A to B, total product is increasing but at a decreasing rate (decreasing marginal productivity of labor), and finally, after B, total product actually decreases implying negative marginal productivity.

For our production function, the marginal productivity of labor is the first derivative of output with respect to labor:

$$Q' = 60L - 3L^2.$$

To find the exact levels of labor at which the marginal productivity of labor is increasing, we take the second derivative of the production function with respect to labor:

$$Q'' = 60 - 6L.$$

Increasing marginal productivity of labor is increasing means $Q'' > 0$, and decreasing marginal productivity of labor means $Q'' < 0$. Since this production function depends only on labor, when marginal productivity is increasing, total product is increasing at an increasing rate and when marginal productivity is decreasing, total product is increasing at a decreasing rate.

Therefore, we set $Q'' > 0$ and solve for L:

$$Q'' = 60 - 6L > 0$$
$$L < 10.$$

For $0 < L < 10$, the marginal product of labor is increasing at an increasing rate. At some point, the marginal productivity of labor becomes negative, and total product falls. To find this point, we set $Q' < 0$ and solve for L:

$$Q' = 60L - 3L^2 < 0$$
$$L > 20.$$

For $10 < L < 20$, the marginal product of labor is increasing at a decreasing rate and for $L > 20$, the marginal product of labor is negative and output falls. This production function exhibits the most common characteristics of production.

The Relationship Between Marginal and Average Productivity

Let's now consider the relation between MP_L and AP_L. Suppose total product, $TP = f(aL)$, where a refers to average productivity. The marginal product of labor is

$$MP_L = dTP/dL = d(aL)/dL.$$

Applying the product rule of differentiation and we obtain

$$MP_L = a(dL/dL) + L(da/dL) \text{ , or}$$

$$MP_L = \text{average productivity} + L(\text{slope of average productivity}).$$

Since average productivity and L are greater than zero (have you heard of negative inputs, or outputs?), we get the following relationships:

1. If the slope of AP_L is less than zero, then $MP_L < AP_L$;
2. If the slope of AP_L is greater than zero, then $MP_L > AP_L$;
3. If the slope of $AP_L = 0$, then $MP_L = AP_L$.

Since the slope of the AP_L is zero at the maximum of AP_L, and $MP_L = AP_L$ at that point, the MP_L curve always cuts the AP_L curve from above.

The average and marginal products for the production function in our last example are:

$$MP_L = dTP/dL = 60L - 3L^2,$$
$$AP_L = TP/L = 30L - L^2.$$

and are shown in Figure 14.6.

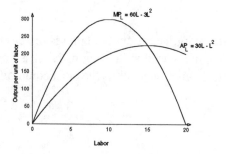

Figure 14.6

Some Common Production Functions

Production functions can come in many shapes and forms. Three simple ones are the following:

Linear Production Function

The production linear function is of the form

$$Q = f(K, L) = aK + bL.$$

For this production process, the marginal product of labor is a constant b and the marginal product of capital is a constant a. This is not used very often because the analysis is too simple.

Fixed Proportion Production Function

Capital and labor must always be used in a fixed proportion. The mathematical form of the production function is given by

$$Q = \min(aK, bL) \quad a, b > 0.$$

where the functional operator "min" means that Q is determined by the smaller of the two values in parentheses. The fixed proportions production function has a wide range of applications. Many machines, for example, require a certain number of people to run them but excess labor is superfluous.

Cobb-Douglas Production Function

The mathematical form of this function was advanced by C.W. Cobb and P.H. Douglas (in 1934) as a law of production for manufacturing industries and is specified by

$$Q = AK^a L^b.$$

Here, Q represents total output, K and L represent capital and labor inputs respectively; A, a, and b are technical constants. It is one of the most widely-used production functions in economics because its characteristics nicely fit the production relationships discussed in the textbook. The Cobb-

Douglas production function also has proved to be extremely useful in empirical applications in economics because it is linear in logarithmic form:

$$\ln Q = \ln A + a \ln K + b \ln L.$$

Here, a is interpreted as the elasticity of output with respect to capital and b is the elasticity of output with respect to labor. We'll consider some of the characteristics of these production functions as we proceed.

Using Calculus and Algebra to Solve the Production Problem

In the geometric presentation, we began with isoquants and isocost curves. In the algebraic treatment of production, we begin with the production function. We will now apply the technique of constrained optimization to the same problem of an entrepreneur who wishes to choose the combination of inputs which will produce the most output for a given budget level, or total cost. Setting this up mathematically, we have a production function, $Q = f(L, K)$, and prices for the two inputs, w and r, where w is the wage rate and r is the rental rate for hiring machinery. The firm can hire the two inputs, L and K, in whatever combination it wants. What we want to determine is the amount of both inputs that it will choose.

Let us choose a generic production function of the form

$$Q = f(L,K).$$

This is the firm's objective function that has to be maximized. The firm is also subject to a cost constraint, which can be written as

$$TC = wL + rK.$$

The left-hand side of the constraint is the total amount of money that the firm has at its disposal. L and K are the two factors of production, and it can hire them at the market prices, w and r, respectively.

Thus the firm's problem is to

maximize $\qquad\qquad\qquad Q = f(L,K)$
subject to $\qquad\qquad\quad\; TC = wL + rK.$

Recall the procedure for solving such problems from the calculus chapter. We can set up the Lagrangean function as:

maximize $\qquad Z = f(L,K) + \lambda(TC-wL-rK)$

with respect to L, K, and λ.

The objective of this exercise is to find the optimal values of L, K at which output of the firm is maximized given a budget constraint.

Recall that in order to maximize the Z function, the first-order conditions require that you partially differentiate Z with respect to L, K and λ and set the result equal to 0:

(1) $\qquad \partial Z/\partial L = (\partial f/\partial L) - \lambda w = 0;$

(2) $\qquad \partial Z/\partial K = (\partial f/\partial K) - \lambda r = 0;$

(3) $\qquad \partial Z/\partial \lambda = (TC - wL - rK) = 0.$

Recall, that $\partial f/\partial L$ is the marginal productivity of labor and $\partial f/\partial K$ is the marginal productivity of capital. Solving equations (1) and (2) for λ, we can set them equal to each other. Doing this, we get

(4) $\qquad MP_L/w = \lambda = MP_K/r.$

We can rewrite (4) as

(5) $\qquad MP_L/MP_K = w/r.$

This equation tells us that to maximize output we must use inputs in a combination so that the ratio of their marginal products equals the ratio of their relative prices.

In the above case, we considered an entrepreneur who wished to maximize production output subject to a cost constraint. Very often in the real world, an entrepreneur has to produce a fixed amount of output; maybe he is subject to a quota, or he has to produce a set of apartment buildings, etc.; but he has to choose the least cost way of doing this.

We will once again apply the technique of constrained optimization to the problem of an entrepreneur who wishes to choose the combination of inputs which will minimize the total cost for a prescribed output level, Q_o.

Setting this up mathematically, we have a production function, $Q_o = f(L, K)$, and prices for the two inputs, w and r, where w is the wage rate and r is the rental rate for hiring machinery. The firm can hire two inputs, L and K, in whatever combination it wants. We want to determine the amount of both inputs that it will choose. Thus we can write the firm's costs that it seeks to minimize as follows:

$$TC = wL + rK.$$

It wants to minimize this total cost while producing some prescribed level of output, Q_o. Thus the firm's problem can be written algebraically as follows:

minimize $\qquad\qquad\qquad TC = wL + rK$
subject to $\qquad\qquad\qquad Q_o = f(L, K).$

As before, we can set up the Lagrangean function as follows:

Minimize $\qquad\quad Z = wL + rk + \lambda[Q_o - f(L, K)]$

with respect to L, K, and λ.

The objective of this exercise is to find the optimal values of L, K at which total costs of the firm are minimized.

   To minimize the Z function, the first-order conditions require that you partially differentiate Z with respect to L, K, λ and set the result equal to 0.

(6) $\qquad\qquad\qquad \partial Z/\partial L = w - \lambda \partial f/\partial L = 0;$

(7) $\qquad\qquad\qquad \partial Z/\partial K = r - \lambda \partial f/\partial K = 0;$

(8) $\qquad\qquad\qquad \partial Z/\partial \lambda = Q_o - f(L, K) = 0.$

Since both equations (6) and (7) are equal to zero, we can set them equal to each other. Doing this gives us

(9) $\qquad\qquad\qquad w/MP_L = \lambda = r/MP_K.$

We can rewrite (9) as

(10) $MP_L/MP_K = w/r.$

Again, this equation tells us that to minimize cost we choose a combination of inputs so that the ratio of their marginal products equals the ratio of their relative prices.

It is important is to note that equation (5) is the same as equation (10) i.e., the optimality conditions to maximize output subject to a cost constraint are the *same* as those to minimize costs subject to an output constraint. This is called the *principle of duality*. We shall discuss it in more detail in Chapter 16.

Thus far we have considered generic production functions. Let us look at some specific functional forms to give some meaning to the above optimality conditions.

An Example

The NorthWest lumber company produces two goods: plywood (x) and logs (y) to be exported to Japan. The State of Washington also mandates that each lumber company produce a minimum combination of goods totaling 84 per week i.e., $x + y = 84$. NorthWest lumber company is a cost minimizer and wishes to minimize its total cost function, $TC = 16x^2 - 2xy + 24 y^2$, but is subject to the above constraint.

To find the optimal combination of goods we set up the Lagrangean function as follows:

minimize $Z = 16 x^2 - 2xy + 24y^2 + \lambda(84 - x - y),$

with respect to x, y, and λ.

The objective of this exercise is to find the optimal values of x and y at which costs of the firm are minimized and the quota is still met.

Recall that in order to minimize the Z function, the first-order conditions require that you partially differentiate Z with respect to L, K and λ and set the result equal to 0.

(11) $\partial Z/\partial x = 32x - 2y - \lambda = 0;$
(12) $\partial Z/\partial y = -2x + 48y - \lambda = 0;$
(13) $\partial Z/\partial \lambda = 84 - x - y = 0.$

Solving both equations (11) and (12) for λ and setting them equal to each other, we get, $32x - 2y = -2x + 48y$, or

(14) $34x - 50y = 0.$

We can now solve equations (13) and (14) as a system of two equations and two unknowns. We find that the optimal combination of x and y are $x^* = 50$ and $y^* = 34$. Substituting these values in the total cost equation we find that total costs are minimized at $TC^* = \$64,344$. From either (11) or (12), the Lagrangean multiplier, λ^*, is $\$1532$. It measures the change in the objective function (total cost), when the constraint (output) is relaxed by one unit — in other words, it is the marginal cost of producing wood.

Exercise 2: For the production function $Q = 40L + L^2 + 10K^2$, and a cost constraint of $\$100$, $w = \$1$, $r = \$.50$, what combination of labor and capital would maximize output?

The Relationship Between the Geometric Solution and the Algebraic Solution

Whether we solved the firm's problem mathematically or geometrically we end up with the same result that in equilibrium, to maximize output (minimize costs) a firm should hire inputs up to a point where $MP_L/MP_K = w/r$; that is, where the cost constraint is tangent to the highest achievable isoquant.

Elasticity of Substitution (σ)

Remember that the isoquant curve tells us those combinations of inputs that maintain a given level of output. But how easy is it to substitute one input for the other? This is essentially a question of the shape of a single isoquant. Along one isoquant it has been assumed that the marginal rate of technical substitution will decrease as the capital-labor ratio decreases. This measure, however, will not be suitable for a measure of the degree of substitutability because it depends on the unit of measurement. Instead, we want a parameter that measures the percentage increase in one input that is needed to substitute for a percentage decrease in another input. The *elasticity of substitution* does just this. It is the percentage change in the capital labor ratio divided by the percentage change in the marginal rate of technical substitution (MRTS):

$$\sigma = [d(K/L)/(K/L)]/[d(MRTS)/(MRTS)].$$

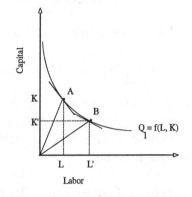

Figure 14.7

In Figure 14.7, the MRTS is depicted by the slope of the lines tangent to the isoquant curve at points A and B. The slopes are falling. The capital/labor ratio is depicted by the slopes of the lines from the origin to each of these points. Their slopes also fall down an isoquant. The elasticity of substitution is defined as the ratio of the proportional changes in these slopes. It is a measure of the curvature of the isoquant.

Elasticity of Substitution of a Cobb-Douglas Production Function

The Cobb-Douglas production function is one of the more popularly used functions in empirical economics. Let us figure out the elasticity of substitution of a such a function. The function can be written as $Q = AL^a K^b$. We know that MRTS $= MP_L/ MP_K$.

Further, $$MP_L = aAL^{a-1} K^b, \text{or}$$

$$aAL^aK^b/L.$$

Substituting Q for $AL^a K^b$ from the production function gives

$$aQ/L.$$

Similarly, $$MP_K = bAL^aK^{b-1} = bAL^aK^b/K = bQ/K.$$

Thus   MRTS $= (aQ/L)/(bQ/K) = aK/bL$.

Using the formula for σ we can then write σ as

$$[d(K/L)/(K/L)]/[d(aK/bL)/(aK/bL)].$$

All terms cancel one another out to get σ = 1. This tells us that all along each isoquant, the ease of substitutability does not change. In contrast, the marginal rate of technical substitution falls as you move down the isoquant of a Cobb-Douglas production function.

Changing the Levels of Output and Returns to Scale

The above analysis was concerned with the short run when one input was being held constant (the concept of MRTS told us what happens when a firm substitutes one factor for the other to produce the same level of output). Let's now consider some issues involved in changing output. Output can be changed in many ways — by changing all the factors of production equally, by changing some of the factors of production but not others, or by changing all factors of production at varying rates. In introductory economics we concentrate on what happens when output is changed by changing all inputs by the same proportion. Economists use the term *returns to scale* to refer to such a process.

To show this mathematically, let the initial production function for the production of cement using L and K be given by $Q_o = f(K, L)$.

Let all inputs be increased by the same proportion, t. This implies that the firm can produce a new level of output, $Q^* = f(tK,tL) > Q_o$. If Q^* increases more than proportionally with the increase in inputs, the firm is experiencing *increasing returns to scale* (IRS); If Q^* increases by the same proportion, t, as the increase in the two inputs, there are *constant returns to scale* (CRS); If Q^* increased but by less than the proportion t, there are *decreasing returns to scale* (DRS).

Returns to Scale and Homogeneity of Production Function

A *homogenous function* is a function such that if each of the inputs is multiplied by a factor, t, then t can be completely factored out of the function. The power t is called the *degree of homogeneity* of the function and is a measure of the returns to scale. If t is factored by a power of one, the function exhibits constant returns to scale and is called *linear homogenous.* If t is factored by less than one, the function exhibits decreasing returns to scale; and if t is factored by greater than one, the function exhibits increasing returns to scale.

An Example

Suppose a production function is of the multiplicative form $Q = KL$. Multiplying each of the inputs by t gives us

$$Q* = (tK)(tL) = t^2KL = t^2Q.$$

Since t can be completely factored out, it is a homogenous function and since it is raised to the power of 2, the function exhibits increasing returns to scale, implying that if the firm were to double inputs ($t = 2$), output would more than double — it would actually *quadruple*!

Let's now determine whether the three production functions discussed earlier exhibit constant returns to scale.

Exercise 3: What are the returns to scale for a production function where the inputs are perfect substitutes?

Fixed Proportion ($\sigma = 0$)

The production function can be written as

$$Q = \min(aK, bL), a, b > 0.$$

Multiplying both factors of production by t gives

$$Q* = \min(atK, btL).$$

Factoring out t gives

$$Q* = t \min (aK, bL).$$

And substituting from the production function gives

$$Q* = tQ.$$

This production function clearly exhibits constant returns to scale. Its isoquants are L-shaped.

Linear Function ($\sigma = \infty$)

The production function is of the form

$$Q = f(K, L) = aK + bL.$$

Multiplying both factors of production by t gives

$$Q^* = atK + btL.$$

Factoring out t gives

$$Q^* = t(aK + bL).$$

And substituting from the production function gives

$$Q^* = tQ.$$

This production function also exhibits constant returns to scale. Its isoquants are straight lines with a constant a slope (or MRTS).

Cobb-Douglas ($\sigma = 1$)

The production function for which $\sigma = 1$ is called the Cobb-Douglas production function and provides an interesting middle ground for the two polar extremes discussed. Isoquants for the Cobb-Douglas production function have the normal convex shape discussed in textbooks. The mathematical form as you recall, is

$$Q = f(K, L) = AK^a L^b ,$$

where $A, a, b > 0$.

The Cobb-Douglas function can exhibit increasing, decreasing or constant returns to scale depending on the values of a and b.

A Numerical Example Let's consider the following Cobb-Douglas production function:

$$Q = 10L^{0.5} K^{0.3}.$$

To see what returns to scale it exhibits, first we multiply each factor in the production function by t:

$$Q^* = tQ = 10(tL)^{0.5} (tK)^{0.3.}$$

Now, factor out the ts:

$$Q^* = t^{0.5 + 0.3} [10 L^{0.5} K^{0.3}]$$

Lastly substitute from the production function:

$$Q^* = t^{0.8} Q.$$

This implies that this function exhibits decreasing returns to scale (0.8<1).

Exercise 4: What returns to scale does the following production function, $Q = 3L^{0.4}K^{0.7}$, exhibit?

Conclusion

We hope that you are able to understand the complexities of production decisions that every firm has to make, whether they involve the production of a pencil or a spacecraft. Production theory is vital to a proper understanding of economics for it links production of goods with the theory of costs (to be examined in the next chapter) and also provides an understanding of how firms hire factors of production, labor, capital and land.

The laws of production, especially the law of diminishing marginal returns, and the law of returns to scale are still as valid today in the era of high technological advancements as in the days of David Ricardo, when it was observed that "but for the law of diminishing marginal returns, the entire world's food supply could be grown in a flower pot."

Problems

1. If the total product line is a straight line through the origin, what do the average product and the marginal product curves look like? What principle in economics would lead you to expect that the total product curve would never have this shape? Explain briefly. Please show the average and marginal product curves in the diagram.

2. A sheep rancher in Australia faces the profit function, $\pi = 200x - 6x^2 - 4xy - 4y^2 + 280y$, where x = amount of meat and y = wool. According to the production process, there is twice as much meat as wool. Find the optimal levels of output that maximizes profits.

3. Do the following production functions exhibit increasing, decreasing, or constant returns to scale? Also, check whether the *marginal product* functions are diminishing, constant, or increasing with respect to K and L. (Hint: you need to take the second partial derivative with respect to each of the two inputs, K and L and check for the sign.)

a. $Q(K, L) = K^2L^2$;
b. $Q(K, L) = 4K^{1/2}L^{1/2}$;
c. $Q(K, L) = K^{1/2}L^{3/4}$.

Answers to In-Text Questions

1. a. MRTS is a constant.
    b. MRTS = 0.

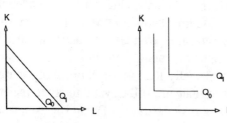

2. $K = 5.85$, $L = 97$.
3. Constant returns to scale.
4. Increasing returns to scale.

15

Costs

The cost function of a firm shows the relationship between output produced and the cost of producing that level of output. Since production is a
function of inputs and technology, and costs are also determined by inputs
and technology, a cost function is ultimately related to a firm's production
function. In the previous chapter we saw how a firm's optimal choice of
inputs depends also on the input prices and so a cost function also depends
on the prices of inputs.

In this chapter we explore costs mathematically, using calculus to show
some of the important relationships and their derivation. We begin with the
algebraic specification of costs functions; then we consider the relationship
between factor productivity and costs.

Cost Functions

Algebraically, we can write the long-run cost function as

$$C = f(Q, T_e, P_f),$$

and the short-run cost function as

$$C = f(Q, T_e, P_f, K^*, T^*)$$

where Q is output of the firm, T_e is technology available to the firm, P_f are
the prices paid for factors of production (or inputs), and K^*, T^* refer to fixed
stocks of capital and land. Generally, at the introductory level we hold
technology and input prices constant, making costs a simple function of
output. That is what is shown in the two-dimensional diagrams developed
in the textbook.

Total Costs for a Cobb-Douglas Production Function

From your chapter on production, you know that one of the most popular functional forms used in empirical research is a Cobb-Douglas function. Suppose that a firm's production function is given by the Cobb-Douglas function, $Q = K^a L^b$ (where $a, b > 0$). The firm can purchase all the inputs it wants in competitive factor markets at rental prices of r and w respectively. The parameters a and b are the elasticities of output with respect to capital and labor respectively.

The firm's problem is to minimize costs. We will show you that costs are minimized where $(wL/b) = (rK/a)$. Recall that a firm's cost minimizing equilibrium has to satisfy the following:

$$MP_L/w = MP_K/r.$$

The marginal product of capital is

$$MP_K = \partial Q/\partial K = aK^{a-1}L^b.$$

The marginal product of labor is

$$MP_L = \partial Q/\partial L = K^a bL^{b-1}.$$

Substituting these values in for the condition for cost minimization we get

$$K^a bL^{b-1}/w = aK^{a-1}L^b/r.$$

Simplifying this expression by dividing both sides by K^{a-1} and L^{b-1} and then cross multiplying we find that

$$wL/b = rK/a.$$

This says that the firm must choose a combination of labor and capital that equilibrates payments to labor and capital divided by their respective elasticities of output.

Once the profit-maximizing level of output is determined, the firm will choose that combination of inputs that minimizes costs. That is, the firm will choose to

minimize $TC = wL + rK$

subject to
$$Q = K^a L^b.$$

This is the firm's cost function. To write this cost function as a function of output, Q, input prices, r, w; and parameters a, and b, we first recall the cost-minimizing condition:

$$wL/b = rK/a.$$

We write total costs as a function of just K, r and a and b and then as a function of L, w, and a and b. Solving the cost-minimizing condition for K,

$$K = waL/br.$$

Substituting K into the cost function we get

$$TC = wL + waL/b.$$

Factoring out wL we get

(1) $$TC = wL(1 + a/b) = wL[(b+a)/b].$$

Doing the same for L we find that

(2) $$TC = rK[(b+a)/a].$$

Stating the level of labor and capital chosen as a function of total costs, we solve (1) and (2) for L and K respectively to get

$$L = [b/(a+b)](1/w)TC, \text{ and}$$

$$K = [a/(a+b)](1/r)TC.$$

Substituting these equations for the cost-minimizing levels of labor and capital into the production function we get

$$Q = K^a L^b = \{[a/(a+b)](1/r)TC\}^a\{[b/(a+b)](1/w)TC\}^b.$$

Distributing the exponents and collecting the TC terms,

$$Q = [a/(a+b)]^a [b/(a+b)]^b[1/(r^a w^b)]TC^{(a+b)}.$$

Now solving this for *TC* we get

$$TC = Q^{[1/(a+b)]}[(a+b)/a]^{[a/(a+b)]}[(a+b)/b]^{[b/(a+b)]}r^{[a/(a+b)]}w^{[b/(a+b)]}.$$

This is the formulation of total costs for a Cobb-Douglas production in terms of output, *Q*, input prices, *w* and *r*, and technical coefficients, *a* and *b*. Input prices and the technical coefficients are assumed to be constant. We can determine total costs given these parameters for any level of output.

An Example

Suppose a firm in Canada produces hockey sticks as given by the following production function:

$$Q = 2(KL)^{1/2}.$$

In the short run, the capital stock is fixed at $K = 100$; the rental rate for capital, *r*, is $1 and the wage rate is, $w = \$4$. We want to determine the short-run total costs as a function of output, or the short-run total cost function. The production function in the short run is

$$Q = 2(100 \cdot L)^{1/2} = 20(L)^{1/2}.$$

We know total costs as function of labor:

$$TC = wL + rK = 4L + 100.$$

To find total costs as a function of output, first we determine labor as a function of output by squaring both sides of the production function and isolating *L* on the left:

$$L = Q^2/400.$$

We can now define total costs as a function of output by substituting *L* into the total cost function:

$$TC = 4 (Q^2/400) + 100 = (Q^2/100) + 100.$$

This total cost function is shown in Figure 15.1. As you can see total costs are increasing at an increasing rate.

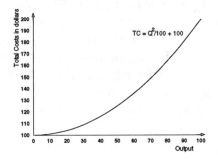

Figure 15.1

The firm can now determine its short-run costs given any level of output. For example, to produce 50 sticks, it would cost the firm $TC = 50*50/100 + 100 = \$125$.

Short-Run Cost Curves

This section emphasizes the underlying relationships of the cost concepts that you have encountered in the textbook.

The Short-Run Total Fixed Cost Curve (STFC)

Total fixed costs are costs incurred on the fixed factors of production, say capital. Since the fixed factor does not vary with output, the level of fixed costs also does not vary with output and can be specified as follows:

$$STFC = C_0.$$

An example is $STFC = \$400$. This cost curve is shown in Figure 15.2.

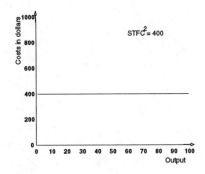

Figure 15.2

The Short-Run Total Variable Cost Curve (STVC)

The total variable cost curve is the expenditure incurred by a firm on variable factors such as labor. By utilizing more of the variable factor in conjunction with the fixed factor, output levels can be expanded. Thus total variable cost is measured by the wage rate times the number of laborers employed. A common short-run total variable cost curve is

$$STVC = AQ^3 - BQ^2 + CQ.$$

This total variable cost curve has a point of inflection reflecting the law of diminishing marginal productivity that governs production. Output increases less than proportionally to input labor and hence the total variable costs increase more than proportionally to increases in output.

The point of inflection can be found by taking the second derivative of *STVC* with respect to Q, setting it equal to zero and solving for Q. Doing so we find that for the general-form *STVC* above, the point of inflection is at $Q = B/3A$.

A numerical example of the above STVC is

$$STVC = (1/3)Q^3 - 10Q^2 + 111Q.$$

This is shown if Figure 15.3. The point of inflection is at $Q = 10$. From 0 to 10, costs rise at a falling rate. Thereafter costs rise at an increasing rate. The law of diminishing marginal productivity begins at $Q = 10$.

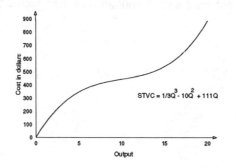

Figure 15.3

The Short-Run Total Cost Curve (STC)

The short-run total cost curve is just the summation of the total fixed costs and total variable costs. For each level of Q, the total cost curve is a vertical summation of the two component curves. Thus

$$STC = STVC + STFC.$$

For our general case,

$$STC = C_0 + AQ^3 - BQ^2 + CQ.$$

For our numerical example,

$$STC = 1/3Q^3 - 10Q^2 + 111Q + 400.$$

This is shown in Figure 15.4.

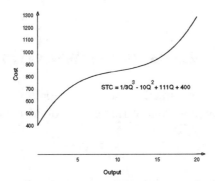

Figure 15.4

The point of inflection remains at 10. The curve has the same shape as the STVC curve, but has been shifted up by $400, the amount of the fixed cost.

The Short-Run Average Fixed Cost Curve (SAFC)

The short-run average fixed cost curve is just total fixed cost divided by amount produced:

$$SAFC = STFC/Q = C_0/Q.$$

Since *STFC* is a constant, short-run average fixed costs declines as output rises. It declines at the same rate that output increases. This implies that it is downward sloping and is a rectangular hyperbola. The function will never touch the axes; instead it asymptotically approaches the quantity axis. For our example,

$$SAFC = 400/Q.$$

It is shown in Figure 15.5

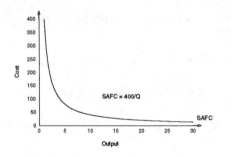

Figure 15.5

The Short-Run Average Variable Cost Curve (SAVC)

The short-run average variable costs curve represents the firm's variable costs per unit of output—total variable costs divided by output:

$$SAVC = STVC/Q.$$

As output level increases, total variable costs also increase. The rate of increase of total variable costs depends on the marginal productivity of the variable input. Up to the point of diminishing marginal productivity, total variable costs increase slowly in proportion to Q, hence AVC decreases; once marginal productivity diminishes, total variable costs increase proportionally more rapidly than the rise in output, and hence AVC rises. Thus the short-run average variable cost curve is U-shaped.

In our example,

$$SAVC = 1/3Q^2 - 10Q + 111.$$

This is depicted in Figure 15.6.

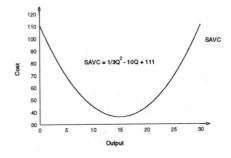

Figure 15.6

The Short-Run Average Total Cost Curve (SATC)

The short-run average total cost curve represents total costs per unit of output. It is the sum of the of average fixed costs and average variable costs:

$$SATC = SAFC + SAVC$$

As the firm's production (Q) increases, the average fixed costs ($SAFC$) declines throughout; however, average variable costs ($SAVC$) declines up to a point and then rises. The minimum of the average total cost curve ($SATC$) occurs to the right of the minimum of the average variable cost curve ($SAVC$). That is because average fixed costs are falling faster than the rise in variable costs. Beyond this point average variable costs are rising faster than average fixed costs are falling and the $SAVC$ gets closer and closer to $SATC$.

In our example,

$$SATC = 1/3Q^2 - 10Q + 111 + 400/Q.$$

This is depicted in Figure 15.7.

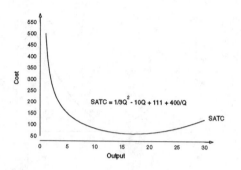

Figure 15.7

The Short-Run Marginal Cost Curve (SMC)

Marginal cost, as you are aware, is the incremental cost incurred by the firm in producing an additional unit of output. Algebraically, the total cost function is

$$STC = f(Q) = STFC + STVC.$$

Marginal cost is the derivative of this function with respect to output:

$$SMC = dSTC/dQ = df(Q)/dQ = d(STFC + dTVC)/dQ.$$

But since total fixed costs do not change $dSTFC = 0$ this leaves us with

$$SMC = d(STVC)/dQ.$$

Like the short-run average variable cost and average total cost curves, the marginal cost curve is U-shaped because of the law of diminishing marginal productivity characterizing the firm's production process.

In our example, marginal cost is

$$SMC = Q^2 - 20Q + 111.$$

This is depicted in Figure 15.8.

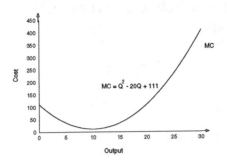

Figure 15.8.

In fact, in the short run, the firm's marginal cost curve is a mirror image of the firm's marginal product of labor (or the variable input) curve, in money terms. Let us see how.

The Relationship Between Marginal Product and Marginal Cost

Let's consider production that is a function of only labor:

$$STVC = wL$$

To calculate short run marginal costs, we take the first derivative of *STVC* with respect to output:

$$SMC = d(wL)/dQ.$$

Since *w* is constant,

$$SMC = w(dL)/dQ = w/(dQ/dL).$$

dQ/dL is the marginal product of labor, so we can rewrite this as

$$SMC = w/MP_L.$$

For the firm in the short run, the marginal cost is equal to wage rate (or the price of the input in general) divided by its marginal product. As the marginal productivity of a factor of production rises, the marginal cost falls. When the firm experiences diminishing marginal productivity, the marginal product curve starts to fall, implying that the marginal cost curve starts to rise. The two curves are mirror images of one another.

The Relationship Between Average Total Costs and Marginal Costs

Recall again,

$$STC = f(Q).$$

Short-run average costs are

$$SATC = STC/Q.$$

We are interested in how SATC changes with respect to output:

$$d(SATC)/dQ = d/dQ\ (STC/Q).$$

Using the quotient rule of differentiation,

$$d(SATC)/dQ = [Q(dSTC/dQ) - STC(dQ/dQ)]/Q^2.$$

Distributing the $1/Q^2$ and then factoring out a $1/Q$,

$$d(SATC)/dQ = 1/Q[(dSTC/dQ)] - (STC)/Q].$$

$(dSTC/dQ)$ is marginal costs and $(STC)/Q$ is average total costs:

$$d(SATC)/dQ = (1/Q)[MC - SATC]$$

Since we constrain Q to be greater than zero,

a. if $MC > ATC$, $d(SATC)/dQ\ >\ 0$ (average total cost curve is rising).
b. if $MC < ATC$, $d(SATC)/dQ\ <\ 0$ (average total cost curve is falling).
c. $MC\ =\ ATC$, $d(SATC)/dQ\ =\ 0$ (average total cost is stationary and at a minimum).

For our numerical example, ATC and MC are graphed together in Figure 15.9.

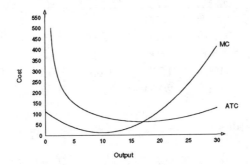

Figure 15.9

Now that you have mastered these relationships, let us apply them to the following example.

A Numeric Example

If short-run total costs are as given for each level of output, what are *STFC*, *STVC*, *SAFC*, *SAVC*, *SATC* and *SMC*?

Q	*STC*
0	500
100	750
200	1100
300	1500
400	2000

The trick to unraveling this puzzle is to first realize that total fixed costs do not change and that when $Q = 0$, $STC = STFC$. Now that you know that $STFC = 500$, you can determine all other cost curves:

$$STVC = STC - STFC;$$
$$SAFC = STFC/Q;$$
$$SAVC = STVC/Q;$$
$$SATC = STC/Q \text{ and}$$
$$SMC = \Delta STC/\Delta Q.$$

The following table shows the values of all the curves for the given levels of output.

Q	*STFC*	*STVC*	*STC*	*SAFC*	*SAVC*	*SATC*	*SMC*
0	500	0	500	-	-	-	-
100	500	250	750	5.0	2.5	7.5	2.5
200	500	600	1100	2.5	3.0	5.5	3.5
300	500	1000	1500	1.66	3.33	5.0	4.0
400	500	1500	2000	1.25	3.75	5.0	5.0

An Algebraic Example

Let us take a specific total cost function to find the functional form of various cost curves. Suppose that the total cost function for a firm producing baseball bats is given by

$$TC = 2000 + 15Q - 6Q^2 + Q^3.$$

The functional forms of the *STFC*, *STVC*, *SAFC*, *SAVC*, *SATC*, and *SMC* are

$$STFC = \$2000 \text{ since } STC = STFC \text{ when } Q = 0.$$

$$STVC = STC - STFC = 15Q - 6Q^2 + Q^3.$$

$$SAFC = STFC/Q = 2000/Q.$$

$$SAVC = STVC/Q = 15 - 6Q + Q^2.$$

$$SATC = STC/Q = 2000/Q + 15 - 6Q + Q^2.$$

$$SMC = dSTC/dQ = 15 - 12Q + 3Q^2.$$

To calculate the various costs at different levels of output, just plug in the level of output for each equation. We leave this to you as an exercise.

Exercise 1: (a) What is the total fixed cost of producing 100 bats? Of producing 1000 bats? (b) What is the average fixed cost of producing 200 bats? (c) What is the total variable cost, average total cost and marginal cost of producing 10 bats?

Exercise 2: For the cost function, STC = a + bQ, *determine the expressions for* STFC, STVC, SAFC, SAVC, SATC, SMC.

Exercise 3: For the cost function, STC = a + bQ - cQ² + dQ³, *determine the expressions for* STFC, STVC, SAFC, SAVC, SATC, SMC.

Shapes of Cost Curves Revisited

All through this chapter we have talked about U-shaped cost curves and have intuitively explained why that may be the case. But can cost functions take other forms? The answer is yes; and here are some typical cost functions appropriate to normal cases:

$$TC = AQ + B;$$
$$TC = AQ^2 + BQ + C;$$
$$TC = AQ^3 - BQ^2 + CQ + D;$$
$$TC = (AQ + B)^{1/2} + C.$$

In order to see where the standard U-shaped cost functions come from, let us go back a step and look at what the total cost function looks like that gives rise to these U-shaped average and marginal costs curves.

We normally use a cubic polynomial function to represent total costs for a firm, because doing gives us a quadratic marginal cost curve, which is the minimum exponent necessary for the marginal cost curve to have a U shape! Cubic functions have the following general specification:

(1) $$C = f(Q) = AQ^3 + BQ^2 + CQ + D.$$

The example we have been using throughout this chapter is of this form where $C = 1/3$, $B = -10$, $C = 111$ and $D = 400$. It is shown in Figure 15.4.

The traditional total cost function $C = f(Q)$ contains two wavy portions that form a concave segment (decreasing marginal cost) and a convex segment (increasing marginal cost). The cubic cost curve has that characteristic. You can see from Figure 15.4 that this total cost function is increasing throughout, which is necessary for it to make *economic sense*, since larger output entails a higher total cost. To see that this is the case, it is essential to place restrictions on the parameters, A, B, C, D to make sure that the marginal cost curves are normally shaped and the total cost curve does not bend backwards.

An equivalent way of stating this requirement is that the marginal cost function should be positive throughout, and this can be ensured only if the absolute minimum of the *MC* function turns out to be positive. Differentiating the total cost function with respect to Q to find marginal cost:

$$MC = f'(Q) = 3AQ^2 + 2BQ + C.$$

The above equation is quadratic, and it plots as a parabola. In order for the *MC* curve to stay positive (above the horizontal axis) everywhere, it is necessary that the parabola be U-shaped (and not an inverse U). Hence the coefficient of the Q^2 term in the marginal cost function has to be positive, i.e., we impose the restriction that $A > 0$. This restriction however is by no means sufficient, because the minimum value of a U-shaped *MC* curve may still occur below the horizontal axis. Thus we next find MC_{min} and ascertain the parameter restrictions for *that* to be positive.

$$d(MC)/dQ = 6AQ + 2B = 0.$$

The output level that satisfies this first-order condition is

$$Q^* = -2B/6A = -B/3A.$$

This minimizes rather than maximizes the *MC* function, because the second derivative of the marginal cost function equals $6A$ and since $A > 0$, $6A$ has to be greater than 0. Since negative outputs are ruled out, and because the law of diminishing marginal productivity is assumed to set in at a positive output level (i.e. the *MC* function is assumed to have an initial declining segment), then for that level of output that satisfies the first-order condition to be positive, B has to be less than 0.

We then substitute the minimizing level of output Q^* into the marginal cost function to determine marginal cost at that point:

$$MC_{min} = f'(Q^*) = 3A(-B/3A)^2 + 2B(-B/3A) + C = (3AC-B^2)/3A.$$

Thus to guarantee that MC_{min} is positive, $B^2 < 3AC$. This last restriction in effect also implies that $C > 0$.

The above discussion has involved the three parameters A, B, C. What about the D in the equation for total costs? At $Q = 0$, $C(Q) = D$. D is the fixed cost associated with production. D must be nonnegative to make economic sense. D determines the vertical intercept of the *MC* curve with no bearing on its slope.

In sum, for a cost function to display the desired shape, the coefficients of a generic total cost function in equation (1) should satisfy the following:

$$A, C, D > 0$$
$$B < 0$$
$$B^2 < 3AC.$$

An Example

The cost function used in the last example, $TC = Q^3 - 6Q^2 + 15Q + 2000$ appears to satisfy these restrictions. The values of A(1), C(15) and D (2000) are all greater than 0; B (-6) is less than 0; and B^2 (36) < 3 AC (3·1·15 = 45). The total cost function is shown in Figure 15.10. And the marginal and average cost curves are shown in Figure 15.11.

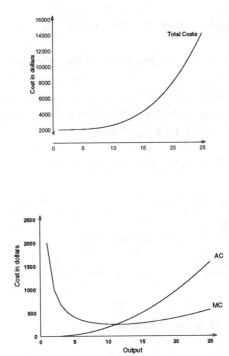

Figure 15.10

Figure 15.11

Cost Curves in the Long Run

In the long run, all factors are variable and so the long-run cost curve is a *planning curve* and is meant to guide the firm's managers in future expansion or contraction of output. From the chapter on production, you are already familiar with the concepts of returns to scale that governs production in the long run. Depending on how fast or slow the costs increase as a result of increases in output, we can trace different long-run total cost functions.

Constant Returns to Scale Production

As factors of production, capital and labor are increased in a certain fixed proportion, output increases by the same proportion. The long-run total cost curve will be a straight line through the origin, with the equation

$$LRTC = aQ,$$

where a is the factor of proportionality and $a > 0$.

Application of Constant Returns to Scale to Total Cost

Recall the production function from the first algebraic example. If that production function exhibited constant returns to scale, that is $a + b = 1$, TC is directly proportional to output, Q. The total cost function is specified by

$$TC = Q^{[1/(a+b)]}[(a+b)/a]^{[a/(a+b)]}[(a+b)/b]^{[b/(a+b)]}r^{[a/(a+b)]}w^{[b/(a+b)]}.$$

Since $a + b = 1$, this simplifies to

$$TC = Q(1/a)^a(1/b)^b r^a w^b.$$

Since input prices and the technical coefficients are both constant, total cost is proportional Q.

Decreasing Returns to Scale Production

With decreasing returns to scale when inputs increase by a fixed proportion, output increases but less than proportionally. Under the assumption of constant factor prices, this implies that costs would increase more than proportionally with output. The long-run total cost curve will start from the origin, and be nonlinear and convex, with a generic equation of the form

$$LRTC = Q^2.$$

Increasing Returns to Scale Production

With increasing returns to scale, when inputs increase by a fixed proportion, output increases but more than proportionally. This would imply that costs would increase less than proportionally with output. The long-run total cost curve will start from the origin be nonlinear and concave with a generic equation of the form

$$LRTC = (Q)^{1/2}.$$

The laws of returns to scale discussed above also affect the shape of the long-run average cost curve. As discussed in the text, the long-run average cost curve is an envelope of all the short-run average cost curves. As production increases, the unit costs decrease due to the economies of scale which the larger plant size makes possible (increasing returns to scale); as production continues to increase, average costs reach a minimum (constant returns to scale, also known as the optimal plant size) and if production increases beyond the optimum size, the firm experiences increasing average costs (or decreasing returns to scale).

Each point on the long-run average cost curve refers to the least cost way of producing a level of output. The minimum point of the long-run average cost curve corresponds to the most efficient level of production. In order to find out that level of output, all you have to do is minimize the long-run average cost function and solve for output (Q).

Conclusion

From this chapter it should be clear that production and costs are really two sides of the same coin. Cost functions are ultimately derived from production functions and, the law of diminishing returns (in the short run) and the law of returns to scale (in the long run) that govern production processes consequently determine the shapes of cost curves in the standard neoclassical analysis.

Problems

1. The production function for a firm producing cricket bats is given by $Q = (KL)^{1/2}$. Derive the expression for total costs given a wage rate of w and rental rate of capital rate of r for hiring labor and capital respectively.

2. Given a total variable cost function, $TVC = AQ - BQ^2 + CQ^3$, show that MC equals AVC at the minimum point of the AVC curve.

3. Suppose the total costs of operating a hotel is given by $TC = 1/3Q^3 - 3Q^2 + 9Q$ where Q is the number of bedrooms (a crude measure of output). Derive an expression for the relationship between the cost per unit of output and the number of bedrooms. How big must the hotel be (in terms of number of bedrooms) to minimize average costs? (Q is measured in thousands).

Answers to In-Text Questions

1.
a.   The total fixed cost is the same whether the firm is producing 100 or 1000 bats and is equal to $2000.
b. $SAFC = \$10$
c.   At $Q = 10$, $STVC = 15 * 10 - 6 * 100 + 1000 = \$550$; $SATC = \$255$; $MC = \$195$.
2.   When output = 0, total costs = total fixed costs. Thus $STFC = \$a$. $STVC = \$bQ$; $SAFC = \$a/Q$; $SAVC = \$bQ/Q = \$b$. $SATC = \$(a/Q + b)$; $SMC = dSTC/dQ = \$b$.
3. $STFC = \$a$; $STVC = bQ - cQ^2 + dQ^3$; $SAFC = \$a/Q$; $SAVC = (bQ - cQ^2 + dQ^3)/Q = b - cQ + dQ^2$; $SATC = a/Q + b - cQ + dQ^2$; $SMC = dSTC/dQ = bQ - 2cQ + 3dQ^2$.

16

Linear Programming

The central problem in economics is how the maximum possible satisfaction can be achieved through proper allocation of scarce or limited resources among competing uses. In the chapter on theory of choice we used calculus to establish a general solution to the problem of choice and derived the optimality conditions. But calculus required us to make specific assumptions about continuity—all functions had to be smooth functions. In the real world many functions are not smooth. In these cases mathematical techniques other than calculus can be used. In this chapter we demonstrate one of those techniques, *linear programming*. It was developed by D. B. Dantzig, an American mathematician, for the purpose of scheduling the procurement activities of the United States Air Force.

Linear programming refers to a technique for the formulation and solution of problems in which a linear function of two or more variables is optimized subject to a set of linear constraints. It is not taught in the introductory course because its solution is neither elegant nor easy, two requirements of any technique presented in that standard course.

Solving real-world linear programming problems requires lots of numerical calculations. Thus it was developed only after the development of computers after World War II. (There are more sophisticated computer software packages and algorithms that handle nonlinear objective and constraint functions; however, we will focus on the linear cases in this chapter.) Linear programming is used extensively in economic decision-making problems in industry because businesses want techniques that work acceptably well. Where production facilities and warehouses should be located with respect to sources of raw materials and markets for the finished product; what mix of ingredients will minimize the cost of producing feed, gasoline or fertilizer; how production can be scheduled to achieve the greatest output of product from plant and equipment are a few of the questions that linear programming can help answer.

When businesses in the real world solve a problem with linear programming, they pull out their software and follow the directions. If they do it right the computer spits back the answer along with various directions about how to check whether that answer is significantly better than other answers. In this chapter we're interested in presenting you with the concept behind linear programming, so that you have an idea of why and how it works. We won't use the computer, but will present a graphical introduction to linear programming with a particular focus on the theory of the firm.

The Firm's Production Decision

As is discussed in the textbook, a firm faces two important production decisions: First, from several possibilities, it chooses one process to produce a commodity or a bundle of commodities. Second, it decides how much of various products it should produce to maximize its profits. Linear programming is a tool to make such decisions given the prices of both inputs and outputs. Thus, in a linear-programming problem it is assumed that the prices for the products and the inputs used will remain constant. Given these prices, linear programming provides an optimal numerical solution to the choice to be made by the firm given the constraints it faces. The optimization can refer to either maximization (as in profits) or minimization (as in total costs). Optimization and choice are thus central to the whole linear-programming framework.

The basic way linear programming works is through modified trial and error. It takes the objective function, and the constraints, plugs in a number, and comes up with a solution that meets both the objective function and the constraints. Then it tries another number, and another, and another. Eventually if it went through all possible numbers it would find the optimal solution, but that would take too long even for a computer. Linear programming groups classes of numbers together and tries only the best of each group, limiting the numbers that need to be tried and leading to a solution relatively quickly.

Concepts of Linear Programming

Before we go through an example, let us familiarize ourselves with some of the basic concepts of linear programming.

Linearity

The principal characteristic of a linear programming problem is that the functions are linear. It is not merely a simplifying assumption, but also a fairly realistic description of the real world. The economic implication of linearity in the context of production is that constant returns to scale prevail and that average and marginal costs are equal and consequently average and marginal products are the same.

Processes

A *process* is a particular method of producing goods that requires various factors of production in fixed proportions. A process is also called an activity or a complex. An essential property of the production process is that inputs must be added in constant or fixed proportions, though it is in stark contrast with the neoclassical approach which assumes easy substitution between factors of production.

Objective Function

An objective function, also called a *criterion function,* describes the determinants of the quantity to be maximized or minimized.

Constraints

The maximization (or minimization) of an objective function is subject to certain limitations, called *constraints.* The budget of a consumer is the constraint on a consumer wishing to consume goods and services to maximize satisfaction. A farmer can produce multiple crops, but each crop has its own unique requirement in terms of fertilizer, water, and labor input, and the farmer begins with certain fixed endowments of these resources.

Feasible Solution

Feasible solutions are those which meet or satisfy the constraints of the problem. It is possible to attain them. The best of all feasible solutions is the *optimum solution*, the solution that will optimize the objective function.

Profit Maximization

Let's consider a firm which is faced with the problem of having to maximize profits subject to resource constraint. The problem can be stated as

maximize $$\Pi = \pi_x x + \pi_y y$$

subject to the following resource constraints:

$$a_{11}x + a_{12}z \leq R_1,$$
$$a_{21}x + a_{22}z \leq R_2.$$

and subject to the following non-negativity constraint:

$$x, y \geq 0.$$

where π_x and π_y are the per unit profit margins and the terms a_{ij} are *technical coefficients*. They tell us how many units of resource R_i are needed to produce one unit of output. R_i is the total amounts of resources available for production. The inequality constraint implies that the levels of x and z in the optimal product mix should not require more than the available amount of labor time, though they may require less. The non-negativity constraint means that the firm produces positive output. Negative output does not make sense.

Recall from Chapter 3 on calculus that we call such a problem a *constrained optimization* problem: the firm is trying to optimize (in this case, maximize) a function (profits), but is constrained by the production process. There are a number of ways to solve this problem. Trial and error is one. A computer program would solve this system of equations by trying some combination of x and y that meets all three constraints and calculate the resulting profit. Then it will vary the values in a way that has been calculated by mathematicians to be the most efficient until it arrives at the best combination of x and z, that is, that combination that maximizes the profit function. Linear programming is simply an algorithm for finding a solution.

We next consider a numerical example and show how to find the solution graphically and then consider the dual problem of cost minimization.

An Example

Think of a firm that has a fixed quantity of three factors of production to produce two commodities, VCRs (call it x) and TV sets (call it z). The firm's problem is to choose the optimal product mix (of x and z) that maximizes the firm's profits given the resource constraints. Assume that the firm has the following quantities of factors of production:

400 units of labor (hours),
300 units of capital (in machinery hours),
1000 units of land (in square feet).

Suppose it takes 4 hours of labor, 1 machine-hour and 2 square feet of land to produce one VCR and likewise it takes 1 hour of labor, 1 machine-hour, and 5 square feet of land to produce one TV set. Suppose that profit margin on a VCR is $200 and profit margin on the TV set is $100. The problem the firm faces is to determine the optimal number of TV sets and VCRs it should produce to maximize profits and also stay within the bounds of the resource constraints.

The Profit Function The profit margins on the VCR (x) and TV sets (z) are $200 and $100 respectively. The firm can produce either all VCRs or all TV sets or some combination of the two. So, we can write the profit function as follows:

$$\Pi = 200x + 100z.$$

The Three Resource Constraints The three factors of production—labor, capital and land—impose constraints on the production process.

The production process requires 4 hours of human labor to produce 1 VCR and 1 hour of human labor to produce 1 VCR and 1 TV. Thus the *labor constraint* can be written as

$$4x + 1z \leq 400.$$

You can similarly write the capital and the land resource constraints as follows:

$$1x + 1z \leq 300 \text{ (capital constraint)},$$

$$2x + 5z \leq 1000 \text{ (land constraint)}.$$

We can now formally write the full statement of the firm's problem as

maximize $200x + 100z$ (profit function),

subject to $4x + 1z \leq 400$ (labor constraint),
                      $1x + 1z \leq 300$ (capital constraint),
                      $2x + 5z \leq 1000$ (land constraint),

$x, z \geq 0$ (non-negativity constraints).

Again, the non-negativity constraints are just to show that negative amounts of TV sets and VCRs do not make any sense in economics.

Intuitively, the sale of a VCR (x) brings in twice as much profit as the sale of a TV set (z). But as you will see, it is not necessary for the firm to produce only VCRs to maximize profits. Recall, VCRs also require more of some inputs, such as labor, than does a TV set.

Solving this problem graphically gives you a picture of the nature of the solution. The graphical solution involves three steps: First, determine the region of feasible solutions; second, determine the graphical presentation of the objective function; and third, combine the two to determine the optimal mix.

Graphical Determination of the Region of Feasible Solutions

The non-negativity constraints mean that the solution must exist in the northeast or the positive quadrant of the coordinate system. We next determine the boundaries or limits set by the technical constraints, i.e. the availability of the different factors of the production.

Bounds Set by the Labor Constraint

The labor constraint was written as

$$4x + 1z \leq 400 \text{ (hours of labor available)}.$$

This constraint can be shown graphically by first determining the z and x intercepts (when $x = 0$ and $z = 0$ respectively). Consider the case where no TVs are produced and solve for VCRs:

$$4x + 0 = 400;$$
$$x = 100.$$

This is the x-intercept. Doing the same for TVs, we can see that if all available hours were spent to produce TVs, 400 TVs could be produced. By connecting these two points we can see the combinations of TV sets and VCRs that satisfy the above labor constraint. We show this in Figure 16.1

as line AB. The slope of this line is the ratio of labor inputs to VCRs and TVs respectively. The firm cannot produce outside the bounds since outside the bounds no labor is available.

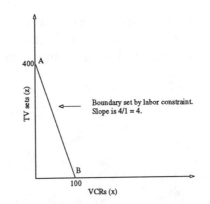

Figure 16.1

Bounds Set by the Capital Constraint

We can similarly derive the boundary set to the production feasibilities by the available quantity of machine hours (*K*). We do this in Figure 16.2. The boundary CD, or the capital constraint, is a straight line whose slope is the ratio of the capital inputs required for the production of VCRs and TV sets, and whose *z*-intercept is determined by the absolute level of capital available.

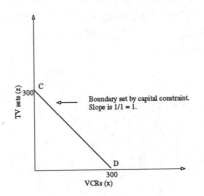

Figure 16.2

Finally, we can solve for the limits set by the land constraint.

Bounds Set by the Land Constraint

The boundary set by the land constraint is shown in Figure 16.3 as line EF. Its slope is the ratio of the land inputs required in the production of TV sets and VCRs, and the z-intercept is determined by the absolute level of land available.

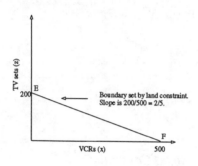

Figure 16.3

Feasibility Set

The region of feasible solutions or the feasibility set is shown graphically by superimposing the three graphs on top of each other. In Figure 16.4, the area OEGB, in which all the constraints are satisfied, is the *feasibility set*. Convince yourself that in this region, all the combinations of x and z lying on the frontier OEGB are technically efficient, i.e., any combination of TVs and VCRs lying on or within this region can be produced by utilizing all three available resources.

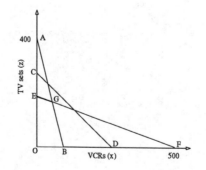

Figure 16.4

Graphical Determination of the Objective Function

Now that you have found the feasibility region, out of all those combinations that are feasible for each input the firm needs to find the optimal combination that will maximize its profits. Recall that the profit function in this example was given by

$$\Pi = 200x + 100z = \pi_x x + \pi_z z,$$

where π_x and π_z refer to the unit profits associated with the sale of a VCR and a TV set.

To present the objective function graphically, we need to construct isoprofit lines, or a set of lines, each of which represents different combinations of x and z that yield the same level of profits.

To graph the isoprofit line, first we solve the profit function for z,

$$z = \Pi/\pi_z - (\pi_x/\pi_z)x.$$

For each constant level Π, there is an isoprofit line whose slope is $-\pi_x/\pi_z = -200/100 = -2$ (or 2 if you look only at the absolute value) and whose z-intercept is Π/π_z.

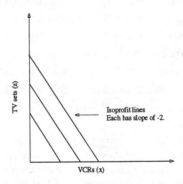

Figure 16.5

The isoprofit lines are parallel, each with a slope of -2, and the higher you go, the higher is the level of profits to be realized.

To determine the optimal solution, superimpose the graphs of the isoprofit lines onto the graph with the feasibility set. We do this in Figure 16.6. The point of tangency of the frontier (outer limits) of the feasibility region to the higher isoprofit line represents the optimal solution. Note that the point G is the optimal solution. This point tells us that the firm in equilibrium will produce 178 TV sets and 56 VCRs to satisfy all the technical constraints and also maximize profits at $\Pi^* = 200(56) + 100(178)$ = \$29,000.

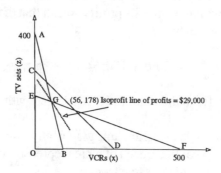

Figure 16.6

The graphical method that you have just seen is intuitively simple and conveys the power of the linear programming approach. However, as you might have figured out, it is impossible to use this method when the objective function has more than two variables. For that, one needs to use the more sophisticated computer algorithms available.

The basic principle of these algorithms is to start with some initial point that satisfies the input constraints, compute the value of the objective function, and then see whether it can be improved upon by iteratively moving from one corner of the feasible region to the other until an optimum is attained. The advancement in computational technology has made it possible to solve linear-programming problems with hundreds of variables and hundreds of constraints in a few minutes.

Exercise 1: The above problems concern maximizing various objective functions. Suppose you had to minimize a function subject to a set of constraints. An example could be a farmer who has to minimize cost of feed for his chickens but has to meet various minimum levels of nutrients. Graphically what would the feasibility set look like in this case?

The Dual Problem and Shadow Prices

The basic problem of profit maximization that you have seen is called the *primal problem*. To each primal problem corresponds a *dual problem* of cost minimization. If the primal problem had been one of minimization, the dual would be one of maximization. The solution to the dual problem provides more information to the firm. We'll show you how.

In the example used above, the firm was maximizing profits subject to three resource or capacity constraints. Recall the general form of the firm maximizing profits given before. This is the primal problem:

maximize $\qquad\qquad\qquad \Pi = \pi_x x + \pi_z z,$

subject to $\qquad\qquad\qquad a_{11}x + a_{12}z \leq R_1,$
$\qquad\qquad\qquad\qquad a_{21}x + a_{22}z \leq R_2.$

The dual for this problem would be to minimize total opportunity costs of producing each. It is usually written in the following manner:

minimize $\qquad\qquad\qquad \Pi^* = R_1 w_1 + R_2 w_2,$

subject to $\qquad\qquad\qquad a_{11}w_1 + a_{12}w_2 \geq \pi_1,$
$\qquad\qquad\qquad\qquad a_{21}w_1 + a_{22}w_2 \geq \pi_2.$

If you look at the primal and dual problems carefully, they involve a mere transposition of terms, but this rearrangement illuminates aspects of the production decision not apparent in the primal problem.

Let us consider each of the steps of the dual formulation in turn. Recall that in the primal problem the firm was maximizing profits, measured in dollars. Likewise Π^* (cost) is also measured in dollars as $R_1 w_1 + R_2 w_2$. R_1 and R_2 refer to the amount of the resources, labor, and capital that the firm has at its disposal, and w_1 and w_2 are some sort of a valuation of that resource. If the firm hired these factors of production from the input market, w_1 and w_2 would be their market price. But in this case the firm owns these resources, so their prices must be imputed. Such prices are called *shadow prices* or *opportunity costs*, also called *dual prices*. They provide information on the opportunity cost of using a particular resource and show which constraints or factors are the crucial bottlenecks to the expansion of the firm and which have some slack. Nowadays, the computer software packages, in addition to the optimal values, provide a set of dual prices, one for each constraint. A positive shadow price implies that constraint is binding on the production process. The shadow price of a factor can be compared to the market price to help the manager decide whether it is profitable to hire additional units of these factors.

Let us now examine the constraints. Consider the first constraint,

$$a_{11}w_1 + a_{12}w_2 \geq \pi_1,$$

where a_{ij} refers to the amount of the ith resource, say R_1, used to produce one unit of good j. The left-hand side of this constraint represents the total opportunity cost of producing one unit of good 1, which is denoted as x in the primal. On the right-hand side, π_1 is nothing but the unit profit margin for good 1. This constraint merely establishes a relationship between the opportunity costs of using a resource and the profit margin feasible, and requires that the opportunity costs for producing the good must not be less than the profit margin for that good (note the $\geq$ sign).

A dual problem can be interpreted as a minimization of the total value imputed for the resources at the firm's disposal while subject to the constraints above. Thus a firm that is maximizing profits to find optimal output levels (primal) is simultaneously minimizing the total opportunity costs of the resources available, with the condition that the opportunity costs for producing each product must not be less than the per unit profit margin from that respective product (dual).

Exercise 2: Given the primal problem in this chapter, set up the corresponding dual problem and provide an economic interpretation. You do not need to solve it.

Conclusion

In Chapter 13, you learned about a firm's production decision in the abstract. In this chapter, you were exposed to a popular technique used in the business world where firms have to make concrete production decisions. Most firms in the real world use multiple inputs to produce multiple outputs. A firm is ultimately interested in maximizing profits and will try to produce that combination of goods that satisfies this objective. To this end, linear programming is a useful tool to arrive at an optimal allocation of scarce resources among competing wants to maximize or minimize a given objective function—which is what most economic decisions are about.

We hope that you appreciate the complexity of decision making in the real world. Given the myriad of alternatives for which resources can be utilized, managers can either go with trial and error or use planning techniques such as linear programming to provide a method of analyzing a variety of alternative decisions.

Problems

1. A specialty metals manufacturer produces two types of a particular metal coded A_1 and A_2. Type 1 requires 2 hours of melting, 4 hours of rolling, and 10 hours of cutting. Type 2 requires 5 hours of melting, 1 hour of rolling,

and 5 hours of cutting. Forty hours are available for melting, 20 hours for rolling, 60 for cutting. The profit margin for type 1 is $24 and that for type 2 is $8.

a. Use the data to *set up* the equations necessary for solving this constrained optimization problem to determine the optimal output mix that would maximize profits.
b. Use the graphical approach to linear programming to solve the above problem and find the A_1* and A_2* and maximum level of profits, Π*. (Use a graph paper and please put A_1 on the horizontal axis.) Shade in the feasibility set. What does that intuitively mean?

2. Fred Flintstone and Barney Rubble, manufacturers of artificial cobble-stones in Bedrock, produce two different kinds of stones: rough (x) and smooth (z). The rough stones require 2 hours of grinding, 5 hours of sifting, and 8 hours of drying. The smooth stones require 6 hours of grinding, 3 hours of sifting, and 2 hours of drying. The profit margin for rough stones is $40; for smooth stones it is $50. Fred and Barney have available 36 hours for grinding, 30 hours for sifting, and 40 hours for drying. You may assume that the objective function and associated constraints are linear functions of x and z.

a. Use the data to *set up* the equations necessary for solving this constrained optimization problem to determine the optimal output mix that would maximize profits.
b. Use the *graphical approach* to linear programming to solve the above problem and find the x* and z* and maximum level of profits, Π*.
c. Shade in the feasibility set. What does that intuitively mean?

Answers to In-Text Questions

1. Suppose a chicken farmer wants to feed his chickens the minimum daily requirements of certain minerals (A, B, C) and is considering different types of feed grains (x, y) based on their nutritional content but also their cost. In such a case the feasibility set is the set of all possible alternatives bounded by the least-cost combination that also satisfies nutritional requirements. The shaded area is the feasibility set for a minimization problem.

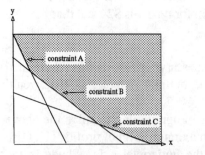

2. The dual problem is to minimize $400A + 300B + 1000C$ subject to $4A + 1B + 2C \geq 200$; $1A + 1B + 5C \geq 100$; and A, B, C ≥ 0.

17

The Firm's Optimizing Decision Under Various Market Structures

In the textbook, you were introduced to four kinds of market structures. Arranged in an increasing order of market power exhibited by a typical firm, they are perfect competition, monopolistic competition, oligopoly and monopoly. The last three are also called imperfectly competitive market structures to distinguish them from the perfectly competitive case. In this chapter we shall consider the mathematics of a typical firm's optimizing decision under the various market structures.

Conditions for Profit Maximization

The firm's objective in each of the market structures is to maximize profits:

maximize $$\pi = TR - TC,$$

where TR is total revenue and TC is total cost and both are functions of the output produced Q.

Profits are maximized at that level of output where the profit of an additional unit is zero. This is where the first derivative of the profit function with respect to output is equal to zero. The standard profit-maximizing condition, therefore, is

$$(d\pi/dQ) = (dTR/dQ) - (dTC/dQ) = MR - MC = 0, \text{ or}$$

$$MR = MC.$$

Now let us consider this general form in relation to the different market structures.

Perfect Competition

Under perfect competition, the firm is a price-taker and MR = average revenue:

$$MR = P.$$

By definition, the demand curve faced by a firm in a perfectly competitive industry is horizontal. A firm in a perfectly competitive market cannot affect price. It receives the same price for each unit whether it decides to sell 100 units or 10, 000 units, implying $MR = P$.

Hence under perfect competition, the necessary condition for profit maximization, also called marginal-cost pricing is

$$P = MC.$$

How close price is to marginal cost is often used as a benchmark against which market structures are judged.

An Example

Consider a perfectly competitive industry, say shoes. Assume the market equilibrium price for shoes is $140. A typical firm in this industry faces a total cost function given by the equation

$$TC = 500 + 50Q - 12Q^2 + 2/3Q^3.$$

We want to determine the profit-maximizing level of output. Since the firm is a price taker, $MR = P = 140$. Total and marginal costs for the firm are

$$TC = 500 + 50Q - 12Q^2 + 2/3Q^3 \text{ and}$$

$$MC = dTC/dQ = 50 - 24Q + 2Q^2.$$

The profit-maximizing condition, $MR = MC$, implies

$$140 = 50 - 24Q + 2Q^2,$$

$$2Q^2 - 24Q - 90 = 0, \text{ or}$$

$$Q^2 - 12Q - 45 = 0.$$

To solve the quadratic expression, we can rewrite the equation as

$$(Q + 3)(Q-15) = 0.$$

Thus possible solutions are $Q = -3$ and $Q = 15$. Since negative output does not make sense, the profit-maximizing output, Q^*, is 15.

Monopoly

In a monopoly, the firm *is* the industry and so the demand curve facing the firm is the industry demand curve. For simplicity we assume the demand curve is linear and specified as

$$P = a - bQ.$$

The total revenue function is a quadratic expression:

$$TR = PQ = aQ - bQ^2.$$

The marginal revenue function is

$$MR = dTR/dQ = a - 2bQ.$$

The demand curve and marginal revenue curves for the monopolist are shown in Figure 17.1.

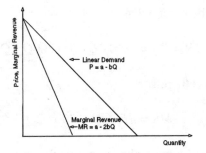

Figure 17.1

Comparing the demand function and the marginal revenue function you can see that they share the same y-intercept term (a) but the marginal revenue curve lies below the demand curve. The marginal revenue function falls twice as fast as the demand function falls. Its slope is $2b$, regardless of the values of $a, b, P,$ or Q. This makes sense since a monopolist must reduce price to sell additional units.

A profit-maximizing monopolist will produce output up to the point at which $MR = MC$. Since the marginal revenue curve lies below the demand curve, this optimal level of output sells at a price, P, where

$$P > MC.$$

An Example

Let's consider a demand curve for a monopolist's product:

$$P = 200 - Q.$$

The total cost expression for the monopolist is

$$TC = 100 + 125Q - 6Q^2 + 1/3Q^3.$$

Again, we want to find the profit-maximizing level of output. To solve for Q^* and P^*, we first must determine marginal cost and marginal revenue for the monopolist. Since the demand curve facing the monopolist is

$$P = 200 - Q,$$

total revenue for the monopolist is

$$TR = PQ = (200 - Q)\, Q = 200Q - Q^2.$$

Marginal revenue is therefore

$$MR = dTR/dQ = 200 - 2Q.$$

Given the total cost function above, marginal cost is

$$MC = dTC/dQ = 125 - 12Q + Q^2.$$

To find the profit-maximizing level of output set $MR = MC$ and solve for Q:

$$200 - 2Q = 125 - 12Q + Q^2, \text{ or}$$

$$Q^2 - 10Q - 75 = 0,$$

$$(Q - 15)(Q + 5) = 0.$$

The solution set to this quadratic is $Q = 15$ or $Q = -5$. Ruling out negative output, the monopolist's profit maximizing output, $Q* = 15$. Substituting $Q* = 15$ into the demand equation we find that the firm charges a price of $185 which is greater than the marginal cost, $170, at this level of output.

Equilibrium under Perfect Competition and Monopoly Compared

You have seen how a typical firm arrives at a profit-maximizing level of output under the two extreme market structures. From the textbook you also know that monopolization of an industry results in costs to society when compared to perfect competition. Let us compare equilibrium prices and outputs under perfect competition and monopoly.

Let's assume a linear demand curve:

$$P = a - bQ,$$

and constant marginal costs:

$$MC = \$A.$$

The linear demand curve of this industry and the corresponding marginal and constant marginal cost curves are given below and shown in Figure 17.2. To maximize profits firms in the perfectly competitive industry set $P = MC$, while the monopolist sets $MR = MC$.

It is obvious from the picture that

$$P_m > P_{pc} \text{ and } Q_m < Q_{pc},$$

where subscript m denotes a monopoly situation and pc denotes the perfectly competitive case.

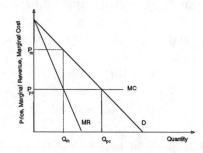

Figure 17.2

The monopolist charges a higher price for a lower output compared to a perfectly competitive industry.

We now demonstrate this result mathematically. Let the equation of the demand curve be

$$P = a - bQ.$$

The expression of the total revenue function for the monopolist is

$$TR = PQ = aQ - bQ^2.$$

And the marginal revenue function is

$$MR = a - 2bQ.$$

Here we assume marginal cost is a given constant, A:

$$MC = A.$$

Under perfect competition marginal revenue equals price and the firms produce where marginal revenue equals marginal cost:

$$P = MC;$$

$$a - bQ_{pc} = A;$$

$$Q_{pc} = (a - A)/b.$$

Substituting Q_{pc} into the demand function we can find equilibrium price:

$$P_{pc} = a - bQ_{pc} = a - b\,[(a\text{-}A)/\,b].$$

Simplifying the expression we find that

$$P_{pc} = a - a + A = \$A.$$

A monopolist produces where marginal revenue equals marginal cost:

$$a - 2bQ_m = A$$

$$Q_m = (a - A)/2b = 1/2\,[(a - A)/b] = 1/2\,Q_{pc}.$$

Thus the monopolist's equilibrium output is half of the equilibrium output under perfect competition.

Exercise 1: Show that $P_m > P_{pc}.$

Measuring Monopoly Power

One of the important distinctions between a perfectly competitive firm and a monopolist is the degree of power or control that the monopolist exhibits in the market. How can this power be measured? For the perfectly competitive firm, $P = MC$; for the monopolistic firm, $P > MC$. An obvious way is to measure the extent to which the profit-maximizing price exceeds marginal costs. Such a measure of monopoly power was introduced by economist Abba Lerner in 1934 and is called the *Lerner's index of monopoly power*:

$$L = (P - MC)/P,$$

where $0 < L < 1$. For a perfectly competitive firm, $P = MC$ so $L = 0$. As monopoly power increases, L gets closer to 1.

An Example

Consider a monopolistic utility company that faces a demand curve

$$P = 22 - 2Q,$$

where P is measured in dollars per unit and Q in thousands of units. The monopolist has a constant average cost of $12 per unit. We want to deter-

mine the monopolist's profit-maximizing price and quantity and then calculate the firm's degree of monopoly power using the Lerner index.

Total revenue and marginal revenue facing the monopolist are

$$TR = PQ = 22Q - 2Q^2, \text{ and}$$

$$MR = 22 - 4Q.$$

Since average cost is constant at $12/unit,

$$AC = MC = 12.$$

The profit-maximization monopolist produces where $MR = MC$. Setting
$MR = MC$,

$$22 - 4Q = 12.$$

and solving for Q^*, we get

$$Q^* = 2.5.$$

Substituting into the demand equation we find that

$$P^* = 22 - 2 (2.5) = \$17.$$

Now calculating the Lerner index,

$$L = P - MC/P = (17 - 12)/17 = 5/17 = 0.29.$$

*Exercise 2: Suppose for the example above, a state level regulatory agency sets a
price ceiling of $14 per unit. What happens to the degree of monopoly power?*

A Rule of Thumb for Monopoly Pricing

A well-known relationship between P, MR (or MC) and the price elasticity
of demand (E_d) is the following:

(1) $$P = MC/[1 - (1/E_d)].$$

This says that as marginal costs increase, the price the monopolist charges
will be higher. Also, the more inelastic is demand, the higher is the price the

monopolist will charge. This makes sense because, since demand is more inelastic, the monopolist does not need to lower price as much to sell an additional unit.

To see the derivation of this relation, consider a general total revenue expression:

$$TR = PQ,$$

where P is the demand function. Taking the derivative of the TR expression with respect to Q using the product rule we get

$$dTR/dQ = d(PQ)/dQ = P(dQ/dQ) + Q(dP/dQ).$$

Since $dTR/dQ = MR$,

$$MR = P + Q(dP/dQ)$$

(2) $$P = MR - Q(dP/dQ).$$

Intuitively, since demand is negatively sloped, the firm must lower its price to sell an additional unit of output. The price elasticity of demand is given by

$$E_d = - (dQ/dP)(P/Q).$$

Inverting this relation, we obtain

$$1/E_d = - [(dP/dQ)(Q/P)].$$

Rearranging terms,

$$-(1/E_d) (P/Q) = dP/dQ.$$

This gives us another way of relating the change in price relative to the change in quantity to the elasticity of demand. Substituting the left-hand side of the above expression into equation 2, we get

$$P = MR + Q [(1/E_d)(P/Q)].$$

Simplifying,

$$P = MR + P/E_d,$$

$$P - P/E_d = MR, \text{ or}$$

$$P(1 - 1/E_d) = MR \text{ or } P = MR /[1 - (1/E_d)].$$

but under profit maximization $MR = MC$, so

$$P = MC/[1 - (1/E_d)].$$

Price Discrimination in Two Markets

A monopolist can charge different prices for the same product in different markets based on differences in consumer's ability to pay in the two markets. This is called *price discrimination*. A firm will charge a higher price for a product whose demand is more inelastic.

Exercise 3: Verify this last statement using equation (1), P = MR - Q(dP/dQ).

An Example

Consider a monopolist whose marginal costs are constant at $100. It sells its product in two markets; in the first market the consumer's elasticity of demand is 2 and in the other it is 4. What is the price it will charge in each of these markets? First we substitute the values for E_d for each market into the equation (1) for monopoly pricing. In the first market,

$$P = \$100/[1 - (1/4)] = \$133.33.$$

In the second market

$$P = \$100/[1 - (1/2)] = \$200.$$

The price of the product in the market with a higher elasticity of demand is lower even though the marginal cost of production is the same in the two cases.

Another Example

Scarlett, the sequel to *Gone With the Wind*, has just been released. Suppose the publisher estimates that the demand for the book in the U.S. is

$$Q_1 = 50,000 - 2,000P_1,$$

where P_1 is the price in the U.S. measured in U.S. dollars. The demand for the magnum opus in England is $Q_2 = 10,000 - 500P_2$, where P_2 is the price in England measured in U.S. dollars.

The publisher who is the sole producer has a cost function

$$C(Q) = \$25,000 + \$2Q,$$

where Q is the total number of copies of book that they produce.

We consider two scenarios: in the first the publishers must charge the same price in both countries and in the second the publisher is able to charge a different price in each country. We want to determine how many copies it will sell and what price it will charge to maximize its profits.

In the first scenario, the publisher considers the U.S. and England to be one market and simply adds the demand curves for each country, proceeding as if it were facing one demand curve. The combined demand curve is

$$Q = 50,000 - 2,000P + 10,000 - 500P,$$

$$Q = 60,000 - 2,500P.$$

Solving for P we get

$$P = 24 - (1/2,500)Q.$$

Total revenue and marginal revenue are then

$$TR = 24Q - (1/2,500)Q^2 \text{ and}$$

$$MR = 24 - (1/1,250)Q.$$

Given total costs above we calculate marginal costs as

$$MC = dC/dQ = 2.$$

To maximize profits the monopolist sets marginal revenue equal to marginal cost and finds that the profit-maximizing level of output is $Q^* = 27,500$. To find the market price, substitute Q^* into the demand equation to find $P^* = \$13$.

In the second scenario, the publisher can charge difference prices in each market. Here we face two monopoly problems. We solve for each separately. In the U.S., the marginal revenue function is

$$MR_1 = 25 - (1/1,000)Q_1.$$

Setting this equal to MC and solving for Q, we find Q^*:

$$2 = 25 - (1/1,000)Q_1.$$

$$Q_1^* = 23,000.$$

Substituting Q^* into the demand equation we find $P_1^* = \$13.5$.
In England the marginal revenue function is

$$MR_2 = 20 - (1/250)Q_2.$$

Setting this equal to MC and solving for Q, we find Q^*:

$$2 = 20 - (1/250)Q_2.$$

$$Q_2^* = 4,500.$$

Substituting Q^* into the demand equation we find $P_2^* = \$11$.

Exercise 4: Determine profits in each scenario and convince yourself that the monopolist makes more money by discriminating than by charging the same price. Recall that profits = total revenue - total costs and take care not to double count your fixed costs.

Real-World Maximization: Profit or Sales?

With the growth of joint stock companies and large corporations, a separation of ownership from the managerial class has emerged. The owners are
the stockholders and the managers are hired persons who run the company.
It has been argued that with this separation, there may also have been a shift
in the optimizing decisions. While profit maximization may still seem to be
the more rational goal, sales maximization may be the more practical one.
After all, the profits of the managers very often depend on the turnover (or
sales volume) of the firm's output. As long as the profits satisfy the owners
(shareholders) and provide sufficient internal finance, it may be in the interest of the managers to increase sales to increase their own bargaining position within the company. This idea was originally proposed by William
Baumol.

How do the solutions to these two scenarios differ? A profit-maximizing firm will set $MR = MC$ while a sales-maximizing firm, by definition,
will produce until the marginal revenue of producing an additional unit is
zero—where $dTR/dQ = 0$.

Let's consider the differences between these two maximization problems mathematically. Consider a linear demand function:

$$P = A - aQ.$$

We want to determine output and price levels that first maximize sales and
second maximize profit. For simplicity, let's assume that marginal costs are
constant, $MC = C$. Given the demand function, total revenue and marginal
revenue are

$$TR = AQ - aQ^2, \text{ and}$$

$$MR = dTR/dQ = A - 2aQ;$$

A sales-maximizing firm will produce until $MR = 0$. Setting MR equal to 0
and solving for Q_S we get

$$MR = A - 2aQ = 0 \text{ or}$$

$$Q_S^* = A/2a.$$

Substituting Q_S^* into the demand equation gives $P_S^* = A/2$.
The profit-maximizing firm sets $MR = MC$:

$$MR = A - 2aQ_\pi = C.$$

Solving for Q_π^* we get $Q_\pi^* = (A-C)/2a$. Substituting Q^* into the demand equation gives $P_\pi^* = (A + C)/2$. Notice that the profit-maximizing level of output is less than the revenue-maximizing level of output and the profit-maximizing price level is more than the revenue-maximizing price:

$$Q_\pi^* = (A-C)/2a < Q_S^* = A/2a,$$

$$P_\pi^* = (A + C)/2 > P_S^* = A/2.$$

An Example

Suppose a monopolistic firm produces mosaic slabs at constant average and marginal costs of \$2. The weekly demand for the slabs facing the firm is given by

$$Q = 50 - 5P.$$

We want to determine output and price levels that first maximizes sales and second maximizes profit. Rewriting the demand function for P,

$$P = 10 - 1/5Q.$$

This implies that

$$TR = 10Q - 1/5Q^2, \text{ and}$$

$$MR = dTR/dQ = 10 - 2/5Q.$$

A sales-maximizing firm will produce until $MR = 0$. Setting MR equal to 0 and solving for Q we get

$$MR = 10 - 2/5Q = 0$$

$$Q^* = 25.$$

Substituting Q^* into the demand equation gives $P^* = \$5$.

The profit-maximizing firm sets $MR = MC$:

$$MR = 10 - 2/5Q_\pi = 2 = MC.$$

Solving for Q_π^* we find that or $Q_\pi^* = 20$ and substituting Q_π^* into the demand equation gives $P_\pi^* = 6$. Notice that the profit maximizing level of output is less than the revenue-maximizing level of output.

Imperfect Competition

Under perfect competition, there are so many sellers that each is small relative to the size of the market, and must act as a price-taker. A monopoly, on the other hand, has only one seller who does not have to worry about competition. In between these extremes exist a number of variations in which there is more than one firm, but not so many that the actions of each firm affect the market. Such market structures are called oligopoly and monopolistic competition. Your text book highlights the various features of these two markets. Here we focus on the interdependency of the actions among firms in such a market structure.

To be successful in today's world of interdependent firms, a manager has to plan a production strategy that takes into account the actions of other firms producing the same or similar products. In addition, he or she must not only anticipate what the firm's rivals have already planned to do but also anticipate how they will react to any change in the firm's own production plan. In more abstract terms, a manager needs to plan a strategy that involves both a planned sequence of moves and a set of reactions to moves that the rivals might make.

Traditionally, oligopoly has been studied by constructing a series of very specific models for specific types of industries, as extensions of the monopoly and perfect competition models. The more modern approach is to model such firms as choosing strategies or playing games with one another. This approach is called (appropriately) *game theory*.

Oligopoly sometimes breaks out into intermittent warfare. In the mid-1800s Cornelius Vanderbilt and Daniel Drew used to cut and recut shipping rates on their parallel roads. By undercutting competitor's prices, John D. Rockefeller used to drive them to the wall or into mergers. When Boeing and Douglas first brought jet planes to market, each had to wonder how high his rival would set the price, asking "What do they think we think they will do?" Now Boeing plays the same game with Airbus Industries of Europe.

Thus we view the manager as *playing a game* with the firm's rivals. This similarity between a manager's strategies and the strategies that might be used in a complicated game such as chess, bridge or poker has led economists to study rivalry among interdependent firms by using a branch of mathematics known as *game theory*. Such a situation, "where two or more free wills each choose strategies that will affect both interdependently," constitutes the essence of the philosophical problems involved in the theory of games.

This theory which sounds playful in its terminology is fraught with enormous significance. At the very minimum, an oligopolistic market structure has to have two players. Early attempts at characterizing interdependent firm behavior focused on a market structure where there are only two sellers called a *duopoly*.

Cournot's Model of Duopoly

Augustine Cournot, a French economist, was one of the earliest economists to write about a market structure with only two sellers. Writing in the 19th century, Cournot focused on two sellers peddling mineral water. Since the water came from the ground, Cournot assumed that the additional costs, after the initial fixed cost was incurred, were zero ($MC = 0$). Furthermore, each seller acted on the assumption that its competitor would not change its output and all it had to do was to decide its own output to maximize profits. Let's discover the final equilibrium in the mineral water market ourselves.

Let the demand function for mineral water be given by

$$P = a - bQ.$$

Let Q_1 and Q_2 be the outputs of the first and second duopolists respectively. Total output, therefore is

$$Q = Q_1 + Q_2.$$

And the market demand function can be rewritten as

$$P = a - b(Q_1 + Q_2).$$

Since costs are zero, the profit functions are equal to the total revenue functions. Total revenue for the two firms is

$$TR_1 = PQ_1 = [a - b(Q_1 + Q_2)]Q_1,$$

$$= aQ_1 - bQ_1^2 - bQ_1Q_2;$$

$$TR_2 = PQ_2 = [a - b(Q_1 + Q_2)]Q_2,$$

$$= aQ_2 - bQ_2^2 - bQ_2Q_1.$$

At equilibrium, $dTR_1/dQ_1 = 0$, or $MR_1 = 0$, and $dTR_2/dQ_2 = 0$, or $MR_2 = 0$. Marginal revenue for the two firms is

$$MR_1 = dTR_1/dQ_1 = a - 2bQ_1 - bQ_2, \text{ and}$$

$$MR_2 = dTR_2/dQ_2 = a - 2bQ_2 - bQ_1$$

Since $MR_1 = 0$,

$$a - 2bQ_1 - bQ_2 = 0.$$

Solving for Q_1,

$$Q_1 = a/2b - (b/2b)Q_2.$$

Simplifying, we find the profit-maximizing level of output for the first firm:

(2) $$Q_1 = a/2b - (1/2)Q_2.$$

Doing the same for MR_2 and solving for Q_2 we get

(3) $$Q_2 = a/2b - (1/2)Q_1.$$

Equations (2) and (3) are the reaction functions of the two duopolists respectively. They indicate how profit-maximizing output depends on the output produced by the rival seller. As was explained earlier, a firm in an oligopoly has to take into account what his/her rival is doing in order to arrive at his/her own profit maximizing levels of output.

The Notion of Equilibrium in Oligopolistic Markets

In perfectly competitive markets and monopolistic markets, the notion of equilibrium was defined as follows: when a market is in equilibrium, firms are doing the best they can and have no reason to change their price or output. Hence a perfectly competitive market is in equilibrium when quantity supplied is equal to quantity demanded and a firm under equilibrium is producing at a level where MR (or P) = MC. Likewise a monopolist is in profit-maximizing equilibrium when $MR = MC$.

In oligopolies, because of the strategic interaction, each firm will want to do the best it can *given what its competitors are doing*. And what should the firm assume that its competitors are doing? Since the firm will do the best it can given what its competitors are doing, it is natural to assume that these rivals will do their best given what the other firm is doing.

Each firm then does the best it can taking its competitors into account, and assuming that its competitors are doing likewise. This may seem abstract at first, but it is logical and gives us a basis for determining equilibrium in oligopolistic markets.

This highly celebrated concept put forward by the Nobel Laureate John Nash, is called the *Nash equilibrium*. Simply put, it is a set of strategies whereby each firm is doing the best it can, given what its rivals are doing, and there is no incentive for either firm to move from its position.

In our model, Cournot's equilibrium can be defined in terms of mutually consistent output levels produced by the two sellers. A pair of output levels, $(Q_1{}^*, Q_2{}^*)$, is called an equilibrium if $Q_1{}^*$ is the output produced by seller 1 when $Q_2{}^*$ is the output produced by seller 2 and vice-versa. Since the Cournot solution and the Nash equilibrium are similar, very often the solution is referred to as the Cournot-Nash solution.

We now want to use equations (2) and (3) to find the equilibrium levels of output for each producer.

Substituting equation (3) into equation (2) we get

$$Q_1 = a/2b - (1/2) [(a/2b) - (1/2) Q_1],$$

Solving for $Q_1{}^*$,

$$Q_1{}^* = 1/3(a/b).$$

This is the equilibrium output of the first seller and is one-third of the competitive output.

By substituting $Q_1{}^*$ into (3) we can also get

$$Q_2{}^* = 1/3(a/b).$$

Exercise 5: Verify that competitive output where MC = 0 *is* a/b.

The Cournot solution is stable. Each seller supplies one-third of the market at a common price lower than monopoly price, but greater than the equilibrium price in a perfectly competitive market. Suppose each of the sellers was not so naive and learned from their previous mistakes. They could have colluded and acted as a joint monopolist, splitting up half the market (since at that quantity, total revenue is maximized) between themselves. The consumers would have had less mineral water and paid a higher price than what they do under the Cournot situation.

Notice that the equilibrium concept is dependent on the firm's expectation of the other firm's reaction. It must be reiterated that the concept of a reaction function is central to the notion of equilibrium in any oligopoly model.

An Example

Let's consider a market inverse demand for mineral water in a small French town,

$$P = 60 - Q.$$

Two sellers, Jacques and Pierre, supply mineral water to the town. Following Cournot's assumption, let $MC = 0$ for both sellers. We want to determine the profit-maximizing quantities for each seller under Cournot equilibrium.

Since there are two sellers, $Q = Q_1 + Q_2$, where subscripts 1 and 2 refer to Jacques's and Pierre's output respectively.

Let us look at Jacques' situation. His total revenue and marginal revenue are

$$TR_1 = 60Q_1 - Q_1^2 - Q_1Q_2$$

$$MR_1 = 60 - 2Q_1 - Q_2.$$

To maximize profits, each seller sets $MR = MC$. Since $MC = 0$ we get

$$60 = 2Q_1 + Q_2 \text{ or}$$

$$Q_1 = 30 - Q_2/2.$$

Doing the same for Pierre we get

$$Q_2 = 30 - Q_1/2.$$

These equations are called *reaction functions* because they tell us how Jacques's output (seller 1) responds to Pierre's output and vice-versa.

The two reaction functions are graphed in Figure 17.3. Solving the two equations simultaneously, we get, $Q_1{}^* = Q_2{}^* = 20$, which is 1/3 the market as we had proved earlier. The total supply of mineral water in the town is 40 units, which is greater than if the two acted as a monopolist (30 units total, 15 units apiece).

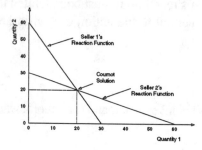

Figure 17.3

You now have an appreciation for how critical strategic interactions are in oligopolistic market structures. The use of game theory has become increasingly popular in studying market structures to precisely look at such strategic situations. Your textbook introduces the basic ideas of a game and some of the more popular games used in economics. Let us refresh your understanding and extend the analysis.

The Payoff Matrix of a Game

Basically, a game in economics consists of a set of players (firms or consumers), a set of alternative strategies available to each player, and a set of payoffs (profits or utilities) obtainable as a function of strategies simultaneously played by all players. For example suppose there are two firms in the town of Middlebury, Vermont - Video King (VK), and New England Video (NEV) - and two possible strategies (set prices = $2 or $3 per tape). The joint strategy diagram can be shown by a two-way table (or payoff matrix) in Figure 17.4.

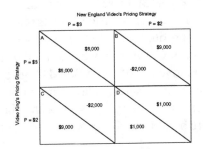

Figure 17.4

The above game is a simultaneous one-shot game. Think of these two firms as having to make up their minds on how to price their tapes. On the first day of the month and they are bound to that price for the rest of the month. Both players are assumed to be rational; they also know the payoff from each possible combination of moves, and each firm wants to maximize its own profits regardless of the outcome for the other firm.

VK picks its strategy by picking a row. NEV's strategy involves his choosing a column. Then in each of the four cells A, B, C, and D the left-hand number denotes row player's (VK) payoff for playing a particular strategy and the right-hand number gives NEV's profit payoff. This game is symmetric in that the payoffs are the same for the two firms across the different strategies.

Thus, in cell A, joint profits of $12,000 are maximized at the common monopoly price, $3. But A is not stable, because if VK knew that NEV would really stay in the first column and price rentals at $3, VK would gain by cutting price to $2 moving down to cell C, to increase its payoff to $9,000. But of course, NEV, now losing $2,000, would prefer to match VK's pricing = $2, taking us from cell C to D. At D where excess profits just happen to be minimal, the competitive solution is stable. But be warned. The competitive solution is not stable against a 'collusive' move from D to A. This might come about by overt agreement or by tacit collusion. The only safe guarantee of competition is thus the potential pressure of numerous sellers (or repeated interaction).

Nash Equilibrium and Dominant Strategies

Cell D is the *Nash equilibrium* solution of the game. That is because each player's strategy is the best given what the other player is doing. To check for other possible Nash equilibria, let us look at other strategy combinations. Let us look at cell A. Suppose VK assumes that NEV will price its videos at $3, does it have an incentive to lower its price? Yes, because it can then reap the higher profits ($9,000 instead of $6,000). So, VK has an incentive to move out of cell A. Likewise, at least one of the players will have an incentive to move out of Cells B and C, given the other player's moves. Thus we come to D. Neither player has an incentive to move and assuming rational behavior by the players and a one-shot game, the solution will be Cell D, where both firms charge $2 for their tapes and each receive $1,000.

Cell D is also a combination of the player's *dominant strategies*. A dominant strategy is a strategy which a player plays *regardless* of what the other player does. As you can see, it is in the interest of VK and NEV to play $P = \$2$, because the profits are higher ($9 > 6$; $1 > -2$) regardless of the other player's choice.

From the above matrix it is obvious that if they cooperate, and both choose $3, they can make more joint profits than with any other individual strategies. A game that has higher joint profits if firms cooperate is a *cooperative game*. If cooperation can lead to higher profits, why don't firms cooperate without explicitly colluding? In particular if you and your competitor can both figure out the profit-maximizing price you would agree to charge *if* you were to collude, why not just set that price and hope your competitor will do the same? If your competitor does the same, you will both make more money. The problem is that your rival might not choose to set price at the collusive level. In fact, it probably *won't* set price at the collusive level because your competitor would do better by choosing a lower price, even if it knew that you were going to set the price at the collusive level.

Prisoner's Dilemma

A classic example in game theory called the prisoner's dilemma illustrates the problem often facing oligopolistic firms. You were introduced to the prisoner's dilemma in your textbook. Oligopolistic firms face a prisoner's dilemma. They must decide whether to compete aggressively, attempting to capture a larger share of the market at their competitor's expense, or to "cooperate" and compete more passively, coexisting with their competitors and settling for the market share they currently hold and perhaps even implicitly colluding. If the firms compete passively, setting high prices and limiting output, they will make higher profits than if they compete aggressively.

Maximin Strategies

A Nash equilibrium depends on individual players being thoroughly rational. In addition, each player also assumes all other players are rational. This need not always be the case as can be seen in the following table.

Let there be two players (*S* and *P*) and the two strategies numbered 1 and 2 respectively. Set the payoff matrix as in Figure 17.5.

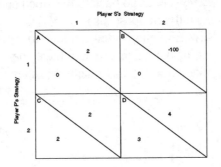

Figure 17.5

Exercise 6: Verify that the strategy combination (P_2, S_2) *is the Nash equilibrium for the game.*

Suppose that you were the *S* player. You had better be sure about player *P*'s rationality. If he were not to play P_2 (as expected) and instead makes a *mistake* and plays P_1, your payoff will be -100 instead of the expected 4. Thus if you were conservative, and you are not sure about *P*'s rationality, you may opt to play S_1 to be at least assured of earning 2 regardless of whether *P* plays P_1 or P_2. A strategy such as this that maximizes the minimum gain is called a *maximin strategy*. If both players used their maximin strategies, the solution would be (S_1, P_2). A maximin strategy is a risk-averse strategy and not a profit-maximizing strategy.

Now in the real world, a *game* is not also always a one-shot deal. Also these games are not always played simultaneously. Most firms set prices and output over and over again, continually observing their competitor's behavior and adjusting their own accordingly. This allows firms to develop reputations from which trust (or fear!) can arise. As a result oligopolistic cooperation and coordination can sometimes prevail. Also, a firm can have what is called a *first-mover* advantage. We now turn our attention to sequential games.

Sequential Games

In all the games considered thus far, the players moved simultaneously. In the real world, firms often have some sort of a first-mover advantage and are able to nose out their rivals in terms of launching a new product, being ahead on research and development etc.

Such games where decisions by the players are made sequentially are called *sequential games*. Let us go back to the video parlor game and analyze the game sequentially. Suppose also that Video King has been around longer and then New England Video decides to open up a branch in Middlebury. The rest of the game can stay the same. The decision-tree (since it does look like a tree and its branches) is shown in Figure 17.6.

Figure 17.6

VK has a first mover advantage and can set price at either $P = \$2$ or $P = \$3$. Once it has made up its mind, and NEV opens shop, it can also set price at either $P = \$2$ or $P = \$3$. Now since payoffs from various strategies are common knowledge to both players, VK would try to get the maximum profits (\$9,000, cell B) and so working backwards, it should price its tapes \$2. But then NEV would not want to set $P = \$3$, for it would get negative profits and would be forced to charge $P = \$2$, thus earning profits of \$1,000 for both, which is a far cry from the \$9,000 that VK wanted. In this case, the first mover does not really have any advantage.

In any of the games given above, you may change the payoffs and see how the outcome of the game changes. Just like for any other game you must be clear about the behavioral rules, the permissible strategies and the number of players. You can create a number of variations that characterize various scenarios found in the real world.

Conclusion

The assumption of profit maximization is often used as the motivation underlying firm behavior in any market structure because it predicts business behavior. This was seen to be true in not only competitive markets but in noncompetitive market structures as well. As we move away from the perfectly competitive markets, we are faced with the exercise of market power by firms who face downward sloping demand curves. A sole monopolist wields the most power. Oligopolistic markets can be characterized by not only the degree of market power but also its power relative to the strategic interaction with other players. This market structure is truly dynamic and often times unstable.

Problems

1. A radio manufacturer produces Q sets per week at a total cost of $TC = (1/25)Q^2 + 3Q + 100$. He is a monopolist and the demand in his market is $Q = 75 - 3P$. Price is $\$P$ per set. What is the monopoly price and quantity in this market?

2. The demand function for World Cup soccer tickets in Europe for a typical game is $Q = 400{,}000 - 20{,}000P$. The marketing manager for the World Cup wishes to set prices to maximize revenue. The main stadium holds 400,000 spectators. What price will generate the maximum revenue? At this revenue, how many seats in the stadium will be left unfilled?

3. An author usually receives a fixed percentage of total revenue as his royalty. As a result, the author will wish to sell his book at a lower price than the publisher. True or False? Explain. You may assume that the publisher is the sole producer of the book.

4. A monopolist can produce output at a constant average and marginal costs of $15 per unit. The monopolist is also able to sell goods in two different markets (with no opportunity of resale between them). The demand curve for the first market is given by $Q_1 = 210 - 6P_1$ and the demand curve in the second market is $Q_2 = 165 - 3P_2$.

a. Suppose the monopolist is able to price discriminate, what are equilibrium price and quantities in the two markets and what is the over all level of profit?

b. How would your answer change if the monopolist is not able to separate the markets and is forced to sell the good at one price in the two markets?

5. Demand for environmentally friendly bulbs is given by $P = 200 - Q$, where Q is in millions of boxes sold and P is the price per box. There are two producers of bulbs: Ecolite (E) and GreenLite(G). They have identical cost functions: $C_i = 20Q_i + Q_i^2$ (for i = E, G) and $Q = Q_E + Q_G$.

Each firm's manager independently recognizes the oligopolistic nature of the light industry and plays by the Cournot rule. What are the optimal values of Q_E, Q_G, and P? What are each firm's profits? What are the respective reaction functions? Draw them making sure to put Q_E on the horizontal axis and indicate the Cournot equilibrium.

6. Terry and Gerry are roommates. Every weekend, they argue about who should go to the super market and purchase groceries. Each of them has two strategies—Shop and Not Shop. The payoffs associated with the strategies reflect changes in utility (measured in utils) from pursuing that activity. Using the payoff information given below, set up the payoff matrix.

T: Shop, G: Shop : 5, 5
T: Shop, G: No Shop: 5, 8
T: No Shop, G: Shop: 8, 5
T: No Shop, G: No Shop: 2, 2

What is the Nash equilibrium in this game? Do either Terry and Gerry have a dominant strategy? Is there a maximin strategy solution for the game?

Answers to In-Text Questions

1. $Q_{pc} = (a$ A$)/b$, $Q_m = (1/2)[(a - A)/b]$. $P = a - bQ$. Under perfect competition, $P_{pc} = a - b \cdot (a - A)/b$. P_{pc} = A. Under monopoly, $P_m = a - b(1/2)[(a - A)/b]$. Simplifying we get $P_m = (a + A)/2$.

2. The new ceiling price is $P = 14$ so the new Lerner index is $L = (14 - 12)/14 = 1/7 = 0.14$. The power of the monopolist has been reduced due to the ceiling.

3. $P = MC/(1 - 1/E_d)$. Let there be two markets with prices P_1 and P_2 and different elasticities E_1 and E_2. Let $E_1 > E_2$. $P_1 = MC/(1 - 1/E_1)$ and $P_2 = MC/(1 - 1/E_2)$. $P_1/P_2 = [MC/(1 - 1/E_1)]/[MC/(1 - 1/E_2)] = (1 - 1/E_2)/(1 - 1/E_1)$. Since $E_1 > E_2$, $P_1 < P_2$.

4. $\pi_{US+UK} = 277{,}500$. $\pi_{US} + \pi_{UK} = 280{,}000$. Profits are higher if the monopolist price discriminates between the two markets.

5. Given the linear demand equation, $P = a - bQ$. Under perfect competition, price is set equal to marginal cost, which is zero in a Cournot duopoly model. Therefore, $P = a - bQ = 0$; $Q^* = a/b$.

6. (P_2, S_2) is a Nash equilibrium because if P knows that his rival's strategy is S_2, she has no incentive to switch from P_2 to P_1 and similarly, if S knows that the rival's strategy is P_2, he has no incentive to switch from S_2 to S_1.

18

Applying the Competitive Model

Most markets in the real world are affected by some form of government intervention. Governments levy taxes; give out subsidies; impose rent controls and other forms of price controls; buy up wheat and other farm products at prices higher than free market price; legislate minimum wages; and protect domestic producers and consumers from foreign competition through the use of tariffs, quotas, voluntary export restraints. There are a host of other ways the government intervenes in the marketplace.

In the textbook we developed the main geometric elements needed to analyze government intervention and went through a number of examples. In this chapter we extend that analysis in two ways. First we present the analysis algebraically, and then we consider some cases not presented in the chapter.

Before we do this, let's review the main elements of the analysis that were presented in the book.

Algebraic Treatment of the Competitive Model

Let's assume that we have linear supply and demand curves specified as follows:

demand: $$Q_D = A - aP_D$$

supply : $$Q_S = -B + bP_S$$

In equilibrium we know that $Q_D = Q_S$ and $P_D = P_S$. This equilibrium condition allows us to solve the two equations to determine equilibrium price and quantity (P^* and Q^*). Government intervention essentially replaces the equilibrium condition with either a price or a quantity restriction. If a price restriction is imposed, quantity demanded and supplied will differ ($Q_D \neq Q_S$). If a quantity restriction is imposed, the price buyers are willing to pay and the price that sellers are willing to accept will differ ($P_D \neq P_S$). The results of the intervention can be determined by replacing the equilibrium condition with an equation that specifies the price or quantity limitation and solving the three equations simultaneously.

First solving P and Q for free market equilibrium, we first set demand equal to supply and solve for P^*:

$$A - aP_D = -B + bP_S,$$

$$P^* = (A + B)/(a + b).$$

Substitute into either the demand and supply equation to find Q^*:

$$Q^* = A - a[(A + B)/(a + b)]$$

$$= (bA - aB)/(a + b).$$

If a price ceiling were imposed, $P_c < (A + B)/(a + b)$, $Q_D \neq Q_S$. Suppose a price ceiling is set $\$C$ below P^*:

$$P_c = (A + B)/(a + b) - C.$$

The quantity demanded at this price will be

$$Q_D = A - a[(A + B)/(a + b) - C].$$

Simplifying we get

$$Q_D = (Ab - aB)/(a + b) + aC.$$

The quantity supplied at this price will be

$$Q_S = -B + b[(A + B)/(a + b) - C],$$

which simplified is just

$$Q_S = (Ab - aB)/(a + b) - bC.$$

Comparing quantity supplied and demanded, the two differ by the second term. Clearly, $Q_D > Q_S$.

Now suppose a price floor were imposed so that $P_c > (A + B)/(a + b)$. A price floor set price above equilibrium, so we assume $P_c = P^* + C =$

$(A + B)/(a + b) + C$. Following the same exercise as with a price ceiling, we find that the quantity demanded and supplied are

$$Q_D = (Ab - aB)/(a + b) - aC,$$

$$Q_S = (Ab - aB)/(a + b) + bC.$$

As expected $\qquad\qquad Q_D < Q_S.$

A Numerical Example of a Price Ceiling

Let the demand and supply for fish be given by the following equations, where price is measured in dollars per pound and quantity is measured in thousands of pounds. The demand and supply curves are specified as follows and are depicted in Figure 18.1:

demand: $\qquad\qquad Q_D = 100 - 5P,$

supply : $\qquad\qquad Q_S = -10 + P.$

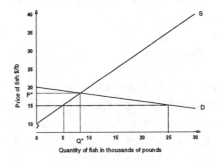

Figure 18.1

Solving for P^*

$$P^* = 110/6 = \$ 18.33/lb.$$

Substitute P^* in either the demand or the supply equations we find equilibrium quantity, Q^*. We use the demand equation:

$$Q^* = 100 - 5(18.33) = 8.35 \text{ thousands of pounds.}$$

Now suppose that the government feels that the equilibrium price for fish is too high and legislates that the price cannot exceed \$15 per pound. Since the intervention price is below P^*, the government has instituted a *price ceiling*. A wedge has been created between the demanders and suppliers (i.e. at $P = \$15$, $Q_D \neq Q_S$). We now replace the equilibrium condition with

$$P = \$15.$$

Now that $Q_D \neq Q_S$ we must calculate Q_D and Q_S by substituting $P = \$15$ into the demand and supply equations respectively:

$$Q_D^{P=\$15} = 100 - 5(15) = 25,$$

$$Q_S^{P=15} = -10 + 15 = 5.$$

At lower-than-equilibrium price \$15, buyers wish to buy 16.65 thousand more pounds and sellers are willing to supply 3.35 thousand fewer pounds ($Q_D > Q_S$). There will be an excess demand for (shortage of) fish in the marketplace. We know from an earlier chapter that with excess demand, prices will be bid up; here, however, the market forces are suspended by the government action.

Price Controls and Monopolies

In the textbook there was a debate about the effect of price controls. The signers of the petition argued that price controls create shortages; Franco Modigliani argued that they don't necessarily. To see Modigliani's argument, let's assume that the market is monopolistic rather than competitive. In that case, the equilibrium condition changes.

Assuming the demand function is

$$P = A - aQ,$$

the total revenue function for the monopolist is

$$TR = AQ - aQ^2.$$

Marginal revenue for the monopolist is

$$MR = dTR/dQ = A - 2aQ.$$

The monopolist will set the quantity produced where marginal cost equals marginal revenue. It then charges the price people are willing to pay for that quantity determined by the demand curve. As long as marginal costs are below the controlled price, there will not be any shortage.

For simplicity let's assume marginal costs are a constant C_0. The firm will produce where

$$C_0 = A - 2aQ.$$

Solving for Q we find

$$Q = C_0/(2a) + A/(2a).$$

It will charge a price

$$P_M = 1/2(A - C_0).$$

Once a binding price ceiling is imposed, the marginal revenue curve facing the monopolist is no longer the marginal revenue curve above, but instead just the price control P_c. The monopolist can no longer set its price. In this case the firm will produce where price intersects the demand curve,

$$Q = (A - P_c)/a$$

so long as $P_c > MC$.

An example of a price ceiling is shown as the price-quantity combination (P_1, Q_1) in Figure 18.2. Still marginal costs are below price, so the firm can earn a profit per unit $(P - MC)$. The firm will choose to produce where the price ceiling intersects the demand curve and produce at a higher level of output. The firm will be willing to do so up to the point where the price ceiling equals the marginal costs at that level of quantity demanded. (Up to Q_c).

In the case shown in Figure 18.2, without regulation, the monopolist would produce Q_m and charge P_m. With the ceiling P_1, it would produce $Q_1 > Q_m$.

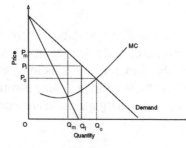

Figure 18.2

The price falls and output increases! Thus whether Modigliani was right depends upon whether markets are competitive or monopolistic.

Pareto Optimality

How can government intervention be evaluated in terms of benefit or harm to society? First, let's review the competitive model. Recall that the demand curve represents the marginal benefit to consumers while the supply curve represents the marginal cost to suppliers. Competitive equilibrium price equates marginal cost and marginal benefits to individual consumers and suppliers respectively. Under certain conditions, the demand (supply) curve represents marginal benefits (costs) to society and competitive equilibrium will be *pareto optimal*. That is, no person can be made better off without making another worse off. The textbook discusses this proof in more detail. Here we want to just restate this proposition to motivate the question, how much welfare is lost with a given deviation from competitive equilibrium? Given this proposition, it is clear that any deviation will make society worse off. Keep in mind, however, that the conditions under which this proposition is true are highly restrictive.

Economists disagree with the extent to which the conditions apply to the real world. Other considerations besides efficiency are important to consider as well. While some economists argue that the loss of efficiency is of paramount importance and that such governmental interventions should be kept at an absolute minimum, others argue that sacrifices in efficiency are necessary and may even be worthwhile if the government can make the distribution of resources and income among members of society more equitable. Again, your textbook describes those arguments in detail. Here, we only consider efficiency. Distribution considerations are beyond the scope of this book. We now present an analytical framework to evaluate the welfare (efficiency) effects of government intervention. We do this in terms of consumer and producer surplus.

Consumer Surplus

In earlier chapters you have been exposed to the notions of consumer and producer surplus. For an individual consumer, *consumer surplus* is the difference between what the consumer would be willing and able to pay for a particular good or service and what she actually pays. Consider the demand curve in Figure 18.3, where equilibrium price P^* is $5. Since the demand curve is downward sloping, the buyer derives greater pleasure from earlier units and would have been willing to pay a higher price for those units than from successive units. In the figure, the consumer has to pay P^* for all units up to Q^*, but was willing to pay more for those earlier units. Take for instance, point A. For this 2nd unit, she was willing to pay $8, but had to pay only $5. The difference, $3, is consumer surplus. Doing this for all points on the demand curve up to Q^*, we can see that consumer surplus is the area below the demand curve and above the equilibrium price. A market demand curve (horizontal summation of all individual demand curves), can be analyzed in the same way: here the units below Q^* represent people who would be willing and able to pay a higher price than they had to pay.

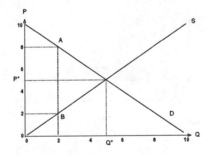

Figure 18.3

Let's consider another example. In Figure 18.4, we show the demand for theater tickets. Price is set at P^*. Consumers are willing and able to pay area $OZEQ^*$ to get Q^* number of tickets. But they only have to pay area OP^*EQ^*. Consumers earn a *surplus* of area P^*ZE; we label this area A. As you can see, consumer surplus, A, is the triangular area under the demand curve over a given price.

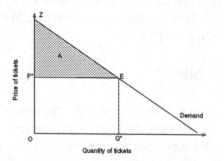

Figure 18.4

An Example

Here we want to calculate the exact value of consumer surplus A. Let the demand for gasoline be given by

demand: $$Q_D = 10 - P,$$

and let the equilibrium price for gasoline be $2/gallon. This is depicted in Figure 18.5.

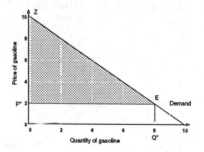

Figure 18.5

Substituting $P^* = \$2$ in the demand equation we find that $Q_D^* = 8$. Consumers are willing and able to pay a sum equivalent to area $\$OZEQ^*$ to get Q^* gallons of gasoline, but only have to pay OP^*EQ^*. We find out the value of each area in dollars respectively. To find the area consumers are willing to pay, we break it up into the sum of areas OP^*EQ^* and P^*ZE. Recall that the area of a triangle is equal to one-half base times height; and the area of a rectangle is the product of its two sides. The triangle $P^*ZE = 0.5 \cdot 8 \cdot \$8 = \$32$ and the rectangle OP^*EQ^*, is $\$2 \cdot 8 = \$16$. Their sum is $48.

This is the sum consumers were willing to pay. In fact, they had only to pay rectangle $OP*EQ*$, the value of which we have calculated as \$16. The difference between these two, \$32, is consumer surplus, the area of triangle $P*ZE$.

Analogously, *producer surplus* is the difference between how much the producer was willing to accept and how much he actually received, the surplus that accrues to a single producer or to all producers in society. Again, consider Figure 18.3, but now focus on the supply curve. The individual supplier at B is receiving $P*$, (\$5), but would have been willing to accept \$2. The difference, \$3, is producer surplus. All quantities sold below $Q*$ are sold at a surplus. Thus the sum of the surplus for all quantities below $Q*$ is producer surplus. Diagrammatically, it is the area above the supply curve and below the price. We leave it up to you to consider a numerical example of producer surplus at the end of the chapter exercises.

Now that we have defined producer and consumer surplus, we can use these tools to see how deviations from competitive equilibrium affect these values. It is the losses and gains in producer and consumer surplus that will be used to evaluate government intervention.

Government Intervention

In this chapter we look at three typical governmental interventions: a price ceiling, a price support and a tariff. Many other forms of intervention exist.

Price Ceilings

A *price ceiling*, if you recall, is a price legally mandated by the government, below the equilibrium price. Examples are *fair price* methods used in many developing countries and erstwhile Socialist countries to distribute essential commodities like rice, sugar, flour, kerosene. Other examples include gas rationing during the late seventies in the U.S., some utilities regulation, and rent controls on urban housing.

When the government decides to impose a price ceiling some members of society lose out, while others gain. Here we are not interested in the distributive effects of price ceilings but the net effect on society's welfare. Consider the supply and demand curves depicted in Figure 18.6. In a free market equilibrium, $Q*$ is bought and sold at $P*$. At price ceiling P^c, however, suppliers are willing to sell only Q_S^c. The difference $(Q*-Q_S^c)$ represents those consumers who now cannot purchase the products because suppliers are willing to sell less at the price ceiling. There are some consumers, however, who can now purchase the products at the lower price. Likewise, $(Q^* - Q_s^c)$ represents a combination of suppliers who are willing to sell fewer goods and now must accept the lower price and other suppliers who just go out of business. To see exactly how buyers and sellers fare, we compare consumer and producer surplus before and after the price ceiling.

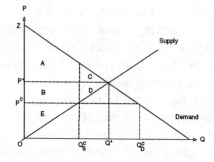

Figure 18.6

Consumer Surplus First we consider consumer surplus. Consumer surplus before the price ceiling is the sum of areas A and C. Consumer surplus after the price ceiling is now the sum of areas A and B. The change in consumer surplus is then,

$$\Delta \text{Consumer surplus} = (A + B) - (A + C) = \text{Areas B - C}$$

Area B represents those people who are able to get the good at a cheaper price (a gain in consumer surplus) and C represents those who are not able to get the good at all (a loss in consumer surplus). The net gain or loss depends on the relative sizes of areas B and C. Clearly, if B is greater than C, there is a net gain, whereas if B is less than C there is a net loss. The size of area C depends upon the elasticity of demand while area B depends upon the elasticity of supply. The more inelastic is demand, the greater is C. This should be intuitively clear since inelastic demand implies buyers would have been willing to pay far more for each quantity.

Producer Surplus How are the suppliers affected by this policy? With a price ceiling, producers will either leave the market or produce less and accept a lower price. Both are losses. We now measure the loss as a change in producer surplus. Recall the producer surplus before the price ceiling is the area below the price level and above the supply curve. This is represented by areas E, B and D. The new producer surplus is just area E. Subtracting the producer surplus with competitive price from producer surplus under the price ceiling we find the change in producer surplus:

$$\Delta\text{Producer surplus} = (E) - (B + D + E) = \text{Areas} -(B + D).$$

Clearly, producers are net losers. Area B represents those producers who now sell goods but now must accept a lower price and area D represents those producers who left the market and a loss in production by those who remained. The more inelastic is supply, the greater the loss.

Net Welfare Effect As you can see, consumers gain areas B at the expense of the producers. This represents a transfer of resources. Producers also lose area D. Consumers lose area C. No one gains either. Thus areas C and D represent the *welfare loss* also called *dead-weight loss*, the loss in resources (or efficiency) from a deviation from competitive equilibrium. Mathematically the net welfare effect of this policy is

$$(\Delta\text{Consumer surplus} + \Delta\text{Producer surplus}) = - \text{Areas } (C + D).$$

A real-world example of a price ceiling are the oil price controls imposed by the Carter administration during the second oil price shock in 1979. Gasoline prices were prevented from rising to world levels. Nonprice rationing determined those people who were not able to purchase gas and was represented by the long hours spent waiting in queues to get gasoline. The long lines represent losses by consumers that were not captured by producers, but lost resources to society.

A Numerical Example

Let us look at the gasoline market that we had referred to in an earlier example. Suppose that the market demand for gasoline is given by

$$Q_D = 10 - P.$$

The market supply curve goes through the origin and has a slope of one:

$$Q_S = P,$$

where Q is millions of gallons of gasoline, and
       P is dollars per gallon.

Competitive market equilibrium is given by

$$Q_S = Q_D.$$

This market is depicted in Figure 18.7.

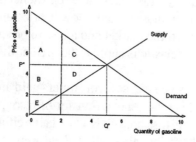

Figure 18.7

Solving for equilibrium price and quantity gives us $P* = \$5/gallon, Q* = 5$ millions gallons. Suppose now that consumers decry the high price of gas and pressure the government to impose a price ceiling, which it does at \$2/gallon. Now instead of solving where $Q_S = Q_D$ we must solve where $P = \$2$. Substituting $P = \$2$ into the demand and supply equations respectively, we find that $Q_D = 8$ million gallons while $Q_S = 2$ million gallons. Hence there is a shortage in the market and non-price mechanisms (such as waiting in lines) will ration the limited supply of gasoline.

We want to measure the change in consumer surplus, producer surplus and the dead-weight loss. You have learned the geometric depiction of these values; here we want to find numerical values for these areas. We do this by first recognizing each area geometrically and calculating their values. We have already labeled the relevant areas A, B, C, D, and E. The following is the calculation of their values:

$$\text{Area B} = b{\cdot}h = (2\text{-}0){\cdot}\ (\$5\text{-}\$2) = \$6$$
$$\text{Area C} = 1/2\ b{\cdot}h = 1/2 \cdot (5\text{-}2) \cdot (\$8\text{-}\$5) = \$4.50$$
$$\text{Area D} = 1/2\ b{\cdot}h = 1/2{\cdot}\ (5\text{-}2) \cdot (\$5\text{-}\$2) = \$4.50$$
$$\text{Area E} = 1/2\ b{\cdot}h = 1/2 \cdot (2\text{-}0) \cdot (\$2\text{-}\$0) = \$2$$

where b is the base and h is height of the area.

Area A is the sum of the area of a rectangle and a triangle. The triangle and rectangles are created by drawing a horizontal line at $P = \$8$ to the demand curve.

$$\text{Area A} = b \cdot h + 1/2 \; b \cdot h' = (2\text{-}0) \cdot (\$8\text{-}\$5) + 1/2 \cdot (2\text{-}0) \cdot (\$10\text{-}\$8)$$
$$= \$6 + \$2 = \$8$$

Now we just need to calculate consumer and producer surplus as sums of these areas before and after the price ceiling. Consumer surplus before the price ceiling is the sum of areas A and C: $8 + $4.5 = $12.5 million. After the price ceiling, consumers can buy gasoline at only $2 per gallon but sellers are willing to sell only 2 million gallons at this price. Consumer surplus with the price ceiling is the sum of areas A and B: $8 + $6 = $14 million. The change in consumer surplus is $14 - $12.5 or $1.5 million. Consumers gain $1.5 million in consumer surplus from this price ceiling.

Let's now calculate the change in producer surplus. Producer surplus before the price ceiling is the sum of areas E, B and D: $2 + $6 + $4.5 = $12.5 million. After the price ceiling producers have to accept a lower price. Some leave the market, others reduce their output. Producer surplus after the price ceiling is area E: $2 million. The change in producer surplus is $2 - $12.5 = -$10.5 million. Producers lose $10.5 in producer surplus.

The change in societal welfare (dead-weight loss) is the sum of the change in producer surplus and the change in consumer surplus, areas C and D: -$10.5 + $1.5 = - $9 million.

In this case, the imposition of a price ceiling benefits some consumers who can purchase gasoline at a lower price (gain of area B); however, a number of consumers are not able to buy gasoline at all or must buy less than with a competitive market (loss of area C). Producers lose by being forced to sell at low prices (loss of area B) or go out of business or sell less than at a competitive price (loss of area D). In our numerical example, society as a whole loses (areas C and D).

Exercise 1: Under what case would a price ceiling produce no dead-weight loss?

Price Floors

We now turn to *price floors*, prices legally mandated by the government, above the equilibrium prices. An example of price floors is the agriculture support system.

Just as with the price ceiling we are interested in the net effect on society's welfare. Consider the supply and demand curves depicted in Figure 18.8. In a free market equilibrium, Q^* is bought and sold at P^*. At price floor P^f, however, consumers demand only Q_D^f. Some consumers are hurt because they now must pay the higher price. Producers are hurt because they can no longer sell as much goods, although some producers are helped who can now sell the products at the higher price. Let's compare consumer and producer surplus before and after the price floor.

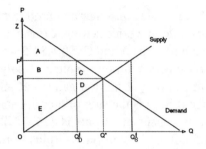

Figure 18.8

Consumer Surplus Consumer surplus before the price floor is the sum of areas A, B, and C. Consumer surplus after the price floor is now just area A. The change in consumer surplus is then

$$\Delta\text{Consumer surplus} = (A) - (A + B + C) = \text{Areas} - (B + C)$$

There is a clear loss in consumer surplus.

Producer Surplus How are the suppliers affected by this policy? Some producers can charge a higher price while others would like to sell their goods but cannot at the higher price. We now measure the loss as a change in producer surplus. The producer surplus before the price floor is the area below the price level and above the supply curve. This is represented by areas E and D. The new producer surplus are areas B and E. Subtracting the producer surplus with competitive price from producer surplus under the price ceiling we find the change in producer surplus:

$$\Delta\text{Producer surplus} = (B + E) - (E + D) = \text{Areas B - D}.$$

The net gain or loss depends on the relative sizes of areas B and D. Clearly, if B is greater than D, there is a net gain, whereas if B is less than D there is a net loss. While the size of area D depends upon the elasticity of supply, that of area B depends upon the elasticity of demand. The more inelastic is supply, the greater is D. This should be intuitively clear since inelastic supply implies suppliers would have been willing to accept far less for each quantity.

Net Welfare Effect As you can see, consumers lose areas B and C. Producers gain area B at the expense of consumers but lose area D. Areas C and D represent the *welfare loss* also called *dead-weight loss*, the loss in resources (or efficiency) from a deviation from competitive equilibrium.

The Case of A Price Floor in Agricultural Markets

Now let's consider a case in which the government has instituted a price floor in agricultural markets to help out farmers. It believes that equilibrium prices in these markets are too low.

In this next case, the government guarantees wheat farmers fixed price per ton of wheat. The government purchases all wheat not purchased by the consumer. In Figure 18.9, P_f is the price floor. At this price, Q_D^f is demanded by consumers and Q_S^f is supplied by farmers. The government purchases the excess, $Q_S^f - Q_d^f$.

Determining consumer and producer surplus should be second nature to you now so our discussion will be brief.

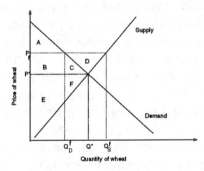

Figure 18.9

In an unregulated market for wheat, consumer surplus is represented by areas A, B and C. With a price floor of P_f, consumer surplus is represented by area A. Consumers have lost areas B and C in consumer surplus.

Now turning to producer surplus, producer surplus in an unregulated market is represented by areas E and F. With the price floor, producer surplus is represented by areas E, F, B, C and D. Producers have gained areas B at the expense of consumers and C and D at the expense of government.

The net gain in welfare is area D. Areas B and C represent a transfer of resources from consumers and government to producers respectively. This analysis, however, assumes that the value of the wheat the government bought is what the government paid for it. More likely, however, the crop purchased will be worth very little. The cost to the government of purchasing the excess wheat will always exceed the value of area D. The extent to which the government can sell the wheat it purchased will determine whether the project will result in a net gain.

Your textbook presents alternative methods of government price supports and the breakdown of gains and losses. We have presented the application of the tools of consumer and producer surplus to just one example.

Exercise 2: Under what case would there be no dead-weight loss with a price floor?

Tariffs and Quotas

Tariffs

Let's now consider a tariff intended to diminish foreign competition and help out domestic producers. Recall, a *tariff* is a tax on imports. A government imposes a tariff on an imported good if it wants to help the domestic producers compete with lower-cost foreign producers.

One of the sacred cows in economics is the extension of the invisible hand argument to the international sphere, i.e., free trade among nations is pareto optimal as well. Two nations would both gain if they traded freely with minimal government intervention. As your textbook points out, U.S. trade policy has not always promoted free trade. A widely-cited example is the Smoot-Hawley Tariff of 1930. The disastrous effects of this and retaliations by foreign countries on world trade convinced most economists that free trade is preferable to government intervention. Today, fierce competition from Germany, Japan, and numerous low cost producers in Latin America and the Pacific Rim have again raised interest in protectionism. Possible tools of protectionism include tariffs, quotas, voluntary export restraints.

Tariffs, by raising the cost of imports, discourage domestic consumption of imports and hence foster domestic import-competing industries. Let us take the case of the sugar market. Figure 18.10 depicts the U.S. domestic sugar market where world price of sugar is below domestic equilibrium price if there were no imports. Assume the free market domestic price of sugar is P_d which is much higher than world price P_w. Hence with free trade domestic producers are willing to supply Q_d at price P_w. Domestic consumption at P_w is Q. The gap between domestic supply and consumption ($Q - Q_d$) is supplied by foreign producers.

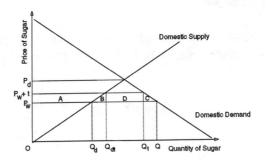

Figure 18.10

Assume that domestic sugar producers successfully lobby Congress to impose a tariff, *t*, on imports. This increases the domestic price of sugar to $P_w + t$. At this higher price, domestic producers are willing to increase their production and supply Q_{dt}. Domestic consumption, however, falls to Q_t. Foreign producers are left to supply a lower quantity, $Q_t - Q_{dt}$. The government collects tariff revenues of $t(Q_t - Q_{dt})$. The government could charge what is called a *prohibitive tariff* that effectively reduces imports to zero. That tariff would be, $t = P_d - P_w$, the difference between the domestic and world price for sugar.

Let's assess this tariff in terms of gains and losses. Here the relevant players are domestic consumers, domestic producers and the government.

Consumer Surplus Recall that consumer surplus is the area under the demand curve and over price. With tariff *t* consumers lose areas of consumer surplus labeled A, B, C and D.

Producer Surplus Recall also that producer surplus is the area over the supply curve and under price. Producers gain area A and lose nothing.

Government Revenue The government gains revenue represented by area D.

The net change in domestic welfare is -(A+B+C+D) + (A) + (D) or -(B+C). This is the dead-weight loss. B represents *production loss* by foreign producers and C represents *consumption loss*.

A Numerical Example

Let's consider a numerical example of a tariff. Suppose the demand and supply curve for coffee beans in the U.S. for 1993 is given by the following equations:

$$Q_D = 400 - 2P,$$

$$Q_S = -50 + P.$$

where P is dollars per ton of coffee,
        Q is thousands of tons of coffee.

The domestic market for coffee is depicted in Figure 18.11.

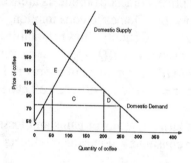

Figure 18.11

The U.S. is a small producer of coffee in the world market where the price is $75/ton. The U.S. Coffee Growers Association would like the Congress to pass a tariff of $25/ton to protect the domestic industry from foreign competition. We want to calculate the gain or loss to domestic consumers, producers and the government if such a tariff were to be levied.

Setting $Q_S = Q_D$, we can find equilibrium price and quantity in the domestic market with no imports. Doing so we find that $P^* = \$150$/ton and $Q^* = 100$ thousand pounds. Allowing imports and free trade, the world price, $75 per ton, becomes the relevant price for domestic consumers and producers. Using $Q_S = -50 + P$, we find that at this price, domestic producers are willing to supply 25 thousand ton and domestic demand is 250 thousand tons. Imports supply the difference: 225 thousand tons.

Suppose the government were to pass a tariff to increase the world price in the U.S. market to $100/ton. Again using the equations for domestic supply and demand, we find that the quantity supplied by domestic sellers increases to 50 thousand tons and domestic demand falls to 200 with a consequent reduction in level of imports. Imports fall to 150 thousand tons.

Let's calculate the change in domestic consumer and producer surplus and tariff revenue numerically.

Consumer Surplus Consumer surplus with free trade is the area under the demand curve above price of $75 per ton: $1/2 \cdot 250 \cdot (\$200-\$75) = \$15,625$. Consumer surplus after the imposition of the tariff is that area below the demand curve but above the new price $100 per ton: $1/2 \cdot 200 \cdot (\$200-\$100) = \$10,000$. The loss in consumer surplus is the difference: $5,625.

Producer Surplus Domestic producer surplus with free trade is the area above the supply curve below price of $75 per ton: $1/2 \cdot 25 \cdot (\$75- \$50) = \$312.50$. Producer surplus after the imposition of the tariff is now that area above the supply curve but below the new price $100 per ton: $1/2 \cdot 50 \cdot (\$100-\$50) = \$1250$. The gain in producer surplus is the difference: $937.50.

Government Revenue The gain in government revenue is imports after the imposition of the tariff times the tariff: $\$25 \cdot 150 = \$3750$.

Net Welfare Loss Producers and government have jointly gained $4687.5. Consumers have lost $5,625. Dead-weight loss is $937.5.

Quotas

Quotas are similar to tariffs in that they restrict trade. A *quota* is a physical restriction on imports. In Figure 18.10 above, after the price rose from the tariff, imports were reduced. Alternatively the government could have produced the same result by restricting imports to Q_t-Q_{dt}. The price would have risen to $P_w + t$. Domestic producers would still produce Q_{dt}. The key difference between the tariff and quota is that while the tariff generates revenue for the government the quota generates increased producer surplus to foreign producers through higher prices. There is no increased revenue for the government with a quota. In our numerical example depicted in Figure 18.11, the government could have used a quota of 150 thousand tons a year to achieve a similar result. Again, there would be no increase in government revenue.

It is unclear which form of government intervention is preferred. Often tariffs generate a significant portion of government revenue for developing nations. In addition, with quotas, the government must distribute the quota permits to the imports which generates the possibility of corruption. On the other hand, a quota in many countries is easier to legislate and has the certainty of placing strict numerical limitations on imports.

Conclusion

From this chapter it is evident that most public policies tend to benefit some sections of society while hurting others. In other words it is difficult if not impossible to implement policies that make everyone universally better-off. It is thus helpful to have a way of assessing the impact of such policies in a fairly objective manner. The concepts of consumer and producer surplus are two analytical tools which will help to assess the impact on society of government intervention in the marketplace.

Problems

1. Consider again the market for fish, which you encountered not only at the start of this chapter but also in Chapter 11. Let Q be the tons of fish and P the dollar price per ton of fish.

Demand: $Q_D = 300 - 2.5\,P,$

Supply: $Q_S = -20 + 1.5\,P,$

Equilibrium $Q_D = Q_S.$

a. Suppose the fishing industry persuades the Congress to save the family fishing industry by mandating a price floor at $100 per ton of fish. When the government imposes a price floor of $100/ton, calculate the gain/loss to consumers and producers of fish.

b. Suppose the Congress realizes its folly after numerous public outcries of high fish prices and so swings the other way and mandates a price ceiling of $50. When the government imposes a price ceiling of $50/ton, calculate the gain/loss to consumers and producers of fish.

c. Based on your answer for (b), a black market might emerge. Graphically demonstrate the black market price and also calculate the dollar price of the fish in the potential black market.

2. The demand and supply for soybeans in the U.S. is given by

$$Q_D = 600 - 5\,P,$$

$$Q_S = -40 + 3\,P.$$

The U.S is a small producer of soybeans in the world markets and is not able to affect the world price of $P = \$60$/ton. The soybean producers lobby the Congress and successfully get a tariff of $20/ton on imports. Calculate the gain/loss to domestic consumers, producers and government from such an intervention.

Answers to In-Text Questions

1. There would be no dead-weight loss with a price ceiling when the demand curve is perfectly elastic at the level of the price ceiling.
2. There would be no dead-weight loss with a price floor when supply is perfectly elastic at the level of the price floor.

Appendix I

Answers to End of Chapter Problems

Chapter 1

1. $652.5 billion
2. 21

Chapter 2

1. Yes, as shown below, this function has a U shape. It is not likely that this function would describe a total cost function of a firm since cost usually rises as output rises. This function initially falls as output rises.

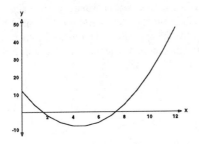

2. The function reaches its maximum at (0, 50) and its minimum at (4, -14).

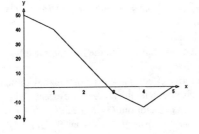

Chapter 3

1. a. $Y' = 20x^3 - 6x$.
   b. $25(5x - 10)^4$.
   c. $6(4x - 5)^3 + 72x[(4x - 5)^2]$.
2. At $Q = 3$, the cost function is at a maximum. At $Q = 8$, the cost function is at a minimum.
3. a. $Q^* = 10$.
   b. $Q^* = 6$.
4. a. $\partial Y/\partial x = 12xz^3$. $\partial Y/\partial z = 18x^2z^2$.
   b. $\partial Y/\partial x = 24x + 36z + 20$. $\partial Y/\partial z = 36x + 60$.
5. Use the Lagrange multiplier method to find the solution $x^* = y^* = 28$, $\lambda^* = -420$.

Chapter 4

1. Extending the model based on equations (1) and (2) in the text, the reduced-form equation is $Y = 1/(1 - b + bt - v - g - x + m)(C_0 + -bT_0 + bR_0 + I_0 + G_0 + X_0 - M_0$ and the multiplier is $1/(1 - b + bt - v - g - x + m)$.
2. Using the multiplier formula $\Delta Y/\Delta X = 1/(1-b+m)$, we know that when exports change, $\Delta Y = \Delta X[1/(1-b+m)]$. Given this change in income, we know $\Delta M = m\Delta Y = m\{\Delta X [1/(1-b+m)]\}$. To prove $\Delta M < \Delta X$ we assume the opposite and prove its falsehood. If $\Delta M > \Delta X$, then $m/(1-b+m) > 1$. Rearranging terms we get $m > 1 - b + m$ or $b > 1$. Since by definition $0 < b < 1$, b $\not>$1. So, $\Delta M < \Delta X$.

Chapter 5

1. a. Yes, Japanese government expenditures will affect U.S. GDP. Government expenditures in Japan will lead to increased income in Japan and then increased imports from the U.S. Japanese imports are U.S. exports which adds to U.S. GDP. The multipliers are $\Delta Y^{us}/\Delta G^j = m^j/[(1 - b^j + m^j)(1 - b^{us} + m^{us}) - m^j m^{us}]$ and $\Delta Y^j/\Delta G^j = (1 - b^{us} + m^{us})/(1 - b^j + m^j)(1 - b^{us} + m^{us}) - m^j m^{us})$.
   b. $121.2 billion in the U.S. and $272.7 billion in Japan.
2. a. The simple multiplier is $1/(1 - b^{us} + m^{us})$. The multiplier with the locomotive effect is $(1 - b^j + m^j)/[(1 - b^j + m^j)(1 - b^{us} + m^{us}) - m^j m^{us})$.
   b. To prove that the multiplier with the locomotive effect is always larger than without the locomotive effect we begin with the multiplier with the locomotive effect: $(1 - b^j + m^j)/[(1 - b^j + m^j)(1 - b^{us} + m^{us}) - m^j m^{us})]$. Then factor out $(1 - b^j + m^j)/(1 - b^j + m^j)$ to get $[(1 - b^j + m^j)/(1 - b^j + m^j)]\{1/[(1 - b^{us} + m^{us}) - (m^j m^{us})/(1 - b^j + m^j)]\}$. Simplifying we get $1/[(1 - b^{us} + m^{us}) - (m^j m^{us})/(1 - b^j + m^j)]$. Since $0 < m^j < 1; 0 < m^{us} < 1$; and $0 < b^j < 1$, $(m^j m^{us})/(1 - b^j + m^j) > 0$ and $\Delta Y/\Delta G$ with the locomotive effect must be larger than $\Delta Y/\Delta G$ without.
   c. With a locomotive effect there is the first-round effect on the domestic economy but since the domestic rise in income increases foreign income which then provides yet another boost to domestic income, the multiplier with a locomotive effect is larger.
   3. The equilibrium level of income for the U.S. is given by

(1) $Y = [1/(1 - b + bt + m)](C_0 - bT_0 + I_0 + G_0 + X_0 - M_0)$.

In a two-country model, exports of the U.S. are imports of Japan. Therefore, $X = M_0^j + m^j Y^i$. We can then rewrite (1) as

(2) $Y = [1/(1 - b + bt + m)](C_0 - bT_0 + I_0 + G_0 + M_0 j + m^j Y^i - M_0)$.

Similarly, the equilibrium level of income for Japan is

(3) $Y^j = [1/(1 - b^j + b^j t^j + m^j)](C_0^j - bT_0^j + I_0^j + G_0^j + X_0^j - M_0^j)$ and since Japan's exports are imports for the U.S.,

(4) $Y^j = [1/(1 - b^j + b^j t^j + m^j)](C_0^j - bT_0^j + I_0^j + G_0^j + M_0 + mY - M_0^j)$.

The multiplier for the U.S. with the trade mechanism feedback can now be constructed by substituting equation (4) into equation (2):

$Y = [1/(1 - b + bt + m)](C_0 - bT_0 + I_0 + G_0 + M_0^j - M_0 + m^j\{[1/(1 - b^j + b^j t^j + m^j)](C_0^j - bT_0^j + I_0^j + G_0^j + M_0 + mY - M_0^j)]\}$.

Simplifying we get

$Y = [(1 - b^j + b^j t^j + m^j)(C_0 - bT_0 + I_0 + G_0 + M_0^j - M_0 + m^j(C_0^j - bT_0^j + I_0^j + G_0^j + M_0 + mY - M_0^j)]/[(1 - b^j + b^j t^j + m^j)(1 - b + bt + m)]$.

Collecting all the Y-terms on the left and factoring out Y yields

$Y = [(1 - b^j + b^j t^j + m^j)(C_0 - bT_0 + I_0 + G_0 + M_0^j - M_0) + m^j(C_0^j - bT_0^j + I_0^j + G_0^j + M_0 - M_0^j)]/[(1 - b^j + b^j t^j + m^j)(1 - b + bt + m) - m^j m]$. The multiplier for a two-country model for an autonomous change in government spending can be written as $(1 - b^j + b^j t^j + m^j)/[(1 - b^j + b^j t^j + m^j)(1 - b + bt + m) - m^j m]$.

4. a. $2150.

   b. The U.S. has a trade deficit of $370.

Chapter 6

1.   If the supply of money were relatively elastic (upward sloping) the LM curve would be flatter than the LM curve derived in the text with a perfectly inelastic supply curve for money. A graphical derivation is shown below:

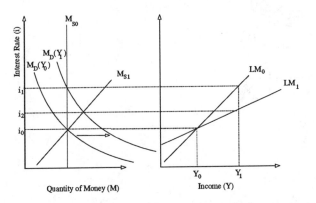

2.   a. If the eonomy of Belarus were to overheat, I would institute contractionary fiscal policy and contractionary monetary policy to reduce national income as in the figures below:

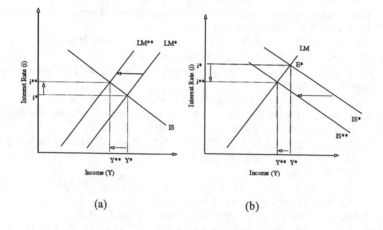

(a)   (b)

b. Since the economy is overheating contractionary policies are required. Contractionary fiscal policy shifts the IS curve to the left, lowering output and interst rates. Contractionary monetary policy shift the LM curve to the left, lowering output and raising interest rates. The rise in interest rates chokes off investment and curbs inflation. Hence monetary policy is more effective in an overheating economy.

c. The steepness or flatness (Classical or Keynesian) of the IS curve has little bearing on the final effect of fiscal policy. However, monetary policy will affect output more with a flat IS curve as shown below. With a flat IS curve, change in interest rates has a larger effect on output through the multiplier process.

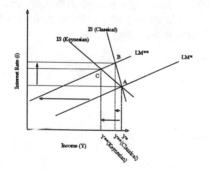

Chapter 7

1. Using equations (1) - (6) from the text and the new equation for consumption, we know $Y = C_0 + bY - bT_0 - btY - di + I_0 - ci + G_0$. To derive the IS curve we rewrite this equation isolating i on the left. Through algebraic manipulation we get $i = (C_0 + I_0 - bT_0 + G_0)/(d + c) - [(1 - b + bt)/(d + c)]Y$. This is the equation for the IS curve.

2. If the money supply curve is $M_s + zi$, then the LM curve is $M_s + zi = j + kY - hi$ or $i = [(j - M_s)/(z + h)] + [k/(z + h)]Y$. This is the LM curve. The elasticity of this LM

curve is $(\partial Y/\partial i)(i/Y)$. For the LM curve here this is $(z + h)/k(i/Y)$. The elasticity of the LM curve with inelastic money supply $(z = 0)$ is $(h/k)(i/Y)$. Since $(z + h)/k > h/k$, the LM curve with the endogenous component is more elastic.

3.   The IS curve in an open economy with trade is $i = (C_0 + I_0 - bT_0 + G_0 + X_0 - M_0)/c -$ $[(1 - b + bt + m)/c]Y$. The reduced-form equation in this model is $Y = [(C_0 + I_0 + G_0 - bT_0 + X_0 - M_0) + (c/h) (M_s - j)/[(1 - b + bt + m)+ (kc/h)]$. The equlibrium value of income in both the goods and money markets is $Y = [h(C_0 + I_0 + G_0 - bT_0 + X_0 - M_0) - c(j - M_s)]/[h(1 - b + bt + m) + ck]$.

Chapter 8

1. $Y_t = [1/(1 - b - v - g)][C_0 + I_0 - (v + g)Y_{t-1} - gY_{t-2}]$.
2.   a. $250 + .75Y_{t-1} - .5Y_{t-2}$.
        b. $Y_2 = 275$; $Y_3 = 406$; $Y_4 = 417$; $Y_5 = 360$; $Y_6 = 311$; $Y_7 = 304$; $Y_8 = 322$; $Y_9 = 340$; $Y_{10} = 344$; $Y_{11} = 338$.
        c. $Y_2 = 312$; $Y_3 = 409$; $Y_4 = 401$; $Y_5 = 346$; $Y_6 = 309$; $Y_7 = 309$; $Y_8 = 327$; $Y_9 = 341$; $Y_{10} = 342$; $Y_{11} = 336$. The differences between the two are small ranging in value of 37 in the first period and -16 in the fourth period.

Chapter 9

1.   a. $3651.39
        b. Yes, you have made a sound investment because the present value, now $5358.92, is greater than the $5,000 purchase price.
        c. Between 12% and 13%.
2.   a. $1.25 million.
        b. $3.3 million.

Chapter 10

1.   a. $N_x + CN_m > C$, where $C = P_m Q_m/eP_x Q_x$.
        b. The interpretation of this case of the Marshall-Lerner condition is that a deprecia- tion is more likely to improve the trade balance if the trade balance is in a surplus. Conversely, a depreciation is less likely to improve the trade balance if the trade balance is in a deficit.
2.   If the exchange rate depreciates, falling from e_1 to e_2, we have a worsening of the trade balance. This is becuase $N_m < 1$ and the Marshall-Lerner condition is not satisfied.

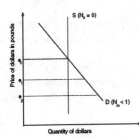

Chapter 11

1. a. $P^* = \$400$ per apartment, $Q^* = 300{,}000$ units.
    b. 50,000 people will be deprived of rent-controlled housing.

Chapter 12

1. a. At 75 cents per ride, $Q^* = 2500$. Total revenue is $1875.
    b. Price elasticity of demand is 0.6 at 75 cents per ride.
    c. The park should raise rates to increase revenue. If price elasticity is less than one, total revenue rises as price rises. If price elasticity is greater than one, total revenue will fall as the price rises.
    d. At $1.00 per ride, $Q^* = 2000$ and elasticity of demand is unitary. The park is maximizing total revenue.
2. $E_d = -1$. Any rectangular hyperbolic demand curve would satisfy this value of elasticity.
3. A linear supply curve that intersects the vertical axis can be written as $P = a + slope(Q)$ where a is the vertical axis intercept. $Slope = (P-a)/Q$. $E_s = (dQ/dP)(P/Q) = 1/(dP/dQ)(P/Q) = 1/[(P-a)/Q[(P/Q) = [Q/(P-a)](P/Q) = P/(P-a)$. Since $a > 0$, $E_s > 1$.
4. Given linear demand curve AB, prove $E_d = MB/AM$.

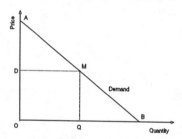

$E_d = (dQ/dP)(P/Q) = (P/Q)/(dP/dQ)$. In the graph above, $E_d = (MQ/OQ)/(MQ/QB) = QB/OQ$. ADM and MQB are similar triangles, therefore, $MB/QB = AM/DM$ and $MB/QB = AM/OQ$. Therefore, $MB/AM = QB/OQ$. But, $E_d = QB/OQ$, so $MB/AM = E_d$.

Chapter 13

1. $MU_x = -(x + 2y)/2x^3$; $MU_y = 1/(2x^2)$; $dU = -[(x + 2y)/2x^3]dx + [1/(2x^2)]dy$. $MU_{xx} = (x + 3y)/x^4$; $MU_{yy} = 0$. Since $MU_{yy} > 0$ and $MU_{xy} > 0$ the utility function does not exibit diminishing marginal returns.
2. Maximize the Lagrangean, $L = x^{1/2}z + \lambda(Y - P_x x - P_z z)$ to find $x^* = Y/3P_x$; $z^* = 2Y/3P_z$. These are the optimal values of x and z. From the expression it is clear that the consumer spends 1/3 of his income on good x and 2/3 of his income on good z.

3. a. The generic budget equation is $Y = Q_B P_B + Q_M P_M$.
    b. Rationing is not optimal, for although the consumer is spending all his income and buying more meat at point F, the indifference curve U_1 lies below U_0. The ratio of the marginal utilities does not equal the the price ratio and the consumer is not maximizing utility at point F.

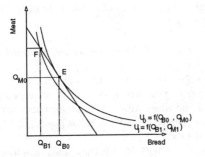

Chapter 14

1.   The marginal and average productivities would be equal and constant. This is depicted graphically by two concurrent horizontal lines. The law of diminishing marginal productivity would lead one to believe that the total product curve is unlikely to have this shape. In our graph below we chose $TP = bL$ as a general form of this production function.

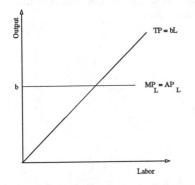

2.   The constraint for the production process is $x/2 = y$ and the values of y and x that maximize output are $y^* = 9.44$; $x^* = 18.88$.

3. a. Increasing returns to scale; marginal products are increasing for both labor and capital.
    b. Constant returns to scale; marginal products are diminishing for both labor and capital.
    c. Increasing returns to scale; marginal products are diminishing for both labor and capital.

Chapter 15

1. $Q = (KL)^{1/2}$. $MP_L = (1/2)(K/L)^{1/2}$, $MP_k = (1/2)(L/K)^{1/2}$. At equilibrium, MRTS = w/r. Thus, $[(K/L)^{1/2}]/[(L/K)^{1/2}] = w/r$, or
    (1) $K = (w/r)L$.
    The equation for an isocost line is given by $TC = wL + rK$. Substituting (1) into the total cost equation and simplifying we get
    (2) $TC = 2wL$.
    We want total costs in terms of Q, w, and L. Solve the production function for L, substitute this into (2) to get $TC = 2(wr)^{1/2}Q$.

2. $TVC = AQ - BQ^2 + CQ^3$; $AVC = A - BQ + CQ^2$; $MC = A - 2BQ + 3CQ^2$. Find that the minimum of AVC is at $Q = B/2C$ by setting the derivative of AVC with respect to Q equal to zero and solving for Q. To find where MC = AVC, set the two equal one another and solve for Q. Doing this you find that AVC = MC at $Q = B/2C$. This is the same point as the minimum of the AVC.

3. The cost per unit of output is the $ATC = 1/3Q^2 - 3Q + 9$. The optimal size to minimize average costs is 4,500 bedrooms.

Chapter 16

1. a. Maximize $\Pi = 24A_1 + 8A_2$ subject to
       $2A_1 + 5A_2 \le 40$,
       $4A_1 + A_2 \le 20$,
       $10A_1 + 5A_2 \le 60$.
    b. The feasibility set is shown in the graph below. It shows that combination of A_1 and A_2 that satisfies all three production constraints.

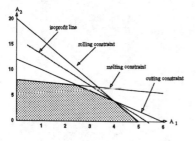

    To maximize Π, draw isoprofit lines with slope -3 and find the highest isoprofit line that touches the feasibility set. This is at point (4,4) for $\Pi^* = 128$.

2. a. Maximixe $\Pi = 40R + 50S$ subject to
       $2R + 6S \le 36$,
       $5R + 3S \le 30$,
       $8R + 2S \le 40$.
    b. The optimal x and z are 3 and 5 units respectively for a maximum profit of $370. The graphical representation is as follows:

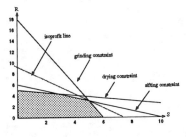

The feasibility set represents that combination of rough and smooth stones that satisfies all three production constraints.

Chapter 17

1. $P_M^* = \$15.10$, $Q_M^* = 29.5$ units.
2.   The price that will maximize revenue is $10. At this price 200,000 seats will be left unfilled.
3.   Marginal cost for the author after the book has been written is zero, but greater than zero for the publisher. Thus, the author wants to maximize total revenue and set quantity sold where MR = 0. The publisher wants to maximize profits and set quantity sold where MC = MR. Since the demand curve is negatively sloped and the marginal revenue falls twice as fast as the demand curve, this implies that price set by the publisher will be higher than the price the author wishes to set.
4.   a. $P_1^* = \$25$, $Q_1^* = 60$ for $\Pi_1^* = \$600$; $P_2^* = \$35$, $Q_2^* = 60$ for $\Pi_2^* = \$1200$. Overall level of profit is $1800.
      b. $P^* = \$28.33$, $Q^* = 120$, $\Pi^* = \$1599.60$.
5. $Q_G = 36$, $Q_E = 36$, $P^* = \$128$. Each firm's profits are $\Pi_G^* = \Pi_E^* = \$2592$. The reaction functions are $Q_E = 45 - Q_G/4$ and $Q_G = 45 - Q_E/4$ respectively. These are drawn in the graph below.

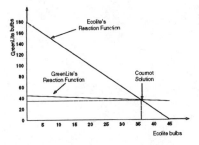

6.   The Nash equilibrium is (Shop, No Shop) and (No Shop, Shop). Neither player has a dominant strategy. The maximin strategy solution to the game is (Shop, Shop).

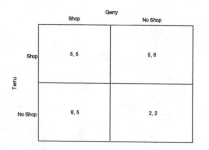

Chapter 18

1. a. The change in producer surplus is area B minus area D which equals $166.67. The change in consumer surplus is loss of area B and area C which equals $1500. This is shown in the figure below.

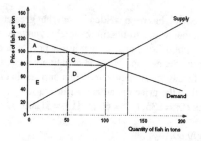

   b. At a price ceiling of $50, producers lose areas B and D. Consumers gain area B and lose area C. Producers lose $2325 and consumers gain $1245.

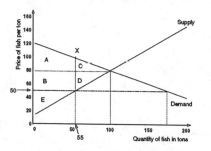

   c. The black market price will be the price consumers would be willing to pay for 55 tons of fish. This is $98, point X on the figure above.

2.   Loss in consumer surplus is $5,000. Gain in producer surplus is $3,400. Since domestic demand is met entirely from domestic producers, government receives no tariff revenue.

Index